RUM

RUM

The Epic Story
of the Drink
That Conquered the World

Charles A. Coulombe, K.C.St.S.

CITADEL PRESS
Kensington Publishing Corp.
www.kensingtonbooks.com

To EILEEN and the late FRANK DILL,
formerly of Roswell, New Mexico, and Winnipeg, Manitoba,
who kept me well supplied with rum-and-Coke
when I was a cadet,
and to ALEX MÜLLERS, of Aachen, Germany,
who initiated me into the mysteries of the Feuerzangebowle,

this book is affectionately dedicated.

CITADEL PRESS BOOKS are published by

Kensington Publishing Corp.
850 Third Avenue
New York, NY 10022

All Kensington titles, imprints, and distributed lines are available at special
quantity discounts for bulk purchases for sales promotions, premiums, fund-
raising, educational, or institutional use. Special book excerpts or customized
printings can also be created to fit specific needs. For details, write or phone the
office of the Kensington special sales manager: Kensington Publishing Corp.,
850 Third Avenue, New York, NY 10022, attn: Special Sales Department;
phone 1-800-221-2647.

CITADEL PRESS and the Citadel logo are Reg. U.S. Pat. & TM Off.

First printing: June 2004
First paperback printing: July 2005

10 9 8 7 6 5 4 3 2 1

Printed in the United States of America

Library of Congress Control Number: 2003112328

ISBN 0-8065-2583-5

Contents

Acknowledgments

As always, to my agent, Jake Elwell; to Richard Ember and Bruce Bender at Kensington; to Stephen Frankini, my Zombie partner; to Matt Hale and the old "Five Zombie Club" at the Nine-Oh; to my mother, Patricia Coulombe, who has just discovered Mai Tais; to Silvana, Rich, and Athanasius Cowden-Guido, and to Virginia and Gary Potter for their hospitality; to Stephen MacDonald; and to the Callahans and the Callaghans for their friendship.

RUM

Introduction

We crouched at the bottom of the trench, abject and trembling. I passed the rum bottle round and took a long swig myself. Rum numbs you at times like these. It gives you Dutch courage and a lurching contempt for danger. You die more or less decently; neither whining nor squealing—which is as it should be.

  —Lance-Corporal Thomas A. Owen,
  "Stand To' on Givenchy Road"

There's nought no doubt so much the spirit calms as rum and true religion.

  —Lord Byron, *Don Juan*

*R*um! The word conjures up all sorts of romantic visions: pirates swigging it down after plundering a walled city on the Spanish Main; languid West Indian planters drinking some rum and fruit juice concoction on a shaded verandah in the tropical heat; Horatio Hornblower and his men thankfully quaffing their rum ration; voodoo priestesses pouring it over an altar to nameless gods; colonial men in knee breeches downing flagons of rum in a tavern, in between puffs from clay church-warden pipes; high rollers downing Cuba Libres in a 1948 Havana casino; or latter-day hipsters imbibing Bacardi Black in Manhattan's latest bar-of-the-moment.

Rum has never been more popular than it is right now. There are about fifteen hundred rum labels bottled in over forty countries around the world. Yet, it is a drink whose roots lie deep in the European colonial experience. Prior to Christopher Columbus's sailing, Europeans were confined to drinking wines, ales, and a number of grain- or tuber-based drinks, from which descend our whiskey, vodka, and gin. In the Far East, rice wine ruled, and in the rest of the world, various potations distilled from everything from cactus to palm held sway. But from the time Europeans in the Caribbean learned to create alcohol from sugar cane (the mid-seventeenth century), rum broke all cultural barriers. Wherever the Europeans went, rum went with them. It owed its origins to the nascent colonial effort; it also acted as a catalyst for further expansion. As with all alcohol, it served to "make glad the heart of man." But it rapidly became a medium of trade, a mark of distinction, and, at last, among some of the peoples it helped to subjugate, a sacramental. But this subjugation itself helped form cultures around the world and became internalized. Many the fiery nationalist in a Third World country, eager to eject every sign of European imperialism, would rather die than give up his rum.

The United States, now the greatest power in the world and arguably the most impressive product of that European imperialism, owes much of its foundation to rum. In time, Americans would see rum as a symbol of all alcohol—at least in its destructive guise, as witness the 1989 novel *Rummies* by Peter Benchley, himself a recovering alcoholic. Without the delicious brew, the political and cultural map of the world would be much different; it may be doubted whether it would be better.

Rum is first reported in Barbados about 1650. Made from cane sugar by British planters (at a time when the new settlers fermented all the new products they found, hence pumpkin-seed beer), it was called "kill-devil," "rumbustion," or "rumbullion." This last is claimed by some to be a Devonshire word meaning "a great tumult"; other authorities maintain that it is a Creole French word for a sort of stew (presumably sugar based). According to the 1911 *Encyclopedia Britannica*—acknowledged to be the best of all that worthy source's editions—the word *rum* derives from the Malay *brum* or *bram*; alas, no definition is given for this exotic term. The same authority assures us that the noun has no connection with "rum," meaning strange, as an adjective. Thus a "rum go" has no apparent connection with intoxication. Whether any of these notions are true, by 1667 the stuff was called "rum." So it has been ever since.

Rum made its appearance as the European powers were covering the Seven Seas with ships and their shores with settlers. Wherever the new arrivals cultivated sugar—the Caribbean, the East Indies, Louisiana, Mauritius and adjoining islands, and later Natal and Queensland—rum was made. Given the unhealthful conditions (to whites) in those places, and the expense of importing the more usual European spirits, it was soon beloved by settlers and natives alike. As a rule, the latter preferred rum to their own creations and would trade practically anything to get it.

Thus, rum became the lubricant of slavery. Stepping back two hundred years, the minor kings of Africa's Guinea coast had, for centuries, been large-scale vendors of human beings to their Muslim neighbors across the Sahara and the Sahel. Not simply to such great interior empires as Mali and Songhay, but even as far as the sultanates of North Africa's Barbary Coast would caravans of slaves wend their way. Not only were hereditary slaves up for sale, prisoners taken in warfare were also fair game and provided great impetus for the never ending struggles between the minor West African rulers. To this day, throughout the region descendants of the sold remain slaves in all but name; in a few places, even the name endures.

But this cozy (for the salesmen) arrangement was threatened in the fifteenth century by the inroads of marauding tribesmen like the Tuaregs. Not only did they besiege many great slave markets such as the glorious city of Timbuktu, they also cut all the caravan lines to the North. From Senegal to Cameroon, local chiefs were deprived of markets for their human wares. But the gods of commerce smiled upon them. For just as economic ruin loomed, the year 1482 saw white sails appear off the Guinea coast. At first, the ships were Portuguese; these were joined by the Dutch, French, British, Danes, Swedes, and, at last, even the Prussians and Courlanders. The newcomers set up castles along the seaside to deal initially for gold. But as settlement proceeded in the tropical areas referred to earlier, and as the locals there proved unsuitable as cheap labor, slaves again became the primary export of the Guinea coast. (This was a pattern repeated in later years elsewhere; the Zulus would not work the sugar plantations in nineteenth-century Natal, South Africa, so indentured servants were brought from India. At the same time, the Queensland aborigines did not do well in the cane fields there, so organized bands of forcible recruiters, the notorious "blackbirders," kidnapped South Sea Islanders—"kanaks"—to work them.) But payment was not primarily in salt, the usual medium of exchange in the Sahara, as it had been with the northern sultans; instead, the Europeans paid for the slaves with the rum they brought from the Caribbean.

The beverage became the standard currency of the slave trade. As the seventeenth century wound into the eighteenth, British colonialism, under the guidance of mercantilism, became more specialized. Jamaica, Barbados, and the rest of the British West Indies, unable to manufacture rum on a large scale, concerned themselves in a more concentrated fashion with raising cane and extracting molasses from it. This in turn was exported to New England. The Yankees were possessed of two important things: the closest thing to an industrial base on this side of the Atlantic, and a large shipping fleet. Apart from using molasses in cooking (think of Boston baked beans), they turned it into tens of thousands of barrels of rum.

Thick, fermented, blackstrap molasses (called "dead wash" after fermentation was complete) was fed into primitive "pot stills"—essentially large kettles. There, the wash was heated until the alcohol began to evaporate. The vapor was piped to a second container, where it condensed: this distillate was rum. Although more modern methods became available in the early nineteenth century, premium rums to this day are still made through pot stilling. Unlike other methods, the pot still cannot produce a rum less than 85 percent alcohol; the rum our forefathers quaffed in such huge quantities was potent, indeed.

Alongside Boston, such ports as Salem and Newport were likewise renowned as centers of rum distillery. Rum was featured in virtually all taverns from Georgia to Maine; the colonists in America consumed twelve million gallons of this liquid spirit per year—almost four gallons per capita. New England ships brought it to Africa, and in turn bought and transported the slaves back to the West Indies. Soon, the great-grandfathers of the abolitionists became the largest slavers in the British Empire. We remember Yankee seamen as China traders and whalers; we forget that the slave trade built New England's maritime supremacy. After the American Revolution, this would become even more striking. Abolitionism only caught on among the Yankees after the Constitution forbade the slave trade to U.S. citizens, beginning in 1808.

When money ceased to pour legally into Boston, Salem, and the other ports from the trade in human flesh, New England's conscience discovered the evil it entailed. Even so, many a Yankee ship plied the route illegally afterward. The last slaver to unload its contraband human cargo in American waters arrived in Mobile, Alabama, in 1859. Its homeport was Portland, Maine. In any case, this was the origin of the famed "Triangle Trade," which contributed so much to the wealth of the thirteen colonies. Inspired by mercantilist theory, which saw colonial empires as single economic units working to the benefit of the mother country (itself in turn responsible for their defense), the British Crown sought for ways to derive some profit from the trade that was creating fortunes for colonial merchants, planters, and shipowners. This was all the more pressing a need, since the enormous financial burden of defending the colonies and their trade fell entirely on the British taxpayer. Thus, taxing American trade made complete sense to the Crown. But attempts to tax molasses, after the French and Indian War ended in 1763, contributed mightily to the unrest that culminated in the American Revolution.

Being both portable and relatively unspoilable, rum soon became a staple aboard ship. Where the traditional beer and wine soon lost their flavor, rum retained its palatability over time. And, in a pinch, merchantmen in any port who found themselves short of supplies could convert their excess rum into cash for emergency rations. Seamen swore by its healthful properties. When Captain William Bligh and his seventeen companions were put into an open boat by the HMS *Bounty* mutineers, Fletcher Christian's conscience forced him to leave his former commander three gallons of rum. On their epic journey over thousands of miles of ocean, navigating solely by the stars, the captain issued each of his men a daily teaspoonful of rum. To this daily ration, he attributed not losing a single man. What Bligh perhaps lacked in human relations skills, he made up for in know-how.

Bligh's knowledge of rum came from his experience in the Royal Navy. From the time of their seizure of Jamaica from the Spanish in 1655, British naval commanders issued rum to their sailors, a practice that became codified in the regulations of 1731. The "tot" of rum, as it was called, became as much a part of naval tradition as the sea itself, and bitterly indeed did the tars (sailors) complain when circumstance forced its replacement from time to time with some other liquor. This state of affairs continued until 1970, when, due to the increasingly delicate and technological nature of modern warships, the daily rum ration was abolished. By that time, the British navy had created a special recipe for its rum. (A latter-day entrepreneur saw his opportunity, and now markets said "blend" under the name Pousser's (Purser's) Rum, a great favorite in British pubs.)

Rum was also issued to the British army, and, as noted in the opening quote, it helped many a frightened Tommy go "over the top" in World War I. In 1740, Admiral Edward Vernon, concerned both for the temperance and the health of his men, originated the custom of adding water, sugar, and limes (for combating scurvy, a real scourge in the age of sail) to the rum ration. Given the admiral's nickname of "Old Grogram," from his waterproof boatcoat, this mixture came to be called "grog." This word, too, has entered the language as a synonym for rum.

But if rum was the staff of life for honest seamen, whether merchant or naval, so, too, did it become for their piratical rivals. Blackbeard, Stede Bonnett, and many other buccaneers became legendary for their consumption of the stuff; many a town looted on the Spanish Main and many a hapless galleon owed the peculiar atrocities they suffered to the drunkenness of the pirates who captured them. By the same token, stories abound of pirates caught ashore by tarrying too long in a rum shop. Rum features prominently in such works as *Treasure Island*, with its "yo-ho-ho and a bottle of rum."

In time, rum's empire extended both to the Dutch East Indies (where the strong-tasting Batavia arrack is still made and consumed in large quantities) and Australia, whose aboriginal population call alcohol of any kind "grog" and enthusiastically consume it in "grog shops." From the first settlement of Botany Bay in 1788, the New South Wales Corps, a special unit raised from English roughnecks to guard the new colony (in strikingly similar fashion to the famed Black and Tans of the Irish revolution), claimed a monopoly of rum sales in the settlement. As everyone on hand—troops, convicts, government officials, and, eventually, free settlers—craved the stuff, this gave the "Rum Corps," as the settlers called it, much greater control than provided for in the King's Regulations. As rum served in place of money, it was difficult for any governor to oppose the corps. When one did, at last, in 1806, it was none other than Captain (now Admiral) Bligh, who never walked away from a fight when it came to defending rules. In this case, it was Bligh who prevailed. On November 6, 1810, Bligh's successor, Governor Lachlan Macquarie, signed a contract with Alexander Riley, Garnham Blaxcell, and

D'arcy Wentworth, giving them a monopoly on the import of rum in exchange for their building the "Rum Hospital." Now named Sydney Hospital, it is Australia's oldest health care institution.

In the thirteen colonies as well as French Louisiana, rum became an essential part of life, and figures strongly in accounts of colonial days. In 1686, Rev. Increase Mather, the Puritan parson, wrote, "It is an unhappy thing that in later years a Kind of Drink called Rum has been common among us. They that are poor and wicked, too, can for a penny make themselves drunk." Edward Burke said around 1750, "The quantity of spirits which they distill in Boston from the molasses which they import is as surprising as the cheapness at which they sell it, which is under two shillings a gallon; but they are more famous for the quantity and cheapness than for the excellency of their rum." As it was to do later in Australia, rum served as an essential medium of exchange in a cash-starved environment. New England militia men were sometimes paid in it, as they were in tobacco in the southern colonies. Despite tobacco's hold over Virginia, it was rum that George Washington used to buy his election to the House of Burgesses in 1765. When the molasses taxes struck too close to home, New England farmers began making whiskey out of rye, thus inventing a drink that would serve as a serious rival to rum until the 1960s.

Rum played its role in the American Revolution. The men who dumped East Indian tea in Boston Harbor gathered first at the Green Dragon Inn to rouse their spirits with the drink. Paul Revere did not begin his famous ride until after he had paused at a rum distillery for a few refreshing noggins. Ethan Allen stopped for some rum at the Catamount Tavern en route to capturing Fort Ticonderoga. Rum punch, the favored drink in Philadelphia taverns when the Declaration of Independence was being debated, far outstripped such colonial rivals as ale, scuppernong wine, and gin. It is easy to think of the signers of the Declaration downing their rum when their work was finished. On the Fourth of July, 1778, Washington directed his army to put "green boughs" in their hats, issued them a double allowance of rum, and ordered an artillery salute to celebrate the day. Even as rum brought colonial America an involuntary workforce, it helped to tame the frontier. The first "firewater" given the North American Indians was rum, thus inspiring this song from New Hampshire's Dartmouth College (founded as a school for Indian missionaries by Eleazer Wheelock in 1768):

> O, Eleazer Wheelock was a very pious man;
> He went into the wilderness to teach the Indians
> Eleazer was the faculty, and the whole curriculum
> Was five hundred gallons of New England rum.

However that may be, the destruction wrought on the eastern tribes by rum was incalculable. It destroyed their will to fight and played no small part in the defeat of those few American Indian leaders who were able to organize pan-tribal alliances: King Philip, Pontiac, and Tecumseh. William Penn wrote to the Earl of Sutherland in 1683, "Ye Dutch, Sweed, and English have by Brandy and Specially Rum, almost Debaucht ye Indians all. When Drunk ye most Wretched of Spectacles. They had been very Tractable but Rum is so dear to them." Distribution of liquor—in the beginning almost exclusively rum—was an inevitable prelude to Indian fighting.

Although rum had to share its supremacy with whiskey, it became the archetypal liquor in nineteenth-century America, where prohibitionists inveighed against "demon rum" and the Democrats were accused of favoring "rum, Romanism, and rebellion." About this time, the slang word for a drunkard, "rummy," came into use, although whether this bears any connection to the card game gin rummy is another, apparently unanswerable, question.

During Prohibition, the ships bringing liquor in illegally from overseas were called "rumrunners." Although whiskey and gin gave rum strong competition on the mainland, it remained supreme in the West Indies. The abolition of slavery and the opening of rival

sugar sources around the world forced West Indian planters—
French, Spanish, Dutch, Danish, and British alike—to go into the
commercial manufacture of rum.

By the dawn of the twentieth century, rum makers had created
brews with as much individuality as wines. A whole school of rum
connoisseurs grew up, and great rum houses—such as Cuba's Bacardi and Barbados' Mount Gay—emerged. At the same time, New
England's rum industry vanished. In many of the islands, sugar
plantations were entirely converted into rum manufacturies, thus
revitalizing areas that had reverted to subsistence farming after the
slaves were freed. Some of the oldest planter families were thus
able to retain their importance into the twentieth century. Meanwhile, the West African coast had not been quiet. Around the
European castles or "factories," groups of mixed blood had arisen.
Rooted in their native lands, they nevertheless identified with the
European side of their ancestry. Rum became a symbol of sophistication and heritage among them, even as it continued to play a part
in the petty wars fought between minor kings. After the slave trade
ended, the Europeans transformed their factories into centers of
colonial power, and the kings were reduced to dependents. A native
rum industry developed, often under the leadership of groups of
mixed blood. Since their independence, these rums have begun to
be exported.

Rum entered the ritual life of West Africa. Among the Ga
people of Ghana, it has become an essential part of birth rituals. As
soon as a child is born, the father and his family are immediately
informed, so that they may go and congratulate both the mother
and the infant. The husband then sends a present to all who assisted
at the birth. The present frequently consists of rum, and therefore
is called *Defomo dan*, the hand-washing rum. Rum became an
essential offering to voodoo, Obeah, and Santeria deities. Moreover,
this sacramental aspect of the drink extends to the American South
and to the west of Africa, to say nothing of ethnic enclaves in some
of our major cities. Baron Samedi, the god of death in Haitian

voodoo, is fond of rum and feasting. He always wears a black tail-coat, a top hat and sunglasses, wields a cane, and smokes a cigar or a cigarette in a long holder. He knows all the secrets of magic and is consulted for advice. The questioner makes a blood sacrifice and asks the priest questions to put to the baron. The god often answers in the patterns of rum drops in the dust.

Rum was always a key ingredient in many versions of that quintessential American invention: the cocktail. From rough colonial libations to sophisticated bar drinks like the Zombie, rum has grown with the country, so to speak. In any foreign bar, Americans will be seen ordering the Cuban rums unavailable in their own nation. Certainly, many a drinker will have had, as his or her introduction to the world of cocktails, a rum and coke. Today, rum manufacture remains an international multimillion-dollar business. According to the Distilled Spirits Council and reported in the trade publication *Impact*, rum sales in the United States hit a modern low of eleven million cases in 1994 after a long decline. But since then, they've ticked upward and could hit 16 million cases in 2004. Between 1999 and 2000, sales improved about 8 percent, the largest rate of increase of any spirit.

This book explores all of these topics: rum's origins in the Caribbean; its naval and civilian maritime lore; its place in colonial expansion; its economic and social role in the growth of the United States; its position in the development of the Caribbean, West Africa, and elsewhere; and its continuing importance in the world today. The expansion of Europe all over the world, which is the great fact of the past four centuries, is inextricably linked with the story of rum. Moreover, it remains an important part of globalization, the dominant theme of our time. What few will recognize is that this process had its start in the expansion of Europe and that rum was a key to it all.

Chapter I

~~~~~~~~~~~~~~~~~~~~~~~~~~~~~~~~~~~~

The Birth of "Kill-Devil"

Barbados was not, of course, the first country in which the
spirit we now call rum was made. It is, however, almost
certainly the country where the name rum was invented
and from which the product was first exported. For this
reason it can claim with some justification to be the country
where the rum industry of the Caribbean had its genesis.
—*Barbados Rum Book*

Our story starts on the beautiful Caribbean island of Barbados. Unlike the other West Indian isles, Barbados had lost
its native inhabitants before the first European settlers
arrived. When the Spanish arrived in 1492, the primitive Siboneys
had been driven by the invading Arawaks into the far west of Cuba
and Hispaniola; but the Caribs were fast pressing the Arawaks in
turn, having pushed up the Lesser Antilles, and were poised to
gobble up (figuratively and actually—the word *cannibal* is derived
from them) the Arawaks in Puerto Rico when Christopher Columbus arrived.

There had been Arawaks on Barbados, apparently. But when
the Portuguese arrived in Barbados en route to Brazil in 1536
(where, ironically, they would begin sugar cultivation and pursue

their own version of rum), the island was deserted. The expedition's leader, Pedro a Campos, dubbed the island "Los Barbados" (bearded ones) after the island's bearded fig trees, a variety of fir. It is believed that either the Caribs had already decimated the Arawaks, or else they had fled before being forced into their tormentors' cook pots.

The Spanish found the Arawaks easy targets (for the most part) and so rapidly conquered the Greater Antilles. But after the immediate bloodshed was over, and such figures as Fray Bartolome de Las Casas, O.P., began complaining to the king of Spain about the treatment his new subjects were receiving, the Crown issued a *Cedula Real* decreeing that the Arawaks must not be enslaved. Although this document arrived too late to do much good for a great number of them, it should be pointed out that the Arawaks were not in fact wiped out, as earlier writers have claimed. The Arawaks were to a great degree assimilated; nevertheless, certain areas in Cuba, the Dominican Republic, and Puerto Rico are known even now as "Indio" sections.

But the Lesser Antilles provided the Spanish with a challenge. On the one hand, there was little in the rocky chain of small islands to appeal to the conquerors. But on the other, after 1511 the savage Caribs were seen as a possible source of slave labor. With their characteristic ferocity, the Carib warriors were able to fend off the Spanish from most of their islands; in Barbados, however, they appear to have failed. By the time a Portuguese expedition arrived there in 1536, the Caribs were all gone. It is perhaps ironic that so many Caribs, who had long terrorized the Arawaks before the arrival of the Spanish, ended their days working as slaves in the sight of their former victims.

Thus, it was an empty land that greeted the body of eighty settlers carefully selected by Sir William Courteen in 1627. Sir William had organized a joint-stock company, similar to the ones responsible for the Virginia, Plymouth, and Bermuda colonies. Within two years, the population of the new colony had swelled to about eighteen hundred people. Sir William provided all the necessities and paid regular wages to his settlers. In return, he was to keep all the profits. While this arrangement served well for the short period it lasted, an unscrupulous and debt-ridden nobleman, the earl of Carlisle, was able to convince Charles I of England to grant the island to him. The incompetence of the representatives Carlisle sent to Barbados resulted in the "starving time," an unpleasant period whose nature may be guessed from its name. After a decade of conflicting claims by various parties, Charles I dispatched a royal governor in 1639. He in turn reestablished order and set up the House of Assembly. Functioning from that time to today, Barbados's parliament thus has the distinction of being the fourth oldest in the English-speaking world, after Westminster, Virginia, and Bermuda.

Parish governments were likewise established. These English-style institutions became so firmly rooted in the country that the proposal by the prime minister to establish a republic a few years ago was laughed to scorn by the majority of Barbadians, forcing the prime minister to drop the idea even before organizing a promised referendum. The arrival of many Royalist refugees from England in the wake of the civil war that broke out in 1642 impressed old England's stamp even deeper on the country.

But how were the settlers to make more than a mere subsistence? At first, in common with the older Virginia and Bermuda colonies, the Barbadians tried their hand at raising tobacco on plantations worked by white indentured servants. But this situation would not last. As the Virginia colony had more powerful friends in London than did Barbados, it was able to induce the mother country to levy a higher tariff on Barbadian tobacco than on Virginian. A substitute had to be found, and so it was: sugar.

What oil is to the modern world, so were spices and other agricultural products to our ancestors. Pepper, nutmeg, mace, cinnamon, ginger, tea, coffee, and, after the discovery of the New World, tobacco and cacao all powered national economies, built private fortunes, and, given human nature, fomented atrocities. So it was, for example, that in 1621 the Dutch East Indian Company leader, Jan Piertszn Coen, massacred almost the entire population of the Banda Islands to prevent them from selling nutmeg to the English. Then as now, greed will drive men to incredible lengths; perhaps the best that can be said for the men of that time is that the commodities they were willing to kill for were far tastier than crude oil. At any rate, foremost among these tropical treasures was sugar.

So far as is known, sugar has been cultivated for at least two thousand years; apparently, it was first grown in Asia. From there it was taken by the Arabs (who were very fond of it) to North Africa, and thence to Sicily and Spain.

Sugar was only discovered by Western Europeans as a result of the Crusades in the eleventh century. Crusaders returning home talked of this "new spice" and how pleasant it was. The first sugar was recorded in England in 1099. The subsequent centuries saw a major expansion of Western European trade with the East, including the importation of sugar. It is recorded, for instance, that sugar was available in London at "two shillings a pound" in 1319. This equates to about $100 per kilo at today's prices, so it was very much a luxury.

In the fifteenth century, European sugar was refined in Venice, confirmation that even then when quantities were small, it was difficult to transport sugar as a food-grade product. By 1420, the Portuguese were growing sugar cane in their newly settled island of Madeira. In the same century, Columbus sailed to the Americas, the "New World." It is recorded that in 1493 he took sugarcane plants to grow in the Caribbean. The climate there was so advantageous for the growth of the cane that an industry was quickly established.

There were more exotic uses of sugar in those days than we are used to now. The Medievals had a decided sweet tooth, delighting in mixing sweet and savory tastes in their cooking in a way their modern descendants would find somewhat bizarre. Not merely pastries, but soups, stews and main meat courses found themselves doused in anything that would sweeten them. Mincemeat, originally as much beef and suet as it was fruit, is typical of this sort of thing. Sugar's taste being far more intense than that of the other sweeteners available, it developed its own culinary market. But sugar was used medicinally as well, to lower fever, stop chest pains, stimulate digestion, and prevent dry lips.

So it was that when opportunity offered yet another source for a hungry market, those seeking riches jumped for it. But importing sugar from exotic locales (and eventually from the New World) was not cheap; it became a luxury item for the wealthy. A byproduct of this expense was that it sent those unable to cultivate cane on a quest for another plant that might be grown in a European clime from which sugar or a sugarlike substance might be derived. A breakthrough came in 1590, when Oliver de Serres discovered the sweet taste of beets, heretofore a humble root vegetable on the order of turnips. Almost two centuries would pass, however, until 1747, when A. Marggraf first derived sugar from beets.

Meanwhile, Christopher Columbus brought the crop to Cuba and Hispaniola on his second voyage, in 1493, and the Spanish quickly spread it to Puerto Rico and Jamaica. By 1554, it was being exported from Cuba to Spain. While the planters fermented the sugar cane juice itself (and happily drank it), they generally threw away the molasses (a by-product of processing sugar) or gave it to their slaves and laborers. As the supply of catchable Caribs ran out (the nastiest remained in the Lesser Antilles), and Arawaks were untouchable (due to the *Cedula Real*), the importation of Africans began. Thus was established the connection between sugar and slavery.

Meanwhile, the Portuguese (who initially had a monopoly of the slave trade), established colonies of their own in Brazil, around Pernambuco and Bahia. These were soon given up to sugar plantations as well. While the Brazilian planters did begin to ferment molasses, they wouldn't touch it themselves, but left it for their slaves. It was to Brazil that Barbadians went to learn about sugar and its cultivation, and there that they learned about molasses and its potential. The first canes were brought to the island in 1637 by Pieter Blower, a Dutchman.

Over the next few decades, sugar rapidly supplanted tobacco, and the foundation of a great industry was laid. Barbados was transformed from an island of small farms to one of great plantations. Many Barbadians immigrated to Charleston, South Carolina, thus establishing the foundation of that region's uniqueness (which would in turn be reinforced by French Huguenots). Some of these were the sons of planters, bringing with them sugar to the Carolinas. But those remaining in Barbados settled down to the business of sugar. Large numbers of slaves were imported, who soon outnumbered the whites on the island. Thus was established the Caribbean demographic pattern that dominates the Lesser Antilles to this day.

Sugar production began with the planting itself. From dawn to dusk (with a two-hour noon break), the slaves worked, tilling the soil with hoes; plows would not spread the essential fertilizer evenly enough. This task accomplished, holes were dug at intervals—three thousand for every acre. Cuttings were brought from neighboring fields and planted in the holes. As they grew, more earth was added and great vigilance was exercised against weeds.

At last came the harvest, the laborious "chopping cane." Slaves with cutlasses carefully cut the stalks low, where they were tough, taking care not to damage the delicate buds, which would be used for the following year's crop. The cane was then loaded on carts and brought to the mill, into which it was hand-carried.

As the windmill turned rollers into which the cane was fed, the stalks were crushed and their juice extracted. So crushed, the stalks were then returned to the field and dried, in order to make their reappearance as fuel in the next step. Fuel and juice were then taken to the boiling house, where the juice was strained through clarifiers. From there, the juice was passed into a series of copper pots. Constantly boiling on a flame fed by the dried, crushed stalks, the liquid passed from pot to pot, leaving ever less amounts of impurities in its wake. Eventually, the journey ended in a vat where the hot fluid waited; as it cooled over several days, the sugar crystals emerged. The contents of the vat were then placed into perforated vessels, from which it would drip syrup into troughs below. This in turn would be boiled; from the first boiling emerged light molasses, and from the second, dark.

Of course, the sugar crystals would be sold as they were; there was a tremendous demand for the stuff, which consequently fetched tremendous prices. For a lot of molasses, also, this step in the process was the end of the road. Much cheaper than sugar, molasses was used as a sweetener almost universally—not just in cakes and breads, but in regular cooking as well. Today's Boston baked beans are typical of one manner of molasses cookery, but there were many others.

The most fortunate molasses, however, was set aside, reboiled, and allowed to ferment. Distilled again, it emerged as an alcoholic spirit; at this early stage in its history, the fluid was always dark. The new liquor had a great deal of competition; most genteel Barbadians preferred Madeira and brandy, so at first the fermented extract was drunk by slaves and poor whites who could afford little else. In 1647, Richard Ligon, a Royalist refugee, arrived in Barbados, and it is to him we owe our first accounts of the drink.

According to Ligon, the drink, called at the time "kill-devil," in tribute to its effects, tasted rather unpleasant. Ligon declared of those who drank it that "it lays them asleep on the ground." As with any rotgut liquor, the hangovers were tremendous, causing the sufferers to pray for death. Christian servants were given one or two drams after their daily ten hours of backbreaking toil had ended. It was used as medicine for slaves who suffered from "any weakness or decay in their spirits or stomach."

At this time, kill-devil began to be sold at two shillings and six pence a gallon. It shortly began to be purchased by planters who had no mills for use by their slaves, by taverns in Bridgetown, the island's capital, for their poorer trade, and by visiting ships; it was soon found to keep better than beer or water, the usual drinks given to sailors in those days. According to Ligon, a planter who owned a still could make 30 pounds sterling a week off the stuff. In short order, the island was producing two hundred thousand gallons a year, and every planter who could afford the equipment was turning it out. Into the early twentieth century, the liquor was distilled on virtually all of the sugar plantations in Barbados.

Kill-devil was not an extremely refined name, however; in 1651, the House of Assembly passed a law regarding the drink, which referred to it simply as "this country's spirits." But according to contemporary accounts, it was already being called "rumbullion" or "rumbustion." As noted in the introduction, the origins of this name are unclear. But soon enough it was being called simply "rum," as noted by the pious Puritans of the Connecticut House of Assembly, who in 1654 passed a law ordering the confiscation of "whatsoever Barbados liquors, commonly called Rum, Killdevil, or the like." Its cheapness and near-universal availability caused the authorities to fear that it would impede the populace's ability and willingness to work (similar fears led Mikhail Gorbachev to attempt to suppress cheap vodka during the final years of the Soviet Union—with as much success). But as rum became an ever more profitable commodity, both colonial governments and the Crown gave up any thought of restricting either its use or manufacture; subsequent legislation was more concerned with pouring some of the money that was made into government coffers. Both in nomenclature and travel, rum was on its way.

Soon, the little English settlements on the Leeward Islands were all forsaking tobacco for sugar and rum: on Antigua, St. Kitts, Nevis, and Montserrat, cane was being planted and slaves imported to work it. More English settlers in Demerara (now part of Guyana) followed suit. In 1655, the English conquered Jamaica from the Spanish.

The Spanish had desultorily raised sugar on the island, but followed their usual pattern with regard to its use. For them, sugar itself was the point of cane-raising; any fermented molasses was given to the slaves for their own use. When they decided to evacuate the island, they freed their slaves and bade them continue the fight against the invader. This the new freedmen happily consented to do, and for several centuries continued, under the name of "Maroons," to wage guerilla warfare against Jamaica's new owners. They still maintain autonomous villages today, long after having negotiated a peace with the English Crown. The English imported new slaves from the Guinea Coast of Africa and settled down to grow more sugar and distill more rum. But another event had already occurred during the conquest of Jamaica: the commander of the English fleet that conquered Jamaica, Vice Admiral William Penn (father of the founder of Pennsylvania), had issued to his sailors what would be the first (but far from the last) ration of rum in the history of the soon-to-be-once-again Royal Navy. This event paved the way for rum to see the world.

The English were not the only busy folk at work, however. The French, too, had seen the utility of sugar for their own colonies in the West Indies. Martinique, settled in 1635, had been used by its colonists for the production of cotton and coffee. But sugar soon replaced these crops, for the same reasons it prevailed in the English colonies—it was much easier to grow and the profits from both sugar and rum were higher. The arrival of a priest, Père Du Tertre, in 1650 revolutionized the industry. The zealous missionary, as worried about the settlers' bodies as their souls, built an apparatus for processing the scum and rough syrup. Thus was born Martinique's rum industry. When, twenty-four years later, the French Crown annexed the island of Guadeloupe, it, too, was immediately turned over to sugar production; rum followed in due course.

In 1693, the Dominican monastery of St. Marie in Martinique received a new member: the missionary Père Jean-Baptiste Labat. Like his predecessor, he worried about his flock's economic well-being. The year following his arrival he invented the alembic, a type of still that allowed French planters to make rum using the method employed in manufacturing cognac. This involved the successive reduction and fortification of that region's wines. The result (which produced a smoother, much more delicious beverage) revolutionized and expanded the rum industry throughout the French empire—not just in the West Indies, but in the Indian Ocean as well. A further boost was the conquest of Haiti from the Spanish in 1697.

The Dutch and Danes were not idle either. Acquiring sugar islands of their own (Curaçao, Aruba, and Bonaire for the Dutch; St. Thomas and St. John for the Danes) during the last half of the seventeenth century, they, too, planted sugar and distilled rum. The New Englanders began distilling their own rum out of imported molasses. In the remaining Spanish Antilles, however, the planters continued to make their low-grade fermented cane juice, or *tafia*. They were not, in any case, interested in trade with the outside world (such trade was forbidden to them by law, anyway). On the Spanish-owned mainland, using somewhat different techniques, the locals distilled a cane "brandy" they called *aguardiente*. Meanwhile, Portuguese planters in Brazil, using a number of methods, came up with a dizzying array of fermented cane drinks: *branquinha, cachaça, caninha, purinha,* and *zuninga*, among others. As the seventeenth century neared its close, the whole New World seemed awash in rum.

Meanwhile, the planters in Barbados were not idle. Forced to import not only foodstuffs, but also barrels from New England and Virginia, they could only pay in sugar, molasses, and rum. As already noticed, the thirst for rum in New England led the locals there to begin distilling their own from the Barbados molasses they imported; unavoidably, a rival had been created.

So the Barbadians worked to perfect their drink and make it more palatable. By 1660, they were adding water to it and aging it in wooden casks. Not content with this alone, the planters experimented with using rum in punch. "Punches" had already had an honorable history in England, where wine, brandy, or whiskey was mixed with water, the juice of lemons or limes, sugar, and sometimes other spices; the result would be served cold or hot, depending on the weather. Using the same sorts of recipes, various rum punches were devised, some substituting milk for water. Still, the island's upper crust preferred a drink made from Madeira and lime juice, the famous "Sangaree."

By the 1660s, in St. Lucy, the northernmost parish of Barbados, several small sugar plantations shared a ridge called Mount Gilboa. Named after their respective owners, Tyrell, Jemmott, Jones, Pickering, and Grey, these establishments were producing rum as early as 1663. Within forty years, they had been consolidated into one: Mount Gay. Throughout the succeeding three centuries, Mount Gay Estate has produced its remarkable dark rum, and so may claim the title of having the oldest rum label in the world. As we shall see, it was the forerunner of a chain of establishments that by our time has circled the world. One of the primary movers in that encirclement was His Majesty's Navy, as we shall see in the next chapter.

Mount Gay Rum Punch
Barbados Recipe

750 milliliter Mount Gay Rum
   Eclipse Barbados
20 ounces lime juice
26 ounces simple syrup (see
   below)

3 ounces angostura bitters
1 ounce nutmeg
40 ounces water

Mix together, shake well, and serve on ice.

Simple Syrup: Dissolve 2 cups sugar in 1 cup water, and bring to boil on stove—the longer it boils, the stronger the syrup. Bottle and save for use.

Chapter 2

~~~~~~~~~~~~~~~~~~~~~~~~~~~~~

Grog and the Navy

The rum in the Navy was unlike anything available ashore
both in taste and in strength, although a couple of brands
came close, in taste only. Each day at noon before dinner
and thus on an empty stomach, we were given half a gill
(one eighth of a pint) of neat rum which was in the region
of 150 degrees proof. This was watered down by two
parts of water to one of rum making three eighths of a pint
of liquid at around 50 degrees proof which is not much
weaker than a tot bought in a pub but certainly a lot more.
After ten years of drinking Navy rum I became quite
accustomed to it and after a night's boozing on Nelson's
Blood I got up to carry out my duties with no more than a
raging thirst. Of course maybe the fact that I had to do my
duty may have had something to do with not having a
pounding head.
—James Buckley, Royal Navy sailor, 1953–1966

The opening up of the globe by the Spanish, Portuguese,
French, English, Dutch, and Danes had a number of unforeseen results. Among them was the necessity of defending
the new colonies from native resistance and above all from rival
colonial powers. This required the maintenance of secure lines of

communication by sea from the motherland. In turn, such maintenance meant the expansion of the national navies from coastal protection forces to fleets capable of spanning the globe.

During the fifteenth century, Europe had not seen such an effort
since the days when the Roman Imperial Navy turned the Mediterranean into "Mare Nostra." Having destroyed piracy in Roman
waters, the navy made possible a perfectly modern transport of
goods and people from Spain to Syria. This transportation was the
key to the spread of Christianity from the Palestine to Europe, as
the voyages of St. Paul make clear.

The fall of the empire in the West, however, and the barbarian
invasions meant a great blow to European maritime expertise; the
lack of naval power in the West (and its increasing debility in the
East) allowed the great success of Vikings and Muslims alike in
extracting the maximum in plunder and slaves from the hapless
inhabitants of medieval Europe. In time, the Vikings would convert
to Christianity and leave off their raiding. But the depredations of
the Barbary pirates continued until the French seized their last nest
in Algiers in 1830. Of course, as good Muslims, these last would
have nothing to do with rum or any other alcohol, unlike the European pirates (whom we will examine in Chapter Four).

Slowly, gradually, through the Middle Ages, the maritime
nations of Europe regained naval knowledge. Here, too, it was a
question of safeguarding commerce; Venice and Genoa were the
first to develop blue-water fleets, precisely to safeguard their merchantmen trading with the Near East from the North African cor-
sairs. The gradual expulsion of the Moors from the Iberian
Peninsula meant that Spain and Portugal would at last have the
leisure time to develop navies of their own. As Portuguese soil was
the first to be entirely freed from the Moors, the Portuguese had a
head start. To the embattled Iberians, such efforts were seen not
merely as commercial ventures, but also as a continuation of their
struggle against the Muslims. It is no coincidence that Prince Henry
the Navigator, founder of the first modern naval school and patron

of the opening explorations of the West African coast, was also grand master of the Order of Christ, a body of knights instrumental in expelling the Moors from Portugal.

Before Christopher Columbus, the Spanish and Portuguese had annexed the Canaries (off the coast of Morocco) on the one hand, and Madeira, the Azores, and the Cape Verdes (in the Mid-Atlantic) on the other. French and English fishermen ranged over to the Grand Banks, off Newfoundland, in search of cod and other fish. All this shipping, to say nothing of the ships of various nations plying the Baltic, the Mediterranean, and the North Sea, required liquid refreshment for the sailors involved. Water, of course, would be provided, but kept in casks below decks, it easily became algae- and disease-ridden, even as it did ashore. Far more precious, to seamen and landlubbers alike, was alcoholic refreshment.

This was no problem for the French, Iberians, and Italians, for their countries had been blessed with plentiful vineyards; while wine might lose some flavor over a long voyage, it would keep. But the northern nations, including the English, relied on beer. While not a problem when the Royal Navy's major concern was to safeguard the English coast, the budding requirements of the seventeenth century to safeguard England's West Indian and American colonies presented a problem. Beer simply would not keep.

Increasing military commitments during the seventeenth century made it all the more essential that the navies of all the imperial powers be better organized and supplied than ever in their histories. Any number of experiments in control and supply were attempted. It is easy to forget, after several centuries' passage, just how revolutionary these efforts were: from them emerged the naval organization common to all nations today. Improvements in ship-to-ship signaling, standardization of uniforms, equipment and organization, and increase of central oversight over the individual ship and captain, turned bands of independent vessels into coordinated fleets.

These nascent blue-water navies would soon be faced with a great challenge. The sevententh century saw what was in reality the first world war (the War of the Grand Alliance; called "King William's War" in North America), involving the combatants in battles not just in Europe, but also in the West Indies, Africa, India, North America, and in all the seas between. Initially, as subsequent world wars would be, this conflict owed its origins to purely European politics. Louis XIV of France had steadily gobbled up pieces of western Germany; moreover, he had fought a war with the Dutch. In response, the Holy Roman Emperor, Leopold I, formed in 1686 the League of Augsburg. This comprised various German states, (notably Bavaria and the Palatinate), as well as Sweden and Spain, both of which countries possessed German territories. The League represented a pan-German attempt to forestall French expansion (although its necessity showed how flimsy the unity of the Holy Roman Empire—as Germany was called then—had become since the end of the Thirty Years' War in 1648).

Taking advantage of three circumstances—his alliance with King James II of England, Scotland, and Ireland; the absence of Emperor Leopold and his great commander Prince Eugene of Savoy from Germany (they were off in Hungary, liberating that country from the Turks); and a succession dispute that broke out in the Palatinate—Louis attacked the latter country, hoping to add it to France. It seemed like an easy victory.

Alas, then as now, wars easily entered into can have unforeseen consequences. The Catholic James II was overthrown by his son-in-law, the Dutch ruler William of Orange; this constituted the last successful invasion of England. James fled to France, and the invading prince took the title William III.

Worse was to follow for Louis the next year, although he did manage to devastate the Palatinate. James's supporters in Scotland were defeated; and a new coalition against the French was formed, consisting of the Pope, the Augsburg allies, William's England, and the Netherlands. It was dubbed the "Grand Alliance." Savoy and Leopold's Spanish Habsburg cousin later joined as well, and the war began in earnest.

In an attempt to keep William from landing an army on the Continent, Louis supported James's attempt to retake Ireland. Although at first successful (the Jacobite armies soon reduced William's hold on the island to the besieged cities of Belfast, Derry, and Inniskilling), the arrival of the usurper himself resulted in the relief of the three towns and the defeat of James at the Battle of the Boyne on July 12, 1690. James fled to France soon after, and although it took two years to completely reduce Ireland, this date is seen as the commencement of Protestant rule there (and, as such, duly celebrated each year by the Orange Order). Certainly, it was the beginning of a long and dreary chapter in Irish history. But when Pope Alexander VIII, William's ally, received the news of the victory, he sang a solemn Te Deum. This both reflects a 180-degree turn from Papal intervention in the Thirty Years' War (when Innocent VIII had supported France, Sweden, and the German Protestants against the Habsburgs), and the abiding ironies of history.

Notwithstanding this setback, the naval war in Europe first saw French victory at Beachy Head in 1690; this advantage was lost, however, by the English victory of La Hogue two years later. The latter engagement saw the first use (in this case, by the English) of fireships—old warships filled with gunpowder and sent, ablaze, against enemy vessels.

On European land, however, the French had it all their own way. Louis and Vauban took Namur in 1692; two years previously Marshal Luxembourg was victorious at Fleurus over the Dutch and at Steenkerke (1692) and Neerwinden (1693) over William III; while the duke of Savoy was defeated at Marsaglia by Catinat that same year. Yet another French army entered Catalonia.

The war was not confined to Europe, however. In America (where the English colonists called the conflict "King William's War"), hostilities broke out between the English and French on Hudson Bay; the Iroquois (allied to the English) and the French fought along the entire area from the Mohawk to the St. Lawrence.

The French and their Indian allies under Governor Frontenac attacked the English colonies all along their northern frontier, raiding Schenectady on February 9, 1690 (in reprisal for the men of that town massacring the women and children of Lachine, Quebec), Salmon Falls, New Hampshire on March 27, and Falmouth (later called Portland), Maine, on July 31. Their Abenaki allies attacked on their own the towns of Wells, Maine (June 21, 1692), Durham, New Hampshire (June 23, 1694), and Haverhill, Massachusetts (March 15, 1697). On the western frontier, Frontenac attacked the Iroquois steadily during the years 1693–96. The only successful colonial operation was the seizure of Port Royal on May 11, 1690 by Massachusetts troops under Sir William Phips (1651–1695). This being recaptured by the French a year later, Sir William's attempt to seize Quebec was foiled, while Frontenac chided the English for overthrowing their rightful king. In the end, Sir William was made governor of Massachusetts just in time to deal with Salem's witch hysteria of 1692. Elsewhere the French contented themselves with seizing most of the English forts on Hudson Bay.

But the colonial action was not confined to North America. In 1689, the French, under Admiral de Grasse, attempted unsuccessfully to seize the Dutch colony of Surinam on the South American coast. That same year, the English on St. Kitts invaded the French sector (the island was divided between them) led by General Codrington. Victorious, he expelled eighteen hundred French settlers to Martinique. The following year, in order to establish a stronghold in Bengal, India, the English under the leadership of John Charnock founded Ft. William at Calcutta. In 1696, under Admiral de Gennis, the French made another unsuccessful swipe at Surinam.

Despite their setbacks overseas, the French went from triumph to triumph in Europe, knocking Savoy out of the war in 1696. But this blow to the Alliance was offset by France's financial straits. Although a wealthy nation, France's government was not sufficiently modern to squeeze the kind of money out of their subjects that the English and Dutch could out of theirs. Both sides were exhausted, and so in 1697 the combatants signed the Treaty of Ryswick. Louis XIV was forced to surrender most of the German territories he had annexed since 1679, with the exception of Strasbourg. Commercial concessions were granted to the Dutch, Savoyard independence was recognized, and William III was acknowledged king of England (except by the Pope, who held his treatment of his Catholic subjects against him). In the colonial world, the status quo was recognized, except that Spain gave the western third of the Caribbean island of Hispaniola, St. Domingue (today's Haiti), to France. This last act would have enormous repercussions on the history of rum, sugar, and slaves.

The War of the Grand Alliance solved little, but it did establish a pattern which would hold through the series of wars ending in 1815: France, under different regimes and in pursuit of differing ideologies, would attempt to take hegemony over Europe. Great Britain (as we must call the country after the union of parliaments of England and Scotland in 1707) would attempt to foil this development, using an ever-changing cast of allies. So the British and Austrians faced off against the French, Spanish, and Prussians in the War of Spanish Succession (1702–13), (called Queen Anne's War in America), and the same cast fought in the War of Austrian Succession (1740–48) (King George's War). In 1755, Great Britain and Prussia became allied in response to the rapprochement between France and Austria, which became a formal alliance the next year. The Seven Years' War (the French and Indian War in America) began shortly thereafter, although fighting had already broken out between the British and the French in North America. Despite the great change in alliances, the pattern of intercontinental warfare, with French land victories in Europe followed by bankruptcy, remained. The War of the Austrian Succession had had its own local name in India, the First Carnatic War; not surprisingly, there the Seven Years' War was dubbed the Second Carnatic War. France lost almost all of her North American possessions, however, thus setting the stage for the American Revolution—ironically, her one victory in almost a century of world wars.

As these conflicts progressed, technology grew, civil and military administration developed, and the shape of the nation state we know today emerged. Through trial and error, the foundations of modern naval and military science were being laid.

One of these trials, as noticed in the last chapter, was the distribution of rum to his men by Vice Admiral William Penn in the Jamaica campaign of 1655. Within a very short time, the rum ration replaced beer to a great extent on all the Royal Navy's ships in the Atlantic and West Indies (in the Indian Ocean, rum was supplemented by rice-derived arrack). This both pleased the crews and radically increased the already enormous demand for rum, providing yet another boom for England's West Indian colonies, generating unheard-of fortunes for the planters, and creating a voracious appetite for the acquisition of yet more sugar islands on the part of the English government.

Life aboard ship in those days was considered barbarous in the extreme. Sir Winston Churchill's dismissal of naval traditions as being merely "rum, sodomy, and the lash" were echoed by Samuel Johnson, who declared prison preferable to sea duty, since in the former case one need not fear drowning and generally met a better class of people.

There was a certain amount of truth to Johnson's gibe. A lack of technology and infrastructure meant that in the seventeenth and eighteenth centuries, it was difficult to maintain a large standing navy. But throughout the eighteenth century, as the War of Spanish Succession was followed by that of the War of Jenkins' Ear, the War of Austrian Succession, the Seven Year's War, the American Revolution, the French Revolution, and the Napoleonic Wars, the navy had to rapidly expand to face the French and allied fleets, and then even more rapidly demobilize on cessation of hostilities. The result was a veritable migraine headache in terms of men and supplies.

To raise the requisite numbers of sailors, the Crown looked to prisons; but this fertile supply area was often not enough to fight world wars in an age of sail. So arose both the law of assessing various towns (particularly ports) a certain number of men, and, most notably, the press gang. The vision of hapless drinkers being rushed off from taverns (or waking up aboard ship after a drugged drink) and finding themselves sailors in His Majesty's Navy has worked itself into the popular mind. Furthermore, with commissions being bought, naval officers were often incompetent. Moreover, in an age that did not understand hygiene, limb wounds often meant amputation, and amputation often meant death. With unwilling crews leading hard and dangerous lives, discipline was (and perhaps had to be) brutal. As such, floggings were given capriciously, even for trivial offenses.

Into this world, rum came like a healing balm. As Jamaica, Antigua, and Barbados were developed into permanent bases, their local products became ever more prized by the sailors. But in the years leading up to the outbreak of the War of Jenkins' Ear against Spain in 1739, it was noted that drunkenness was responsible for perhaps as many griefs as the griefs it cured. Drinking their rum neat after twice daily rations of it, the men would often get violent or derelict in their duties, so floggings multiplied.

At the same time, the many wars and the need to prepare for them had begun to create a new class of professional officers. Perhaps the best known of these was Edward Vernon. Of good background and well educated, he was loved by his men for his humanity toward and affection for them; his command respected him also for his prowess as a tactician. His career was made by an engagement during the War of Jenkins' Ear.

Few conflicts have ever had such silly origins as did this one. Back in 1731, a Spanish coast guard sloop off Havana boarded the English privateer *Rebecca* as it voyaged to London from Jamaica. The Spanish were unable to find evidence of privateering (although that is in fact what the ship's Captain, Robert Jenkins, had been doing, by his own later admission). Jenkins claimed that he had been repeatedly tortured, and that a Lieutenant Dorce sliced off his ear with his cutlass and told him to take it to King George as a token of what the Spanish intended for the king. Whatever the truth of this tale, seven years later Jenkins was invited by a certain party of war-mongers to display his pickled ear to Parliament, thereby inflaming British and American colonial opinion against Spain. Tensions were already high between the two countries: Despite the nominal peace between them, privateers like Jenkins preyed on Spanish shipping, British loggers and others had illegally squatted on the Honduras coast, and border disputes between British Georgia and Spanish Florida were perpetual. The government of Hugh Walpole duly if reluctantly declared war, and the press could not resist naming the war for its theatrical beginning. It would go on until being absorbed by the War of Austrian Succession.

Vernon was a vice admiral at the time, and led a fleet in the suc-cessful attack on Porto Bello, Panama. This was a key target for the British (as we must now call them, England having united Parlia-ments with Scotland in 1707), because it was the major entrepôt for the Spanish treasure fleet. Following the town's capture, Vernon did two remarkable things: he forbade molestation of the town's inhabitants, and he directed that the enormous plunder of the place be divided equally among the crews of the ships, in violation of contemporary regulations. Such was the magnitude of his victory that the Admiralty ignored the infraction. But it also made him a demigod to the average sailor. He would need this status when enacting his next reform.

As already mentioned, sailors took their rum ration neat, that is, a half-pint in one gulp. This led to many accidents in the rigging, as well as all sorts of problems ashore, on those rare occasions when shore leave was granted (the presence of so many pressed men in the ranks ensured that a proportion would not return to the ship once safely back on dry land). One alternative was the ferrying of prostitutes aboard ship whenever a fleet docked in a harbor—a practice that met with little favor on Vernon's part. In any case, in the aftermath of his victory at Porto Bello, Vernon turned his attention to the rum question.

While anchored at Port Royal, Jamaica, on August 21, 1740, Vernon ordered that henceforth the half-pint of rum should be mixed with a quart of water (although the men were to receive still every drop due to them), and the sailors were encouraged to further mix sugar and lime and lemon juices with the potation. This was done to prevent scurvy, that age-old plague of long distance sailing (use of limes for this purpose by British sailors led to all Englishmen being dubbed "limeys"). As a further health precaution, he ordered that water be taken from the casks and stored in open scuttled butts (half-barrels); not only would it be fresher and sweeter, but also the men would have access to it at all times. From their congenial practices while drawing water, these sailors gave the name "scuttlebutt" to gossip.

Another slang word was to emerge from these new regulations of Vernon's. His habitual outer garment was a waterproof cloak made of a stiff and heavy material called "grogram." From this habit, he himself came to be called by his men "Old Grogram." They swiftly applied this to the drink for which he was responsible, "grog." Thus was coined the naval term that has survived to our own day. Moreover, due to the nautical nature of the first settlement there (to say nothing of the prominent role played by naval rum in the country's history), grog passed into Australian speech eventually as an expression for any liquor—a term surviving today among the Aborigines of that country, whose addiction to it is proverbial. As with many native peoples, they had nothing so intoxicating before the Europeans arrived, and alcoholism quickly became (and remains) one of the chief causes of death among them.

Another colonial connection may be tied to Vice Admiral Vernon. Among his troops were three thousand volunteers from the thirteen North American colonies; one of these was the half-brother of George Washington, Lawrence. Upon his return to

Virginia, Lawrence named his new estate after his old commander, "Mount Vernon." This was also the first time in which such colonials were called "Americans," rather than "Provincials."

In any case, only the great esteem in which his men held him allowed Vernon to impose these new rules with little unrest. The results were encouraging, and Vernon went on to regularly petition the Lords of the Admiralty to apply his reforms to the entire navy. At last, in 1756 new regulations were issued ordering all the ships in the navy to mix rum with water. The call to "Up Spirits" sounded aboard Royal Navy ships for more than two centuries thereafter. The mixture seamen used for grog was named by compass points. Due North was pure rum and due West was water alone. WNW would therefore be one-third rum and two-thirds water, NW would be half and half, etc. If a seaman had two "nor-westers," he'd had two glasses of half rum and half water. But it would be some years before the Admiralty would condescend to call the drink grog officially, no doubt in part because Vernon's blunt language to his superiors (which in the end condemned him to a shore command, despite his record) did not please them.

In any case, twice daily the jolly tars would gather for their grog ration, an event that inevitably made them jollier. Of course, such issue only occurred after the still-continued beer rations were exhausted; thus, grog was reserved for warships on duty away from home waters. But of course, these were precisely the locations of the great British naval victories of the eighteenth and early nineteenth centuries: Cape St. Vincent, Les Saintes, Trafalgar, and the rest. Throughout this history, grog became an integral part of the Royal Navy's identity and tradition. Manliness as well as solace were sought from it by sailors, and its consumption was a jealously guarded right. But various thinkers constantly questioned grog's utility from the standpoints of health, efficiency, and morality (at first concerned with drunkenness as giving rise to illicit behavior, it came on the part of the "high minded" to be seen as an evil in itself). Successive naval regulations would fiddle with proportions of rum to water, amounts served, serving times, and the like. But at bottom, both government and the Admiralty feared to toy too much with the grog tot for fear of mutiny or worse. Certainly, whatever might be said, the period when the tot was issued was also the time of the Royal Navy's greatest glory. If it did the sailors any harm, it would be hard to prove by their record in wartime.

Rum played its role in most mutinies, not least the most famous of all, that on HMS *Bounty*. William Bligh, noted in popular legend as a cruel martinet, had been born in Cornwall in 1754. He served as master of the HMS *Resolution* under Captain James Cook, on that noted explorer's third voyage, in the course of which they discovered Hawaii. After Cook was murdered by the locals, Bligh skillfully sailed the ship back to Britain.

In 1786, he was seen as the obvious choice for captain (although he was in fact a lieutenant) when Joseph Banks, president of the Royal Society, planned an expedition to Tahiti. Banks had sailed to that island with Captain Cook back in 1768, and there had discovered the breadfruit. A great food source for the Tahitians, Banks felt that it could do as well for the slaves on the West Indian plantations. Bligh had married the daughter of the Isle of Man customs collector; as a result, he was known by the gentry on that island. A number of sons of such families volunteered for the voyage: two of these were Peter Heywood, fourteen, and Fletcher Christian, twenty-three. The *Bounty*'s mission was sail to Tahiti and gather breadfruit pods. These duly taken, the ship was to sail to Australia and map the Endeavour Straits, after which they were to move on to the West Indies and offload the pods.

Bligh was a short man and a strict disciplinarian, with very little tact. But he was also an extremely able navigator and kept abreast of all the latest developments in medical science. Aware of the necessity of exercise, he ordered obligatory dancing (strange as it may seem, this was a major reason for the sailor's hornpipes and reels we are familiar with today); fearful of scurvy, he added lime juice and sauerkraut to the ship's diet. Having set sail in December 1787, the *Bounty* arrived at Tahiti on Halloween, 1788.

Although it took a mere six weeks to gather the required bread-fruit, by that time the winds had turned against them. Bligh resolved to wait in Tahiti for favorable weather. The result was that the journey was not resumed until April 4, 1789. While this prolonged stay had allowed Bligh to study Tahitian culture rather carefully, it had also ruined his men's discipline. The Tahitian women had been free with their favors, and the return to shipboard routine, coupled with Bligh's severe temper (made even more so by his men's behavior on the island), raised tension to the proverbial fever pitch. On April 24, after Christian had been accused of dis-obedience and cowardice by the captain, and after the crew had guzzled its rum, the famous mutiny broke out. Bligh and seventeen loyal crew members were set adrift. But Fletcher and the other mutineers' consciences got the better of them, and they placed three gallons of rum in the boat.

Freed of their captain, the mutineers sailed on to Tubuai, where they lived until their demands on the local women caused the resi-dent warriors to drive them off. Then they returned to Tahiti; from thence, Christian with eight mutineers and eighteen Tahitians set off to find an uninhabited island where they might be safe from the Royal Navy.

In January 1790, they reached Pitcairn Island. Christian made his home there with his Tahitian "wife," Maimiti, her English name being Isabella, named after his cousin, Isabella Curwen. Christian wanted the land to be divided into nine equal parts (the number of the mutineers) and ordered that Christianity was to be observed. He used to vent his grief in a cave, still called Christian's Cave. Fletcher Christian died on Pitcairn of natural causes on October 3, 1793.

By the time naval authorities found the island in 1808, all but one of the remaining mutineers and the Tahitian men had murdered each other. The lone survivor dwelt with four Tahitian women and the many offspring of the slaughtered men. From these few people descend the inhabitants of both Pitcairn and Norfolk Islands (the latter lying between Australia and New Zealand, and having served as a refuge when Pitcairn became overcrowded). The bloodiness of their early history instilled a love of order and discipline in the mutineers' descendants: Pitcairn remains Britain's only colony in the Pacific, and Norfolk (now a territory of Australia) voted over-whelmingly to retain the monarchy in the 1999 referendum, which defeated the creation of an Australian republic.

Meanwhile, Bligh and his men sailed by the captain's dead reck-oning west to Australia, mapping the Endeavour Straits in accord with the original mission. Key to this superhuman feat was the daily administration of a teaspoonful of rum to each crewmember; it was in fact credited by both contemporaries and historians with preserv-ing the lives of all hands on the forty-one-day voyage. Back in Eng-land, Bligh was rewarded with a promotion to captain (he had in fact still been a lieutenant all through his adventures) and given the command of HMS *Providence*. At the helm of this ship, he returned to Tahiti, gathered the breadfruit, and duly brought it to the West Indies. Nor did he stint on that crew's grog rations. The breadfruit, in its turn, became the staff of life that Joseph Banks foresaw.

Captain Bligh, on his second voyage to Jamaica and St. Vincent in 1793, brought breadfruit trees, which were planted in the Hope Botanical Gardens in Kingston and in government botanical gar-dens in other parishes of Jamaica; he planted other trees in the St. Vincent Botanical Gardens. Intended to provide a supply of cheap food for slaves, breadfruit was unpopular for the first fifty years and was fed to pigs. But in time it caught on and is used today for puddings, drinks, wines, chips, and flour and for potato-like salads. The blossoms are used to make tasty preserves. Thus, the West Indies gained an important food source in return for their gift of rum to the world.

Although naval regulations became ever more standardized during the late eighteenth century, precise application of those reg-ulations continued to vary from squadron to squadron and from ship to ship. Among the practices pretty much left up to the discre-tion of each captain was the proportion of water to rum when mixing grog. Admiral Vernon had ordered that a half-pint of rum be added to a quart of water (four to one). In time, this was decreased to three to one.

Rum aquired the nickname "Nelson's Blood" after his victory— and death—at Trafalgar in 1805. Lord Nelson's body was placed in a barrel of rum for preservation. It is said that when the sailors learned of this, they drank the rum. From that time on, grog was also called "Nelson's Blood."

After the Napoleonic Wars, when Britain found itself possessing not only new West Indian lands and extended tracts of land in India, but also of the Cape, various Indian Ocean islands, and Australia, the Royal Navy had to become more professional and well organized. Part of the problem facing the peacetime navy was the ever more commented on problem of drunkenness with both officers and men. Already the problem had been attacked, during the conflict, by Admiral Lord Keith, who advocated a reduction in the rum ration. His voice was echoed by many others. At last, in 1824 the Admiralty ordered that the rum ration was to be halved to a quarter-pint, with the difference made up in tea and cocoa. Moreover, sailors' pay was to be raised by two shillings and their meat ration increased as compensation. Despite widespread fears, the men accepted the change more or less without complaint. Slowly, however, old ways returned.

As the navy continued to centralize, the Lords of the Admiralty acquired more centralized control of the navy's various supporting facilities. In 1832, new reforms passed control of the various civilian-supporting departments—including victualing (the supplying of food)—to the Admiralty. The latter operation was taken over by a sea lord with the new title of controller victualing, who ran every aspect of the sailors' food and drink, which included determining the strength, color, and taste of naval rum. From this time forward, the navy would have a more or less standard style and taste of the beverage unique to itself; moreover, with the ending of beer rations the previous year—even for ships in British home waters—rum was now supreme aboard ship.

Already in 1784, exclusive brokering rights for rum to the Royal Navy had been awarded to James Man, a merchant trading with the West Indies. He and his sons after him imported the liquor and sold it to the navy; naval officials in turn had it transported to the vats at the newly built naval yards in Gosport and Devonport. So pleased was the navy with the Man family's work that the rum brokerage remained in their hands as long as the service required the drink. As the Royal Navy ballooned in the nineteenth and twentieth centuries, the Man operation expanded and became as worldwide as the force it served by dealing in goods from around the British Empire. Incorporated in 1860 as E. D. and F. Man (being the initials of the family members then in charge), the company survives today—sort of.

Operating as a partnership until 1994, the renamed Man Group was floated on the London stock exchange; in addition to trading in molasses and spices (having left the rum trade when its principal client, the Royal Navy, did), Man had also gone heavily into financial services and general investments. But in 2000, the Man Group separated into two parts: the financial services division retained its listing on the stock exchange as Man Group PLC; and the agricultural products division returned to the status of a private company owned by its employees under the name ED&F Man Holdings Ltd.

While the mid-nineteenth century progressed, the ritual of taking one's rum tot became standard. Sailors had a particular love for King William IV, the "sailor king." Being the second son of George III, the duke of Clarence (as William was then called) was not expected to inherit the throne; he was thus allowed to pursue an active naval career. As a midshipman, William had visited New York City during the American Revolution, the first member of the Royal family to travel to North America. During his stint as a naval commander, he shared his men's travails and earned their affection.

After his brother, George IV, died without offspring, William IV was crowned king and the mutual regard between the new sovereign and his navy continued. When the ration-drawing routine became formalized, the sailors would doff their hats in honor of "their" king before drawing grog from the tub. On the tubs themselves it soon became standard to inscribe the words "The King God Bless Him," which were (and are) the standard phrasing for the loyal toast after dinner.

It is a long-standing custom that in officers' messes aboard British ships this same loyal toast is offered seated (as opposed to standing, which is the case at similar functions ashore, and for military and civilian dinners). There are several theories proposed for this strange custom. One is that William IV (as lord high admiral, before his accession) himself bumped his head on one occasion, while rising for the toast; another version ascribes this occurrence to Charles II. A third variant declares that George IV, when serving as prince regent, was at a dinner aboard one of the naval vessels. as the officers prepared to rise, the regent supposedly said, "Gentlemen, pray be seated, your loyalty is above suspicion."

While such ritual prevailed (and continues to do so) in officer territory, the men were summoned to the tub by the call "Up Spirits." This was played on the bosun's pipe. Supposedly, the call itself is older than the navy; it has been alleged that the call goes back to the days of the Phoenicians, about 1200 B.C. Since so many essential orders were played on the bosun's pipe, no one was allowed to whistle while aboard ship, for fear of a whistled tune being confused with a command. The one exception in the days of sail was the ship's cook, who was expected to whistle while making "plum duff," the Royal Navy's traditional raisin pudding. This would prove that he was not eating raisins on the sly!

In 1850, in response to recurring complaints of the ill effects of drunkenness among the men, the Admiralty decided to reduce the rum tot yet again. It was to be cut by half, and the noon ration was eliminated. There would be compensation in food and cash, and more money for those willing to forego the tot completely. Underage sailors (those under the age of twenty), who had no choice in the matter, lost their rum as a group.

But for the rum drinkers who remained, the Admiralty needed to ensure that the remaining eighth of a pint was the best possible.

From this time on, the Man Company began to blend Trinidad and Demerara rums in a particular formula that pleased both naval noses and palates. Seamen, however, preferred dark to light rum; this was a bit difficult, since the same refining processes that produced superior taste and bouquet turned out a pale product. A solution was found by adding caramel and/or burned sugar to the brew. The exact blend was a closely guarded secret; as a result, sailors always complained about civilian rums!

Another major reform that followed in 1851 was the regularization of the office of purser aboard ship. This functionary, who time out of mind had been responsible for provisioning the crew, was a hated individual. Familiarly called the "pusser" (through the same naval linguistic alchemy that turned the forecastle into the "foc'sle" and the boatswain into the "bosun"), he was often suspected, since he was an independent agent, of making his money from commissions by siphoning off supplies and selling them. But in 1851, he was given a regular salary and placed under the Admiralty. Now called the paymaster, he became a regular wardroom officer; all of the abuses connected with the position swiftly disappeared. Henceforth, the rum ration would never be watered more than rules required.

In the wake of new regulations and the Crimean War, the Royal Navy gradually became a modern, all-volunteer force. Floggings were discontinued and provision was made for libraries and education aboard ship. Whatever the position of sodomy might have been, the lash was gone and rum was tamed, as Britain's imperial noon progressed. As sail made way for steam, protection of far-flung possessions required that coaling stations be available wherever possible. Securing such (often over the objections of local rulers) became a paramount objective of British foreign policy. Permanent squadrons were deployed in the East Indies, the China Sea, and the Cape of Good Hope. At the same time, the concern for morals which characterized the Victorian era was extended to seamen. Whereas in earlier times, chaplains were few and a ship's

captain conducted Sunday and burial services himself, their numbers began to multiply. In 1827 the senior chaplain at Greenwich
Hospital was recognized as "Head of the Naval Chaplains" with
the title Chaplain of the Fleet. This rank was made equivalent to a
rear-admiral. The title and scope of his authority was widened in
1888 to Chaplain of the Fleet and Inspector of Naval Schools. Shipboard education increased tremendously, both in quality and in for-
mality of curriculum. Seafaring became a respectable profession,
and the navy, as guardian of the empire, became more popular
among the civilian population. Naval officers became heroes in the
popular mind.

As such, more began to be expected of them. Above all, their
drinking habits came under serious scrutiny. Since officers were
able to drink in private, the temptation to overindulge was always
present. Moreover, in addition to the rum ration they shared with
the enlisted men, wines were served in their messes. The result was
a high proportion of alcohol-related offenses in officer country. At
length, in 1881 the Admiralty deprived commissioned officers of
their rum ration. Warrant officers, who had often risen through
the ranks, managed to hold on to theirs until 1918. But at last the
inverted snobbery that demanded better behavior from officers
prevailed in their case as well.

But the common seamen were not forgotten by the forces of temperance either. As wooden ships changed to iron and then steel,
Jack Tar was offered an ever increasing set of cash compensations
for renouncing his tot. Amazingly, although alcohol-inspired
offenses continued to decline, a large core of sailors preferred booze
to money. Even so, rum was plainly in decline after the advent of
the twentieth century.

Luckily for the liquor (and for E. D. and F. Man, presumably),
World War I gave naval rum a new lease on life. The combination
of restricted shore leave and the deployment of a large number of
warships in the cold North Sea helped to reverse the gradual
decline of seamen's rum consumption since the new century

opened. The rapid expansion of the navy's numbers required larger quantities of rum, which requirement was fulfilled heroically by the Victualing Department. This last accomplishment was in itself a victory of sorts; supplying a navy with ships in every ocean despite wartime restrictions was a superhuman task. The department would prove its mettle again by achieving the same task during the 1939–1945 war.

In the course of that latter conflict, however, supplies became so limited that the traditional blend had to be adulterated with rums from Cuba and Martinique. In the Far East and the Indian Ocean, inferior rum from Natal was substituted entirely, much to the disgust of the sailors. They frequently took Australian beer as a substitute. Submariners, meanwhile, lessened the water in their grog: one to one became the undersea formula.

After the war, when the Royal Navy first demobilized and then began (with the rest of the British nation) its long retreat from empire, the rum tot was not at first threatened. But the increasing complexity of naval technology, coupled with the reduction in storage space, led to a continuing barrage against the tot. The Admiralty feared the effect of alcohol on sailors dealing with highly delicate navigational equipment and weapons systems; the ever present moral "reformers" simply hated rum for its own sake.

Through the 1960s, the battle raged in the press and in Parliament. The antidrunk driving lobby weighed in, warning against sailors taking to the roads on leaving after polishing off their grog. At last, on December 17, 1969, the Admiralty decided to abolish the rum ration, three centuries after its birth. Citing technological and health issues, it was ordered that in compensation, officers and men of age would be allowed to buy spirits of all kinds, up to one-eighth of a pint a day, in their messes. By way of compensation, a new fund was set up and endowed by the Admiralty to the tune of 2.7 million pounds sterling. This Sailors' Fund would be administered by the enlisted and have as its objectives the recreation of seamen and the welfare of their dependents. The rum ration and compensating grog money for those who had abstained were to be abolished on August 1, 1970.

As might be expected, the average sailor was none too pleased at this announcement. The outrage of past and present seamen was noted by the House of Commons, where the "Great Rum Debate" took place on January 28, 1970. The Labour government of the day, presided over by Harold Wilson and bearing a long record of tradition-smashing, sided with the Admiralty. Two years previously, the Wilson government had ordered the abandonment of all British bases east of Suez (save Hong Kong), and a corresponding reduction in the Royal Navy. Later that year, an election swept the Tories under Edward Heath back into power. But in this, as in other areas, the new cabinet did not see fit to alter course. The fact that the Admiralty supported the change clinched it.

On July 31, 1970, "black tot day," the last rum ration was issued. On Royal Navy ships across the globe, mock funerals were held, black armbands worn, and the tot buried. Thus ended the practice begun by Vice Admiral Penn in 1655; as rum had been present at the birth of the British Empire and the expansion of its navy across the globe, so its demise as an item of issue coincided with the end of that empire and its global reach. For many, the end of Britain's might and that of the tot were likewise positive developments. One cannot help but think, however, in light of subsequent developments, that they were unmixed blessings. Certainly, in many parts of what is now the Commonwealth, neither human rights nor the infrastructure have done well since independence. As to grog— well, one may question how much better off the Royal Navy is today than are the few fleets that still retain some sort of liquor ration.

But while the empire passed away, naval rum did not vanish entirely. The tot was gone, but the ceremony of "splicing the main brace" remained. This consisted—and continues to consist—of issuing an extra one-eighth of a pint of rum to all the ship's company over the age of twenty who wanted it (lemonade was given the teetotalers). The rum is mixed with water into grog for all ratings below the rank of petty officer. This extra issue may be given only by the queen, a member of the Royal family, or the Admiralty itself. Splicing the main brace is the only occasion when officers may be issued with service rum.

The title comes from the reward given in sailing ships to men who carried out the task of splicing the main brace, that is, the brace (a rope used to hold the direction of a sail) attached to the main yard of a sailing ship. The main brace, being one of the heaviest pieces of running rigging in a ship, was seldom spliced if damaged, but was replaced instead. As the main brace was led through blocks, a long splice (as opposed to a short splice or a knot) had to be made in it when repair was necessary, and the ship had to remain on the one tack—that is, that given direction—until the job was completed. Thus, the work had to be done at great speed and in whatever conditions prevailed at the time since the ship could not be steered effectively with a broken main brace. The ship's best able seamen were normally chosen to do the work under the supervision of the bosun. Splicing the main brace has come to be the name for any nautical party, naval or civilian. Perhaps the most memorable order given in recent times to the entire Royal Navy was that on June 4, 2002, the Golden Jubilee of Queen Elizabeth II.

But after 1970, the rum specially made by E. D. and F. Man for the navy ceased production. As noticed earlier, it was a unique blend and its demise was mourned by rum connoisseurs the world over. At 95.5 proof, this special "Pusser's" rum was unique. Fortunately for lovers of the drink, an American ex-marine named Charles Tobias went into partnership with the Man Company and opened a distillery on Tortola, in the British Virgin Islands. Using the closely guarded naval recipe, he opened Pussers Ltd., which now bottles and distributes Pusser's Rum. For every case sold, Tobias donates $2 to the Royal Navy Sailors' Fund; in return, Pusser's now graces every main brace splicing!

As the British Empire gave birth to the Commonwealth, so the Royal Navy gave birth to several daughter fleets. These adopted their parent navy's traditions as a whole; among these was the rum ration. But modern conditions forced them to deal with the same problems the Royal Navy had. Although Canada became an independent dominion in 1867 (retaining the British Sovereign as its own), the Royal Canadian Navy (RCN) was not formed until 1910. The rum tot continued to be issued aboard RCN ships until March 31, 1972, when the Trudeau government, citing Royal Navy practice, abolished it. The Royal New Zealand Navy became independent of the Royal Navy in 1941, and kept up the rum tot tradition until March 1, 1990, being the last of Her Majesty's fleets to abandon it. The Royal Australian Navy (RAN) has never had a rum ration; when it was formed in 1909, the temperance movement was very powerful there. Instead, the ships of the RAN were and are issued two cans of beer a day, officers not excepted.

But if Her Majesty's navies have all abandoned the tot, at least one republican Commonwealth fleet retains it. In 1947, the Empire of India was given independence as two dominions: India and Pakistan. The former became a republic in 1950 (Pakistan retained the Queen until 1956), and in that year the Royal Indian Navy dropped its first adjective. But many British traditions were retained: in the officers' messes, Indian naval officers still sit when toasting their president, and the men still receive their tot.

But where the Canadian, New Zealand, Australian, and Indian navies all received their independence peacefully with their countries, the most successful child of the Royal Navy, like its nation, was born of a revolution. Nevertheless, the U.S. Navy retained many traditions of its parent: among these was the alcohol ration. On November 28, 1775, the congress at Philadelphia, even before independence, ordered the creation of a navy. One of the first authorized rules was that each seaman should receive a half-pint of rum per day. Although the U.S. Navy was dissolved after the war, it was revived in 1794 to fight the Barbary pirates. A daily half-pint of "spirits" was duly authorized, to be substituted with a quart of beer if necessary. Although rum was preferred at first, by the mid-nineteenth century, rye whiskey had taken its place. So matters rested until September 1, 1862, when President Abraham Lincoln ordered that it should cease. He expressed the pious wish that something similar could be done to the army, given that it was busy with the War between the States. However, the soldiers were left unmolested. The Confederate navy continued to issue grog to its sailors until the surrender of its last ship, the CSS *Shenandoah*, in 1865.

As the temperance movement gathered strength in late nineteenth-century America, the navy could not be unaffected. In 1881, the Department of the Navy ordered that while officers might have wine and beer in their wardrooms, "spirituous liquors" were forbidden. This was often gotten around by labeling whiskey bottles "wine." But the forces of Carrie Nation were to have their victory in the end.

In 1912, Princeton president and Presbyterian minister Woodrow Wilson was elected chief executive of the United States. With him came a new secretary of the navy, Josephus Daniels. A teetotaler and North Carolina resident, the new secretary looked askance at the consumption of alcohol by anyone, let alone seamen; but he controlled the lives only of the latter. He issued an order on April 1, 1914, forbidding alcohol aboard ship. Daniels declared later that he had made the order "convinced after a year's reflection that the cause of both temperance and democracy demanded it." While the former interest was obviously served, it is hard to see how the latter was, given the opposition of most sailors to it. But such considerations have rarely counted for much with government officials.

Nevertheless, one unforeseen casualty of the order aboard ship was the American version of the loyal toast. The U.S. Navy had substituted the word *president* for *king*, and until 1914, U.S. naval officers happily practiced loyal toasting both ashore and afloat. But Daniels's order ended formal onboard dinners. The center of naval social life moved from the wardroom to the officers' club, where it has sat ever since.

The two other major navies to emerge from the seventeenth-century race for empire were the Dutch and the French. From 1692 on, Dutch crews were issued daily rations of jenever (Dutch gin). This continued until 1905, when the jenever ration was abolished, and two bottles of beer substituted. Since 1979, drinking during "business hours" has been strictly forbidden. The French navy has, from antiquity, served wine at all major meals; apparently, it has not lost any efficiency over it. In recent years, French servicemen have supplied both bootleg liquor and Catholic Masses to their American counterparts serving in Muslim nations.

In any case, rum's supremacy at sea has vanished. Ironically, however, grog does retain a slight hold on land in the American forces. There yet remains one official ration of rum administered by a quasi-naval authority: the Commandant of the United States Marine Corps. Every New Year's Day since 1804, the Marine Band has serenaded the Commandant of the Marine Corps at his quarters in Washington, D.C., receiving a tot of hot rum punch and breakfast in return. This is the last surviving official issue of grog in the U.S. armed forces.

But there are also a couple of unofficial uses. In keeping with their British and nautical roots, the United States Marines also use rum punch at their formal "Mess Nights." Most of the after-dinner toasts are drunk in port. Those completed, however, the President of the Mess announces "The floor is now closed for toasting." He then says to the Vice-President (who is charged with carrying out his orders), "Mr. Vice, bring forth the rum punch." At this the stewards then give each Marine some rum punch which is made with four parts dark rum, two parts lime juice, one part maple syrup, and a small amount of grenadine, and chilled with ice. When everyone has their glasses charged the President says, "In 1776, one of the first recruiting posters ordered recruits upon enlistment, 'Take courage then, seize the fortune that awaits you, repair to the Marine rendez-vous, where in a flowing bowl of punch, and three times three, you shall drink.' Long live the United States, and success to the Marines. Mr. Vice, a toast to the Corps and Country." The Vice-President of the Mess then toasts: "Marines, a toast: Long live the United States, and success to the Marines." The Mess members then repeat the toast, drain their glasses of rum punch, and place them on the table upside down. The tradition of using rum punch comes from the U.S. Marines' origins at Tun Tavern, Philadelphia, in 1775. This was a typical eighteenth century rum house. As a result, the recipe used at such events is called "1775 Rum Punch" and is also used to toast the Corps at all celebrations marking the Marines' birthday on November 10 each year.

There remains one other use for "grog," in the American military, in name if not in content. Fittingly, it also occurs at formal Messes, or "Dinings-in," as they are called in other branches of the service. At each of these events, a large bowl is set up, in view of the assembly. In it the President—sometimes before the Mess begins, sometimes (depending on the unit) as a part of the function, accompanying his task with humorous narration—pours alcoholic but distasteful ingredients. These he mixes together into a drink which, though called "grog,"is certainly nothing Admiral Vernon or his men would have recognized. At such a mess, violations of etiquette are punished either by a fine (which is then put toward the open bar after the event finishes) or else, depending upon their nature a visit to the grog bowl. Such infractions as may warrant a trip to the grog bowl are noted at any time during the proceedings by the President, Vice President, or any member of the mess. Such infractions are brought to the attention of the President by raising a point of order. If the validity of the charge is questioned, members vote by tapping their spoons on the table.

When the President directs a violator to the grog bowl, the individual is to proceed to the bowl promptly. The bowl is usually located on or near the Vice's table. Upon arriving at the grog bowl, the violator does an about-face and salutes the President; does another about-face to the bowl and fills the cup; does yet another about-face and toasts the mess; and then empties the contents of the cup without removing it from his lips, placing it inverted on his head to show that it is empty. He then does an about-face, replaces the cup, about-faces again, salutes the President, and returns to his seat. With the exception of the toast, "To the Mess," he is not permitted to speak during this process. Few mess members are able to make it through an entire evening without at least one such visit. Alas, often enough in these soft times the grog is nonalcoholic, albeit just as foul-tasting. But in those fortunate messes where tradition yet reigns, many an evening ends as pleasant for the participants as ever grog-drinking did for the tars of Admiral Vernon's time.

This is fitting: For whether they know it or not, by emulating their eighteenth-century forebears, such participants are honoring the memory of men who truly made the evening possible. This is not just because those old tars originated the rituals to some degree. It is because the Royal Navy safeguarded the dreaded "Triangle Trade" of colonial times, without which the United States, as we know them, simply would not exist. So it is that we must now consider that trade, and the vital role rum played in it.

Hot Grog

1 shot rum   Squeeze of lime juice
1 teaspoon sugar (preferably   Cinnamon stick
    superfine)   Boiling water

Stir all ingredients, adding enough boiling water to fill a mug or glass.

Chapter 3

Triangle Trade

Rutledge:
Molasses to rum to slaves, oh what a beautiful waltz
You dance with us, we dance with you
Molasses and rum and slaves

Who sails the ships out of Boston
Ladened with bibles and rum?
Who drinks a toast to the Ivory Coast?
Hail Africa, the slavers have come
New England with bibles and rum

And it's off with the rum and the bibles
Take on the slaves, clink, clink
Hail and farewell to the smell
Of the African coast

Molasses to rum to slaves
'Tisn't morals, 'tis money that saves
Shall we dance to the sound of the profitable pound
In molasses and rum and slaves

Who sails the ships out of Guinea
Ladened with bibles and slaves?
'Tis Boston can coast to the West Indies coast
Jamaica, we brung what ye craves
Antigua, Barbados, we brung bibles and slaves!

Molasses to rum to slaves
Who sail the ships back to Boston
Ladened with gold, see it gleam
Whose fortunes are made in the triangle trade
Hail slavery, the New England dream!
Mr. Adams, I give you a toast:
Hail Boston! Hail Charleston!
Who stinketh the most?
—Sherman Edwards, "Molasses to Rum" (1776)

he famed Triangle Trade, which the above song so wittily describes, was born of three components and one doctrine: slaves, molasses, rum, and mercantilism. Its lifeblood was shipping, its defense the Royal Navy, and, like that navy, the ships who conducted it used rum as a lubricant.

Let us look first at mercantilism. This was the doctrine, popular throughout the seventeenth, eighteenth, and into the nineteenth centuries, that a country was economically sound insofar as it was self-sufficient. The possession by the national treasury of as much gold and silver as possible was key to this health. The expansion of the colonial powers into the Americas, Africa, and Asia resulted in their attempts to build up empires that would be self-sustaining economic units. The colonies would provide raw materials for the mother country; its merchants in turn would either sell them directly to consumers or else to nascent industrialists. The wares of these latter would, in turn, get sold back to the colonial settlers. In return for the metropole defending and sustaining the colonists, the colonists would pay the metropole's keep, and all would profit. To protect these arrangements, trade with outside powers would be forbidden, and navies of the sort that we saw in the last chapter would be raised.

For the English, this meant that, once the initial hopes of gold and silver being found had passed them by, they must look to their colonies for agricultural goods of various kinds, timber, and furs.

Little or no manufactures could be permitted in order that the colonies would remain a market for British manufactured goods. Hence, with their oldest colony, Ireland, after the Battle of the Boyne in 1690, no effort was spared to restrict any sort of industrial growth. Until after the famine of the 1840s, most of the Irish were confined to farming; this, together with the anti-Catholic penal laws, succeeded in stoking a bitterness that has not faded.

In any case, in accord with mercantilist thought, a series of laws were passed by Parliament during the seventeenth and eighteenth centuries regulating commerce between Great Britain and its colonies. The Corn Laws put heavy duties on grain (abundantly raised in the thirteen colonies) to protect British farmers from colonial competition. But colonial tobacco, sugar, lumber, and naval stores were encouraged by liberal excise taxes—and forbidden by law to be traded with foreigners. Initially, much of the trade between England and the empire was carried on by Dutch ships. To stamp this out, the Navigation Act of 1651 was enacted by Oliver Cromwell; it required that all commerce between England and its colonies (and between each colony) be carried only in English or colonial ships. Goods brought into Britain from foreign nations must be carried either in British ships or those of the country of origin, thus excluding the Dutch.

It was necessary for Charles II, after regaining his father's throne in 1660, to cultivate the same wealthy merchant class that had been the backbone of Cromwell's regime. Thus, in the year of his return, the king enacted another Mercantile Act that reaffirmed Cromwell's. It went further, however, in enumerating articles that could only be sold within the British Isles and the English colonies. Among the "Enumerated Articles" (a phrase that found its way into law) were sugar, tobacco, ginger, cotton, wool, fustic, and other dyewoods. Three years later, another act forbade direct trade on foreign ships to the colonies. At the time, these laws had the effect of stimulating both the home and colonial economies, and went far toward accomplishing the goals of their authors. The colonial economies, based upon agricultural production, found an ever-hungry market in Great Britain; British manufacturers had guaranteed colonial sales for their wares; and British and colonial merchants profited from the two-way traffic. It was the perfect accomplishment of mercantile theory.

An important consideration at the same time was the need of cheap labor to work the Caribbean plantations. At first, this labor was an equal opportunity profession. Cromwell's wars in Ireland and Scotland provided many captives for the lord protector; always anxious to make money, Cromwell sold the unfortunates to plantation owners in the West Indies. Many of the Irish went to the tiny island of Montserrat in the Leeward Islands. These exiles had an enduring effect on the island's culture. Marrying black slaves, they bequeathed their surnames to their descendants, and Irish names are most prevalent among the Montserratians to this day. The shamrock became Montserrat's emblem and graced Government House (residence of the island's governor) until that historic mansion's destruction by volcanic ash a few years ago. Catholicism plays a more prominent role in the island's life than it does in most of the Anglophone West Indies, and despite the havoc wreaked by the volcano, it is called "the Emerald Isle of the Caribbean."

The Scots and Irish who were sent to Barbados also left a lasting mark. Their poor white descendants in the Scotland District and elsewhere on the island occupy the same role in the island's social structure as do the Appalachian hillbillies in the United States. Resettlement programs by the Crown in the nineteenth century (intended to help the poor whites to establish a new life for themselves where they faced no social stigma) established enclaves of these folk on Becquia in the Grenadines, St. Vincent, and Grenada; they did well there, and their descendants on those islands have fared much better than most of those who remained in Barbados.

Combined with these people was a steady stream of white indentured servants who came to the Americas voluntarily or otherwise throughout the eighteenth century. A graphic reference to the latter is made in Robert Louis Stevenson's novel *Kidnapped*. Indentured servants endured a slave-like way of life for a stated term (five to seven years), after which they were free.

But neither in numbers nor in stamina could these unfortunates provide for the labor needs of the plantations. Another alternative was found in captured New England Indians, following the Pequot and King Philip's Wars. While this source was insufficient as well, it resulted in the establishment of an American Indian settlement on St. David's Island, Bermuda, which has endured to the present. In 2002, a reunion was organized that brought a large number of Connecticut Pequots to meet their distant cousins in Bermuda. Both sides were astonished at the physical and cultural resemblances that had survived three centuries of separation. Taken as a whole, however, the American Indian experiment was also a failure.

This left the other great source of labor, of which we spoke in chapter 1: African slaves. In 1660, the Crown chartered the "Company of Royal Adventurers Trading to Africa." Mismanaged at first, in 1663 it was completely (and successfully) reorganized. At this point, it was clearly stated that the company would engage in the slave trade. The company was granted a monopoly on the trade.

As a result of the Second Ango-Dutch War, however, the company collapsed in 1667. But from the wreckage came the Royal African Company. Founded in 1672, the new company was granted a similar monopoly in the slave trade. Between 1680 and 1686, the company transported an average of five thousand slaves a year. Between 1680 and 1688, it sponsored 249 voyages to Africa.

But pressure from English and colonial merchants mounted. In 1698, Parliament yielded to their demands and opened the slave trade to all. With the end of the monopoly, the number of slaves transported on English ships increased dramatically—to an average of over twenty thousand a year. Key to this development were the sea captains of New England. Already the provinces of the region had outstripped the English West Indies in production and quality of rum, although they remained dependent on Caribbean molasses for production.

These three factors—plentiful rum from New England, the need for slaves in the West Indies, and the demand for molasses by rum-makers in Massachusetts and Rhode Island—led to the development of the Triangle Trade. As recounted in the song opening the chapter, ships from such ports as Boston, Salem, and Providence set sail for the West African coast, loaded with rum. Once there, the growing thirst of the African kings was slaked in return for slaves. From thence the New England ships bore their captives in the so-called Middle Passage back to the West Indies. The human cargo was sold, and the molasses was loaded for the return voyage home.

Early on, the Portuguese and Spanish had traded various wines and brandies for slaves; these European drinks came to be much preferred by the locals to their own palm wine, which soured after a few weeks. But after the Brazilians began making *gerebita*, a sugar-cane brandy made from the foam skimmed off the second boiling of cane juice, they became very successful, indeed. A pipe of gerebita bought ten slaves in Angola by the end of the eighteenth century.

So, too, did rum become highly demanded. Even under the Royal African Company's monopoly, the drink gave the English an edge. In 1679, the Frenchman Jean Barbot arrived at the great slave entrepôt of Cape Coast; he found "a great alteration: the French brandy, whereof I had always had a great quantity abroad, being much less demanded, by reason that a great quantity of spirits and rum had been bought on that coast . . . which obliged them all to sell cheap."

New Englanders were not the only ones to benefit. Frederick Philipse, the great New York manor lord, augmented the rents from his Hudson valley estates with profits from the slave trade. He began his involvement in 1685. It was then that his ship, the *Charles*, sailed from Amsterdam to Angola to exchange weapons and other goods for Africans. In 1698, Philipse's ship, the *Margaret*, set sail for the Guinea coast with sixteen casks of rum; this became a major product for his fleet thereafter. Ever mindful of bargains, Philipse was one of several New Yorkers who circumvented the official routes for the importation of slaves by dealing with a colony of pirates who used Madagascar as a base of operation. These illicit partners led to his near downfall, however; during a Royal crack-down on piracy, one of his captains narrowly escaped hanging. Philipse lost a ship and two valuable cargoes; and he and his son were barred from holding provincial office for years, a blow that severely threatened the family's commercial power base. But although kept from the slave trade thereafter, the Philipses retained their wealth and position. Philipse Manor Hall in Yonkers and Philipsburg Manor in Sleepy Hollow, New York, remain as testimonies to the great, if brief, role rum played in their builder's fortune.

But if the Philipses had to bow out of the trade, innumerable others remained. Although the Royal African Company had lost its monopoly, profits on the Guinea coast were so great that it was able to survive the competition. In 1721, its chief factor at its headquarters, Cape Coast Castle, reported to the directors that rum had become the "chief barter," not merely for slaves, but for gold as well.

Rum played its part as well on the Middle Passage. The horrors of that journey are well known; but these horrors varied from nationality to nationality and ship to ship. As mentioned in the last chapter, seagoing of any kind was difficult in those days, and generally at least a fifth of a ship's crew would die over the year's time that an entire triangle voyage generally took. The French, Portuguese, and Spanish authorities laid down rigid regulations on the numbers of and care for slaves being transported; these rules were observed as well or as poorly as those regulating the care of seamen. But profit required in any case that as many slaves arrive alive as possible. Thus, their rations were generally the same as those of the seamen (leading unscrupulous sailors to try to steal the slaves' food "even from their mouths" when food was short). Often, as exercise, the slaves were brought out on deck to dance, and the best dancers were rewarded with rum or other spirits. The ship's surgeon, who was responsible for bringing as many alive to the Americas as possible (and so had a great voice in choosing the healthiest slaves at the mart before the voyage began), prescribed rum as medicine for the captives as often as he did for the crew.

By this time, the demand by New England for molasses to manufacture rum had outstripped the ability of the British West Indian planters to produce it. Partly, this was the result of soil exhaustion, partly because of their loss of capital. This last, paradoxically, was brought on by mercantilism itself. The British planters were less and less able to compete with their French rivals, who were able to trade with the whole of Europe.

Liberal trade laws enacted by the French Crown in 1717 allowed the planters on Haiti, Guadeloupe, and Martinique to sell their wares to the entire European continent much more cheaply than could the British; this in turn increased the demand on the part of their European clients. With the increased flow of money, French planters could keep abreast of all the latest agricultural developments and apply them to their own sugar production.

The New England merchants, for whose sake the home government had imposed the damaging restrictions on the British planters in the first place, saw their opportunity. They began buying molasses not merely from the French West Indies, but from the Dutch, Danish, and even Spanish as well. Before long, trade with foreign planters exceeded that with British. Sugar growers in Barbados, Jamaica, and the other British islands began appealing for relief to Parliament.

Many of the West Indian "nabobs," as they were called, had close friends at Westminster. The result of their lobbying was the Molasses Act of 1733. This measure placed heavy duties on all sugar, molasses, rum, and spirits imported into the North American colonies from foreign-held sugar islands. For the New Englanders, the act, if enforced, would have meant ruin. The fish and lumber they sold to the foreign islands for molasses would have no outlet, and the faltering supplies of the syrup from British islands would have wrecked their rum manufacture, and so the slave trade.

Fortunately for the New Englanders, several factors worked against the act's solid enforcement. Government officials were few on the ground in the colonies. In addition to the Royal governors (whose upholding of imperial decrees was tempered by the provision of their salaries by local assemblies) and regular soldiers (usually too busy with their military duties to worry about other things), the Crown was directly represented only by the customs officials. Under a surveyor-general of the customs in the American colonies, there were in each province a collector of the customs and however few deputies he might be pleased to appoint; the entire customs staff never amounted to more than ninety individuals for all forty-nine colonial ports during the entire prerevolutionary period. Thus, customs collections depended to a great degree on the good will of the local colonials. Apart from the personnel problem, the Crown also faced pressure from northern English manufacturers whose production was dependent on the transport of raw materials from the colonies by New England traders. Ignoring the act seemed easier than insisting on it.

Moreover, Parliament came at last to the aid of the British West Indies. Acts were passed in 1739 and 1742 that removed sugar from the list of enumerated articles. Now able to sell their product directly to Europe, the financial position of the planters improved tremendously. Their fortunes saved, they no longer pressed the Crown to enforce the Molasses Act. Regardless, it remained on the books.

The result was to make smuggling a respectable profession in New England. Such moneyed men as John Hancock were to owe much of their fortunes to smuggling, which became a uniquely honorable profession in Massachusetts and Rhode Island. The result was that when Britain and its colonies were locked in a life and death struggle with the French and Spanish during the Seven Years' War (called the French and Indian War in North America), many of the most prominent New England shipping families happily traded with the enemy. This act of what could only be called treason would not be forgotten in London; in turn, Britain's reluctance to enforce its laws—thought of as weakness—was remembered in New England. Both attitudes would have later repercussions.

Meanwhile, Yankeedom's legal trade in rum with West Africa continued to expand, rum bottle by rum bottle. Distilleries flourished in Massachusetts and Rhode Island; Newport produced a specially strong "Guinea Rum," meant purely for trade. It eventually drove out most of the West Indian rum, as well as European gin, brandy, and liquor. By carrying eighteen hundred hogsheads (i.e., barrels that hold sixty-three gallons, or 238 liters) of rum to the African coast every year for more than twenty years (1740 through 1760), Rhode Island destroyed the French brandy trade with the African coast and discharged one-third of its annual debt to Great Britain. Even Liverpool got into the act, with two distilleries opening in that city in 1765. By 1770, rum represented four-fifths of New England's exports, and it is estimated that eleven million gallons of Rhode Island rum were traded for slaves between 1709 and 1807.

As the years progressed, however, the West Africans required ever more rum for slaves. In 1755, Newport captain Caleb Godfrey traded 799 gallons of rum, as well as meat and other items, for four men, three women, three girls, and a boy. Twelve years later, the standard at Cape Coast Castle was 130 gallons of rum per man, 110 per woman, and 80 per girl. By 1773, the price had risen to 210 to 220 gallons per slave.

Money poured into the New England ports, and fortunes built on rum and slaves enabled their holders to "play the macaroni" (i.e., live lavishly). In Boston and Newport, huge mansions and country seats were built, extravagant entertainments were offered, and the latest fashions were worn by the Hancocks, Whipples, and the like. On his profits from the Triangle Trade, the Huguenot merchant Peter Faneuil built Faneuil Hall in 1742 and gave it to the people of Boston. More than a marketplace, its halls also served (and still do) as the headquarters of the Ancient and Honorable Artillery Company and as the location of the Boston Town Meeting (until that body's abolition in 1830). As a backdrop for many political meetings during the decade leading up to the American Revolution, Faneuil Hall has won the nickname "Cradle of Liberty." But the origins of the money that paid for it have led to a popular saying of the time: "the Cradle of Liberty rocks on the bones of the Middle Passage."

When the rupture between the mother country and the American rebels broke out, the Triangle Trade suffered tremendously.

The closing of the Port of Boston in response to the 1773 Boston
Tea Party, the town's occupation until 1776, and its blockade until
the end of the war, ruined many a fortune; so with Newport's occupation by the British in 1778. The economic sufferings of the
wealthy merchants have entered our folklore.

But problems were not restricted to New England. While British
slavers continued to visit the marts on the Guinea coast, they had to
do so with West Indian rum, which the locals considered vastly
inferior to the New England product. Complaints were regularly
made to London by the local factors, and the West Africans jacked
up the price in rum.

When the war ended, the Triangle Trade did not resuscitate; for
several years afterward, the Navigation Acts were applied against
now-foreign American vessels. This forced merchantmen to seek
other venues; so originated the China Trade, which brought such
ports as Salem into prominence. But the slave trade resumed; once
again New England distilleries produced rum for the Africans; but
now American slavers headed for Charleston, New Orleans, and
Havana, rather than Bridgetown and Kingston.

The doom of the slave trade was impending, however. In 1789,
the framers of the constitution at Philadelphia agreed that the trade
should become illegal in 1808. In Great Britain, a wave of aboli-
tionist fervor had swept the country by the 1780s. The English poet,
William Cowper, contributed to the antislavery movement by writing ballads that could be set to music and sung in the streets. One of
these ballads, published in 1791, was titled "The Negro's Complaint," and sought to get the people of Great Britain to abstain
from West Indian sugar and rum so as to abolish the slave trade.
Here is an excerpt:

> Why did all-creating Nature
> Make the plant for which we toil?
> Sighs must fan it, Tears must water,
> Sweat of ours must dress the soil.

Think ye Masters, iron-hearted,
Lolling at your jovial Boards,
Think how many Backs have smarted
For the Sweets your Cane affords!

In 1807, a bill in the English Parliament abolishing the slave trade became law (although slavery itself continued in the Empire until 1833). But the British went even further than outlawing the slave trade; they also set up their navy to seize slavers on the high seas. Eventually, France and Spain followed suit. Thus, in time New Englanders would have to evade the fleets of three nations in order to smuggle their human cargo into the South—and their also having to escape detection at the hands of local police. Existing slaves were still property and would be until the Civil War, but the importation of new ones was strictly forbidden after 1808.

The price for apprehension was great; a slaver could lose his ship, his cargo, and, depending on how stiffly he and his men resisted, possibly his life. In turn, the slaves themselves were generally released at the nearest friendly landing. There are a number of villages in the Bahamas, Jamaica, Sierra Leone, and elsewhere, whose inhabitants descend from such dramas. There is even one such settlement, Africky Town, near Mobile, Alabama, whose ancestors were dropped off by a Portland, Maine, based ship eluding government pursuers in 1859. It was the last such attempt ever made in North America. The last surviving member of that cargo lived long enough to be interviewed by noted author Zora Neale Hurston, as recorded in her 1942 autobiography *Dust Tracks on a Road*.

As slave trading became riskier and less profitable, New England merchants understandably withdrew from the practice. As they ceased to profit by slavery, their consciences reemerged—the more so because the southern slaveowners became greater rivals for economic and political power. So it is in exact proportion that as Yankee slave trading declined, Yankee abolitionism arose.

But this was not the end of New England rum trading. Its export to the Hawaiian Islands and the addiction of that country's King, Liloliho, to the stuff was instrumental in the establishment of Yankee Congregationalist missionaries there. This paved the way for the reverend gentlemen's descendants to take over the islands completely.

Nor did the trade with Africa cease, although the end of slavery as a result of the Civil War forced it into more benevolent channels. The Chase distilleries in Somerville, and the Lawrence distilleries in Medford, both in Massachusetts, continued to make rum for export. Together with Bibles, the liquor arrived on the West African coast, and in turn bought palm oil for the Lever brothers and black mahogany for various manufacturers.

Alas, even this pleasant and beneficial trade would meet its doom at the hands of what some claimed was another kind of slavery: Prohibition. The Volstead Act of 1919 and the Eighteenth Amendment to the Constitution the following year closed the last remaining New England distilleries. The last gasp of the Triangle Trade went unnoticed as bootleggers and "untouchables," jazzmen and flappers set about making the 1920s roar.

Spicy Baked Beans with Rum and Molasses

2 cups raw pea (navy) beans
3 tablespoons butter
2 cups chopped onion
3 cloves crushed garlic
¾ teaspoon salt
2 teaspoons dill weed
1 teaspoon allspice
lots of fresh black pepper
4 tablespoons dark (Dijon or Poupon) mustard
4 tablespoons dark molasses

3 cups tomato juice
¾ cup dark rum
2 teaspoons tamari (or soy sauce)
1 cup water
2 tablespoons fresh lemon juice
1 or 2 diced carrots
1 or 2 stalks minced celery
1 chopped bell pepper
1 teaspoon freshly grated ginger (optional)

Place the beans in a large kettleful of water. Bring to a boil, then partially cover, and cook over medium heat until the beans are tender (1 to 1½ hours). Check the water level from time to time during cooking and add if needed. When tender, drain, if necessary.

While the beans are cooking, sauté the onions and garlic in the butter and salt till the onions are soft.

Add the spices and liquids to the onions, and simmer, covered for about 45 minutes.

Preheat the oven to 300°. Combine the cooked beans, the sauce, and the raw chopped vegetables in a large casserole. Cover tightly and bake for an hour or two.

Serve topped with sour cream, with a green leafy salad and some cornbread.

Chapter 4

ⵥⵥⵥⵥⵥⵥⵥⵥⵥⵥⵥⵥⵥⵥⵥⵥⵥⵥ

Yo-Ho-Ho: Rum and Piracy

"Doctors is all swabs," he said; "and that doctor there, why, what do he know about seafaring men? I been in places hot as pitch, and mates dropping round with Yellow Jack, and the blessed land a-heaving like the sea with earthquakes— what do the doctor know of lands like that?—and I lived on rum, I tell you. It's been meat and drink, and man and wife, to me; and if I'm not to have my rum now I'm a poor old hulk on a lee shore, my blood'll be on you, Jim, and that doctor swab"; and he ran on again for awhile with curses.
—Robert Louis Stevenson, *Treasure Island*

Just as there have been burglars since humans lived in houses, and robbers since they began traveling, so humanity's first venture on the water soon created pirates. They were the scourge of the Mediterranean at the dawn of recorded history; the Cilician pirates of southern Asia Minor were particular banes of the Roman navy, and their clearance went far to establish that empire's supremacy over "Mare Nostra." Centuries later, North Africa's Barbary pirates held the same sea in a reign of terror. Combining a thirst for plunder (without, however, drinking the liquor banned by Islam) with a jihad against the Christians, they ranged as far as the coasts of Ireland and Iceland in a neverending search for slaves and loot. Their final suppression by Europeans during the opening decades of the nineteenth century led, on the one hand, to U.S. Marines arriving at "the shores of Tripoli," and on the other, to the beginning of the 130-year-long French adventure in Algeria.

In our own time, bands of hereditary pirates continue to prowl the shipping lanes of the South China Sea, and in recent years a new breed has begun freeing narcotics-bearing yachts of their wares in the waters around Florida. Most recently, the latter breed of sea dogs have begun attacking small craft in the West Indies, regardless of cargo. The newly independent island microstates there are incapable of providing security, the Royal Navy is long gone from Caribbean waters, and the Americans have other fish to fry.

But when one uses the word "pirate," it brings to mind none of these ancient or modern freebooters, but the "brethren of the coast," who terrorized the Spanish Main (and many other places) from the sixteenth to the seventeenth centuries. Thanks to Robert Lewis Stevenson's *Treasure Island*, and Disney's "Pirates of the Caribbean" rides, few boys raised in American seaports (and even a number raised inland) have not dreamed of being pirates at one time or another. Images of gold doubloons, silver pieces-of-eight, and talking parrots haunt many such a lad. No matter what the reality was, these pirates are more often seen as fun-loving rogues than as the seagoing criminals of contemporary accounts.

But if rum was the lubricant of the slave trade, it was the lifeblood of piracy. "Yo-ho-ho and a bottle of rum" may have been fictional verse, but Stevenson was quite correct in his portrayal of the rum thirst of pirates. The old buccaneer who boards with young Jack Hawkins and his mother at the Admiral Benbow is willing to sacrifice his life to the liquor Dr. Livesey says will kill him. So it often proved in real life.

The Spanish in the Americas were great city builders, an achievement often forgotten today. But such towns as Cartagena, Colombia, Vera Cruz, Mexico, Panama City, Panama, and our own

St. Augustine, Florida, stand as testimonies to their ability to create civilization out of little. It was gold that permitted this—gold that, apart from paying for local building, was shipped home to Spain in huge quantities.

Envious of the flow of wealth, the Protestant nations of northern Europe—the English, Dutch, and French Huguenots—took to the seas to seize some of it for themselves. As with the Barbary pirates, such men as Sir Francis Drake could invoke the sanctity of a religious crusade for their plunder.

As the Spanish cities became bigger and wealthier, and as the British, French, Dutch, and Danes set up New World colonies of their own, piracy expanded in both scope and organization.

Among the first English privateers was Sir Francis Drake. In 1567, he and his cousin John Hawkins had tried to break the Spanish monopoly of the African slave trade to the Americas. When they arrived off the coast of New Spain (Mexico) the following year, the Spanish opened fire and they were driven away. Drake turned his hand instead to licensed piracy.

This sort of activity was called privateering, a trade with an ancient past. However, as noted in the last chapter, organized national navies were a relatively recent development. During the Middle Ages, governments hired ships from private owners to form fleets, licensing them in wartime to raid enemy commerce. The international law that was developing at that time recognized licensed raiders (known in English as privateers), but outlawed unlicensed raiders as pirates. Legitimate sovereigns alone could license privateers and issue the necessary "letters of marque and reprisal." These licenses to plunder are first mentioned in English law in 1354. They specified the names of the ships to which they were issued, their officers' names, and which sorts of ships they could seize. The licensing ruler's admiralty courts regulated privateering, sold the captured ships as prizes, and distributed the proceeds as prize money; government, captain, and the crew all received designated shares.

As national navies appeared, their commissioned officers came to regard naval service as a more virtuous calling than privateering. But as control of the sea required disciplined navies, competition also grew for seamen, who often found privateering more lucrative. Worse still, when wars ended, privateers often turned to piracy; turning their hands against all comers, they were as likely to prey upon ships of their own country as those of any other.

Queen Elizabeth I, whose legitimacy was, in Catholic eyes, rather spotty (the more so since she had reneged on her promise to abide by her sister Mary's return of England to the Church, and who in 1571 had been declared deposed by Pope St. Pius V as a result), encouraged privateers such as Drake to raid the wealth of the Spanish trade. Since the two nations were at peace, this was considered by the Spanish to be particularly heinous. In response to their protests, Elizabeth pretended to the Spanish that she could do nothing to stop the "sea dogs." In addition to damaging the Spanish, the piracy encouraged by the queen provided a ready source of revenue for her. Licensing the privateers to rob Spanish ships brought in huge sums to her exchequer.

Drake set sail for the Strait of Magellan in 1577, eventually raiding Peru and the west coast of America (where he claimed California for his queen) before circumnavigating the world and returning to England. Elizabeth's cut of the take enabled her to pay off the entire national debt. Drake was given £10,000—an enormous sum in those days—for himself alone. The crew had to settle for nothing.

In the meantime, Sir Walter Raleigh, who was a generation younger than Drake, established himself as a major backer of privateering expeditions. As one of Elizabeth's innumerable lovers (her nickname "Virgin Queen" was something of a joke to her contemporaries), he bolstered his personal prowess by ruthlessly suppressing a Catholic rebellion in Ireland. There, in 1580, he butchered six hundred people, including women and children, on a site still called the "field of skulls." Sir Walter, at his house near Youghal called Myrtle Grove (which still stands), was able to build up an enormous fortune through his monopoly on wine sales and cloth granted to him by the queen. His privateering licenses also helped a great deal. Elizabeth benefited from her share of the profits; but perhaps in reparation for his dealing with the Irish, he introduced potatoes into the country from America and also stimulated the nascent colonial economy by popularizing tobacco. This did not endear him to Elizabeth's successor, James I, who had Sir Walter executed in 1618. Of course, the tobacco-hating James (who wrote the first anti-smoking tract) had other reasons for annoyance with him.

During the world wars of the seventeenth and eighteenth centuries, the distinction between privateering and piracy became very slight, especially in the Caribbean. There, buccaneers (the name comes from *boucan*, a rack used by the Caribs to cure beef) united as "Brethren of the Coast." Initially headquartered on the island of Tortuga, just north of Hispaniola, these buccaneers illegally plundered Spanish commerce in peacetime. In time of war, however, they did so under easily obtained French, Dutch, or English letters of marque. During the War of the Grand Alliance, as we have seen, the French at first triumphed over the English due to their victory at the Battle of Beachy Head in 1690, but the English and Dutch in turn defeated the French two years later at the Battle of La Hogue. Louis XIV was assembling an enormous army, some 400,000 men, at the time. The tremendous expense involved, as well as the defeat at La Hogue, caused him to abandon further large-scale naval action; he would fight the naval war on the cheap, with privateers. The navy was laid up to cut costs, while privateers were licensed on a grand scale. Doubtless to their mutual chagrin and/or amusement, buccaneers and French regulars served side by side.

As might be guessed, however, the governments of Europe were not unaware of what had been unleashed on the Seven Seas by the indiscriminate use of privateers. After the Peace of Ryswick in 1697, the courts of Europe decided to end the increasingly savage piracy spawned by their wars. The most famous casualty of this "get tough policy" was Captain Kidd. The darling (for a time) of New York

society, Kidd was an Englishman who had been licensed as a
privateer in 1696; he had previously spent over a decade bucca-
neering against Spanish ships, thereby earning the money needed to
win friends in Manhattan. But he turned to piracy when the war
ended in 1697, attacking British ships in the Indian Ocean. Seized
and convicted, he was hanged in 1701 on Execution Dock, London.
He left behind him a ton of legends, particularly as regards his
treasure. There does not seem to be a beach on the Atlantic or
Indian Oceans where children (and others) have not searched for it.

Had Captain Kidd evaded capture for another couple of years,
however, he would have been back in legitimate trade. When the
War of the Spanish Succession broke out in 1702, the good inten-
tions of the Powers to abandon privateering were swiftly forgotten.
As the war progressed, Britain acquired the strategic points of
Minorca and Gibraltar from Spain. She took Nova Scotia and
Newfoundland from France (unbeknownst to anyone, the sad stories of the Florida Minorcans and the Louisiana Acadians would
stem from these acquisitions). In addition, the grant of the Asiento
de Negroes gave the British a thirty-year monopoly on exporting
slaves to Spanish America. In 1708, Parliament passed the Cruisers
and Convoys Act. This measure bound the Royal Navy to protect
British merchantmen from privateers—an employment that would
occupy two thirds of the navy by the close of the war. By that time,
as a result, Great Britain's foreign trade had increased tremendously
over both that of her rivals and the Dutch. For two hundred years
to follow, despite challenges from the French and other powers,
the Royal Navy would be supreme at sea.

Privateering continued through the wars of the eighteenth century and the Napoleonic Wars. During the War of 1812, 526 American vessels were commissioned as privateers by Congress under
the authority of Article I, Section 8 of the U.S. Constitution. While
Britannia ruled the waves, commerce raiding was the desperate
response of a weaker naval power. Although the Paris Conference
of 1856 issued a declaration that abolished privateering, the United

States did not subscribe because it would require amending the Constitution. During the American Civil War, the Confederacy licensed privateers; in 1898, at the opening of the Spanish-American War, Spain and the United States, neither of which had signed the Declaration of Paris, agreed not to license privateering. It was not until the Hague Convention of 1907, which refined the prohibition of privateering and set rules for taking prizes by warships, that the United States officially renounced the use of letters of marque and reprisal. The United States now outlaws privateering through a federal statute rather than a constitutional amendment, and has abolished prize money as well. Interestingly enough, in the wake of the terrorist acts of September 11, 2001, some have advocated granting letters of marque against al-Qaeda, who started out as our "privateers" in Afghanistan.

Some early, anti-Spanish privateers, such as Sir Henry Morgan, having made a fortune from the foreign foe, turned legitimate, and were rewarded by their sovereigns. In Morgan's case, he was made governor of Jamaica by Charles II in 1674 and spent the rest of his life fighting the trade that had made him rich. His reputation, both as a pirate and a drinker, survived him, however, and he has given his name to a very popular modern rum; an ironic note, surely, as he is said to have "died of drink."

But a piratical fraternity—the afore-named buccaneers—developed, its hands against every nation. Certain places, like the island of Tortuga, north of Haiti, became pirate strongholds. There, free from any government supervision, however light, they could indulge whatever pleasures they wished. Money exhausted, they would take to the seas once more. The invention of rum gave them an enormous incentive.

Where rum was carefully rationed out to naval and merchant seamen, pirates expected a steady flow. At times, the crews got so drunk that they were unable either to capture a ship or defend themselves against attackers. William Dampier, one of the few buccaneers who kept journals, wrote, "We weighed before day, and all got out of the road except Captain Swan's tender, which never budged; for the men were all asleep, when we went out, and the tide of flood coming on before they awoke, we were forced to stay for them till the following tide." The same Captain Swan later complained that his crew had been so drunk on another occasion that it was unable to attack a merchantman. These events are all the more remarkable because Captain Edward Davis, in overall command of the company to which Dampier and Swan belonged, was renowned in piratical circles for his sobriety. Unable to manufacture the stuff themselves, the pirates rejoiced whenever they captured a vessel with a large supply.

Because of this, and because of the fear of fire at sea, many "ship's articles" (a sort of piratical constitution—each pirate vessel had its own) required that all drinking be done on deck.

Pirates of the seventeenth and eighteenth centuries often compared their "freedom" to what they considered the slavery of legal crews. According to contemporary accounts, the drinking of rum was not merely a relief from the crushing boredom of long voyages (for under sail, by the early eighteenth century they were ranging as far as the Guinea coast and the Indian Ocean in search of plunder), but in itself symbolized their liberation from authority. No pirate captain, to our knowledge, ever tried to rein in his crew's drinking. In all likelihood, any such corsair officer foolhardy enough to try would himself have been made to walk the plank.

All sorts of strange mishaps occurred as a result of this unbridled rum use. Captain William Snelgrave, a slave trader captured by pirates off Sierra Leone in 1719, wrote in his *A New Account of Some Parts of Guinea and the Slave Trade*, one of the best contemporary accounts of pirate life:

> About half an hour after eight o'clock in the evening, a Negro man went into the hold to pump some rum out of a cask, and imprudently holding his candle too near the bunghole, a spark fell into the hogshead and set the rum on fire. This immediately fired another cask of the same liquor, whose bung had been through carelessness

left open. And both the heads of the hogsheads immediately flying out with a report equal to that of a small cannon, the fire run about the hold. There were twenty casks of rum, with as many barrels of pitch and tar, very near where the place where the rum lay that was fired, yet it pleased God none of these took fire, otherwise it would have been impossible for us to escape.

While Snelgrave's captors managed to avoid this mishap, exploding rum barrels ignited through carelessness were a grave danger on pirate ships, whose standards of maintenance were often slapdash, to say the least.

One way in which pirates of the eighteenth century mimicked society in general was their devotion to toasts. At that time, toasting was considered analogous to a prayer, and all the more sacred for being consecrated in liquor and good fellowship. After the deposing of the Catholic Stuart, James II, from the English throne in 1688, a few of his followers sought refuge under the jolly roger. Given the severe persecution meted out to Jacobites (as the Stuart followers were called) by the British government, many more pirates declared themselves Jacobite out of sympathy, or at least to annoy the authorities. The following passage, by Captain George Roberts, relates a drinking bout that took place on a pirate ship shortly after its crew captured him in 1722:

> After supper, a bowl of [rum] punch and half a dozen of claret being set on the table, Capt. Russel took a bumper and drank success to their undertaking; which went round, I not daring to refuse it. Next health was prosperity to trade meaning their own trade. The third health was the King of France. After which, Russel began the King of England's health; so they all drank round, some saying "The King of England's health," others only "The aforesaid health," until it came round to me; and Capt. Russel having emptied two bottles of claret into the bowl as a recruit, and there being no liquor that I have a greater aversion to than red wine in punch, I heartily begged the captain and the company would excuse my drinking any more of that bowl and give me leave to pledge the health in a bumper of claret.

Hereupon Russel said, "Damn you, you shall drink in your turn a full bumper of that sort of liquor that the company does." "Well, gentlemen," said I, "rather than have any words about it, I will drink it, though it is in a manner poison to me; because I never drank any of this liquor, to the best of my remembrance, but it made me sick two or three days at least after it." "And damn you," says Russel, "if it be in a manner or out of a manner, or really rank poison, you shall drink as much, and as often, as any one here, unless you fall down dead, dead!"

So I took the glass, which was one of your Holland's glasses, made in the form of a beaker without a foot, holding about three quarters of a pint, and filling it to the brim, said, "Gentlemen, here is the aforesaid health." "What health is that?" said Russel. "Why," says I, "the same health you have all drank. The King of England's health." "Why," says Russel, "who is King of England?" I answered, "In my opinion, he that wears the crown is certainly king while he keeps it." "Well," says he, "and pray who is that?" "Why," says I, "King George at present wears it." Hereupon he broke out in the most outrageous fury, damning me and calling me rascally son of a bitch; and abusing His Majesty in such a virulent manner as is not fit to be repeated, asserting with bitter curse that we had no king.

I said I admired that he would begin and drink a health to a person who was not in being. Upon which, he whipped one of his pistols from his sash and I really believe would have shot me dead if the gunner of the schooner had not snatched it out of his hand.

Contemporary accounts are almost universal in describing this sort of drunken schizophrenia; one moment, the pirates are courteous to their captives, and the next brutal, or vice versa. Almost always, the catalyst was the rum bottle.

Certainly, rum made its mark on the careers of some of the best known of the buccaneers. Edward Teach (better known as Blackbeard) was as well known for his drinking as his cruelty. Operating primarily off the Carolina coast during the early eighteenth century, Blackbeard engaged in any number of rum-inspired high jinks. At one point, he informed his crew on the *Queen Anne's Revenge* that they should "make a hell of our own, and try how long we can bear it." That said, the captain and three of his men went down into the hold and closed up all the hatches. Then they set aflame pots of sulphur. At last, when the three others started shrieking for air, Blackbeard opened the hatches, happy that "he held out the longest."

One night, Blackbeard, Israel Hands, the master of the ship, and another pirate were drinking heavily below decks. The captain drew out a pair of small pistols and cocked them under the table; at this the third man excused himself. Blackbeard then blew out the candle, crossed his hands, and fired. Hands had a bullet through his knee, and was lamed ever after. Painful as this little joke was, it served Hands well. He left Blackbeard's service, and although arrested after his former chief's demise, was thereby able to prove his innocence of all subsequent crimes performed by his former shipmates and allowed to turn King's evidence against them for those preceding his desertion.

As might be guessed from these two episodes, rum played a strong role in Blackbeard's downfall. The captain's demise started with a booze-soaked beach party. In September 1718, the celebrated Charles Vane—at the time the most wanted pirate prowling the Atlantic—hailed the *Queen Anne's Revenge* at Ocracoke Inlet, North Carolina, and landed on the south end of the island with ninety crewmen. The two pirates got on well; the resulting jamboree lasted for days, with pigs and cows barbecued on the beach and, of course, much rum drinking.

News of the festivities reached Lieutenant Governor Alexander Spotswood of Virginia, who heard in Williamsburg that Blackbeard intended to turn Ocracoke into a pirate haven. His Excellency intended to bring an end to Blackbeard's reign of terror. A few weeks later, two sloops commanded by Lieutenant Robert Maynard caught the pirate undermanned at his hideout on Oracoke, a harbor on the south end of the island still called Teach's Hole. Whether or not Blackbeard knew of the intruders as night fell, he spent most of the night drinking rum with the master of a trading sloop visiting his ship.

In the morning, emboldened by drink, Blackbeard chose fight over flight. One of the bloodiest battles ever fought on the deck of a small ship followed. Having lured the Royal Navy sloops through a narrow channel where they ran aground, he turned and blasted them with a volley from his eight cannons, killing or wounding twenty men on Maynard's ship and stopping the second dead in the water. Seeing only Maynard and his helmsman still standing on a smoke-filled deck strewed with bodies, Blackbeard and fourteen of his men boarded with pistols and cutlasses drawn. Maynard in his turn fooled Blackbeard by ordering all his surviving men to hide below until the pirates were on board. A savage melee ensued as they poured out on a deck already slick with blood. Blackbeard and Maynard squared off, the lieutenant finding his mark with a pistol, the pirate fighting on despite suffering wound after wound from the battle raging around him. Snapping off Maynard's sword with a blow from his cutlass, he was about to finish off the lieutenant when a seaman came from behind and delivered a mortal slash across his neck. When he finally fell dead along with eight of his crew, Maynard recorded "five pistol ball and 20 cutlass wounds" on Blackbeard's body. But there is no record that he ever killed anyone until the day he died, November 22, 1718. Blackbeard's head was cut off as proof of his death and hung from the bowsprit of Maynard's sloop. When they arrived in port at Hampton Roads, it was staked on a pike at the mouth of the harbor as a warning to other pirates. At least in regard to rum, it was a warning heeded by few.

Where Blackbeard's career was marked by violence and a bloody end, that of Edward England was just as rum soaked, if more peaceful in both its course and its end. England's life as a pirate began when the sloop that he was a mate on was taken by a Captain Winter during a trip from Jamaica to Providence. England was so well regarded by the pirates that he was soon given command of a sloop of his own sailing out of New Providence in the Bahamas. He held this position until the island was settled by the English and the local pirates accepted the amnesty offered by Royal Governor Woodes Rogers in the name of the Crown.

England then sailed for the Guinea coast, where he and his men captured the ship *Cadogan*. Next, England took a ship called the *Pearl* and exchanged it for his sloop, renaming it the *Royal James*, in keeping with the aforementioned Jacobite sentiments of many of the pirates. The Guinea Coast was a fertile hunting ground for pirates, because of the heavily laden slave ships. As with any other stolen cargo, slaves were a valuable and easily sold commodity. With slaves going in one direction and rum in the other, the Triangle Trade was as much a boon to piracy as to any other profession involved.

Seizing a number of other ships, England and his pirates operated in West African waters until 1720. They then set off for Madagascar and then the Malabar Coast of India, seizing ships as they went.

On this voyage, England and his men encountered three vessels: two were owned by the British East India Company; the third was in the employ of the Ostend Company (this was an imperially chartered trading concern from the Austrian Netherlands that had started in 1719 and managed to acquire two Indian ports and a fair amount of business before being shut down in 1731, as the result of a treaty). The captain of the English ship *Cassandra* put up a fierce fight. He and his men so damaged the pirates' captured ship, the *Fancy*, that the pirates kept the *Cassandra* and gave the battered *Fancy* to the English captain. The other English ship, the *Greenwich*, and the Ostender deserted the *Cassandra*. Captain England, impressed by the Englishman's bravery but fully knowing his crew's bloodthirstiness, got his men drunk on captured rum and persuaded them (under the influence) to release the captain with the *Cassandra*. The doughty Englishman made good his escape.

Sobering up, the crew was angry, to say the least. They marooned England with three others on the island of Mauritius and sailed off under Captain John Taylor.

England and his men made a small boat of scrap wood and sailed it to St. Augustine Bay, Madagascar, near the present city of

Toliara. Here, England survived for a short while off the charity of other pirates, which consisted primarily of rum. As with the captain staying at the Admiral Benbow, it was alcoholism that finally killed Captain England in late 1720 or early 1721.

By that time, the pirate settlements in Madagascar were flourishing, and with them, the need for rum. In response, sugar planters in Mauritius, Reunion, and finally Madagascar itself began distilling the stuff and soon found it their major cash source. To this day, the areas of rum manufacture and consumption in Madagascar tend to center around old pirate settlements such as Nosy Be, Diego Suarez, Toliara, and the Ile Ste. Marie, off the east coast of the island. To this day, Nosy Be's Dzamandzar Distillery remains the largest and best known in the country.

The pirates in many such settlements also left behind mixed-blood descendants. But where the fathers had been outcasts and criminals, the sons became respectable, churchgoing pillars of local society. When, in time, the French began to colonize Madagascar, they found these people to be loyal allies.

In Ile Ste. Marie (or Nosy Boraha, to give its little-used Malagasy name), the English pirate Thomas White married Betsimsaraka, a native princess. This union gave rise to a mixed-blood royal dynasty, the Zanamalata. Their son, King Ratsimilaho, extended his rule over a good piece of the east coast of Madagascar. In 1750, he presented his domain to the king of France, thus opening the way for French colonization, which would end in the 1890 annexation of the island.

Today, the inhabitants of the Ile Ste. Marie continue to drink their rum, to attend Catholic Church, and to revere as their founder the pirate captain who put their settlement on the map.

But rum and piracy have had other unforeseen consequences in this part of the world. The planters of Mauritius, who found themselves under British rule after the Napoleonic Wars, were in search of new lands in which to cultivate sugar and produce rum. Their status as British subjects allowed them to settle in the newly acquired colonial territory of Natal, South Africa. There, the more enterprising planters introduced sugar plantations, rum distilleries, and the Catholic Church. Since the archbishop of Durban, a century and a half later, was to play a key role in the struggle against apartheid (which role the usually abstemious Afrikaners might be forgiven for seeing as a local incarnation of "rum, Romanism, and rebellion"), both South Africa's flourishing rum industry and its present constitution owe much to the buccaneers of the Spanish Main—a result that Morgan could not possibly have predicted. But such is the nature of history.

Bombo

A drink much favored by both pirates and regular West Indians.

Tall glass filled with ice cubes   ½ ounce sugar syrup
2 ounces Pusser's rum

Fill the glass with water, stir, and garnish with an orange slice and cherry. Sprinkle nutmeg and cinnamon on top.

West Indian Rum Beef Stew

4 cups coarsely chopped onion
2 pounds prime rib of beef, roasted to medium rare, trimmed of fat and gristle, and cut in ¾-inch cubes (or roast pork or lamb)
1 green bell pepper, seeded and cut in ¼-inch julienne
1 red bell pepper, seeded and cut in ¼-inch julienne
1 yellow bell pepper, seeded and cut in ¼-inch julienne
2 fresh tomatoes, coarsely chopped

2 teaspoons pressed garlic
1 tablespoon sugar
1 teaspoon freshly ground pepper
1 bay leaf, crumbled
1 cup water
⅓ cup tomato paste
1 teaspoon Tabasco sauce
1 teaspoon Pick-a-Pepper sauce
⅓ cup stuffed olives
¼ cup dark rum

Preheat the oven to 325 degrees F. Grease a baking pan.

Layer the onion, beef cubes, peppers, and tomatoes in the baking pan and sprinkle with the garlic, sugar, ground pepper, and bay leaf.

Combine the water, tomato paste, Tabasco, and Pick-a-Pepper sauce in a small bowl and pour over the ingredients in the pan. Cover and bake for 35 minutes.

Remove from the oven and stir in the olives and rum.

Makes 6 servings.

Chapter 5

Planter's Punch: Rum in the West Indies

Ireland was permitted to import directly from the Plantations all goods, of the growth, production or manufacture of the said Plantations, except sugar, tobacco, indigo, cotton, wool, molasses, ginger, pitch, turpentine, tar, rice, and nine or ten other specified items—which, stripped of its facetious verbiage, just means that Ireland was permitted to import West Indian rum. This aided the planters and rum makers of the West Indies, at the expense of Irish farmers, distillers, and their collective constitutions.

—Martin McMahon, *I Cry for My People*

IV. And be it further enacted . . . that from and after . . . [December 25, 1733,] . . . no sugary paneled syrups or molasses, of the growth, product and manufacture of any of the colonies or plantations in America, nor any rum or spirits of America, except of the growth or manufacture of his Majesty's sugar colonies there, shall be imported by any person or persons whatsoever into the kingdom of Ireland, but such only as shall be fairly and bona fide loaden and shipped in Great Britain in ships navigated according to the several laws now in being in that behalf, under the penalty

of forfeiting all such sugar, paneles, syrups or molasses,
rum or spirits, or the value thereof, together with the ship
or vessel in which the same shall be imported, with all her
guns, tackle, furniture, ammunition, and apparel. . . .
        —Molasses Act, May 17/28, 1733

Rum has always been the lifeblood of the Caribbean. As we
have seen, in its origins, in its distribution by the Royal
Navy, in its place within the Triangle Trade, and in its use
by the pirates of the Spanish Main, it has remained a huge part of
the image of the West Indies down to our own time. Americans
aged sixty plus will immediately think of the song "Rum and Coca-
Cola" when the Caribbean comes to his or her mind.

Nor is this image far off; rum is universally consumed in the
region and on every imaginable occasion. But although the drink's
supremacy has never been challenged, producing it at a profit has
often been problematic for its producers. Bound up as it is with
sugar production, it has served alternately as a curse and a blessing
for sugar planters.

Sugar and rum, as we have seen, depended on slavery for their
production. The new unwilling arrivals, however, came with their
own ideas—religious, social, cultural, and culinary—that pro-
foundly affected the places where they were forced to live and work.
It is a strange irony of the horrors of the Middle Passage that without the arrival of African muscle and culture, the countries and cultures of the New World would be immeasurably poorer today.

For a start, the slaves brought us peanuts, okra, and yams. We
owe all of the Western Hemisphere's beans and rice mixtures to
them, from the Hoppin' John (black-eyed peas and rice) of the
American South, to the *Moros y Cristianos* (black beans and rice) of
the Spanish Caribbean. We also owe to them the origins of all sorts
of preserved hot pepper sauces and dishes like gumbo. Alongside
these dishes, rum was served in as copious amounts as the slaves (or
their masters) could procure.

The music and dances of West Africa were also brought over and similarly transformed under European influence and supervision—the baboula and many others. But such European dances as the mazurka and the beguine received in their turn tremendous alteration at the hands (and feet) of the slaves and are still popular in various corners of the West Indies, long after having been virtually forgotten in Europe. An important factor in the celebrations that sparked all this dancing was, of course, rum.

Religiously speaking, it was presumed that the new arrivals would accept the faiths of their new masters (Catholic, in the case of the Spanish, French, and Portuguese; Protestant among the British, Dutch, and Danes). While civil law in most colonies required that the planters instruct their acquisitions in the local form of Christianity, such teaching was often sketchy, particularly among the British and Dutch. The memories of the gods and rituals of the Guinea coast continued to haunt the Africans; over time, many of them identified the former gods with the saints of Catholicism. In Protestant regions, such deities tended to continue under their own names. But the hybrid faiths that inevitably arose—voodoo, obeah, Santeria, candomble, macumba, and so on—remain an important factor in all the tropical areas colonized by African slaves. As we shall see in chapter 9, rum plays a great part in the ceremonial aspects of these religions.

Depending on the particular area and the period, masters and slaves, living and working together in close proximity, forged closer relationships than one might expect. The children of slave owners, raised in large part by slave women, picked up stories, bits of language, and other fragments of culture from these women. Slaves, in turn, observed their masters, absorbing and adapting a variety of their customs. To a greater or lesser degree, the slaves took part in their masters' festivities, not merely as servants, but as participants. Christmas, carnival, and Easter all took on a particularly local color, and all involved rum.

The hybrid culture that evolved from the meeting and mixing of native, European, and African elements (alongside Asiatic ones introduced later by East Indian and Chinese immigrants) came to be called "Creole"—a word that can be applied to people, dialects, livestock, and even vegetables. In the Americas, the "Creole Zone," at its widest extent, might be said to include the coastal regions of the American South, those parts of Mexico, Central America, Colombia, and Venezuela touching the Gulf of Mexico or the Caribbean, the Guianas, northeastern Brazil, various pockets elsewhere in Latin America, and, of course, all of the Greater and Lesser Antilles. In time, similar cultures that grew up in West Africa, certain islands in the Indian Ocean, the East Indies, and the Philippines acquired the same title.

However close individual relationships between masters and slaves might be, one great fear haunted Europeans throughout the Creole Zone until emancipation: slave revolt. The specter of a mass rising by the Africans shaped legal and military procedures for centuries; sometimes, often fueled by rum, such fears came to life. Whenever such outbreaks occurred, the colonial authorities acted swiftly. One particularly vicious rebellion broke out in Barbados in 1732. So close to victory did the slaves come on that occasion that the Royal governor was forced to appeal to neighboring colonies for aid. The governor of New Jersey dispatched his best militia unit, the crack Jersey Blues, to help put down the revolt. In this they were successful; the Blues became very proud of their distinction as the only militia unit to be sent out of the thirteen colonies on imperial service. Even so, as today's 2nd Battalion, 113th Infantry, New Jersey National Guard, it does not feature "Barbados 1732" as a battle streamer!

In the House of Commons, the planters of Jamaica and the British Lesser Antilles were wealthy enough to buy votes, even as various wealth interests can do in our Congress today. From time to time, as we saw in chapter 3, they were able to inspire the Crown to fits of protectionism.

Their opposite numbers in the French West Indies needed little such support at the court of Versailles, as successive French kings saw the necessity of keeping their sugar planting subjects in the

Caribbean competitive. This was as much a matter of foreign policy as of economics; the dependence of New England and New York on molasses from St. Domingue (later Haiti), Martinique, and Guadeloupe helped drive a wedge between London and New England.

In the Spanish West Indies, while planters did deal in sugar, there was more money to be made from such things as cattle and tobacco. But, as elsewhere, a great deal of rum was distilled for local use. As such, the center of rum production in the Caribbean remained in the British Lesser Antilles.

So things stood for most of the eighteenth century. In response to the French Revolution, however, the situation altered wildly. An ultimately successful slave revolt in St. Domingue had results that altered the face of West Indian rum forever. While many white planters were slaughtered, far more fled the island. Eventually, the world's first independent black republic was formed: Haiti.

In Haiti itself, although a large number of estates owned by *gens de couleur* (the mixed-blood descendants of Frenchmen and slave women) survived, most of the plantations were divided into small plots by their laborers, who turned to subsistence farming. As Haitian sugar and rum production collapsed, the country descended into an abyss of poverty from which it has yet to emerge.

The white refugees, on the other hand, soon carved out new lives for themselves. Many fled to such American ports as Norfolk, Charleston, and Savannah. These émigrés brought to their new homes cultural and religious traditions that survive there today. Most notably, they swelled the numbers of the recently legalized Catholic Church, founding parishes that still remain (Sacred Heart, Norfolk; Old St. Mary's, Charleston; and St. John the Evangelist, Savannah) and establishing a reputation for gracious living. *Gone with the Wind* fans will recall that Scarlett O'Hara's mother was described as the daughter of such folk; Pierre Toussaint, likely to be the first canonized African American, came to New York as the servant of his refugee mistress.

But many more fled to Spanish territory. In Louisiana, they swelled the numbers of the *Creoles blancs* (white Creoles), adding to

New Orleans's reputation for gracious living. A large group joined the Royalist émigrés in St. Martinville, which soon came to be called "petit Paris." Even today, the French spoken there, by white and black alike, is a refined eighteenth-century speech, quite distinct from the rustic Cajun patois spoken in the rest of rural southern Louisiana.

Trinidad, which had been a colonial backwater during most of the Spanish rule, was revitalized by the new arrivals. They introduced sugar cultivation and rum distilling on a large scale and soon put the island into the front row of the world's sugar producers.

The French and their slaves began to arrive in Trinidad as early as 1777 under the Spanish military governor Don Manuel Falques. In addition to Haitian refugees, the Royal Cedula of Population brought thousands of French and African people from the Lesser Antilles in the 1780s and '90s. One of these was St. Hilaire Begorrat from Martinique. Born in St. Pierre on that island in 1759, Begorrat was the grandson of the treasurer of La Rochelle, France. His father, Pierre, had emigrated to Martinique as a teenager. Setting up as a merchant in St. Pierre (then the capital of the island, and by report, a pleasant place until the volcanic eruption that destroyed it in 1902), St. Hilaire saw his business flourish. When he came of age, he was sent back to La Rochelle, where he became an engineer. Upon returning to Martinique, St. Hilaire found that his mother, Anne, had died. Since his older brother was old enough to take over the business in St. Pierre, the twenty-four-year-old St. Hilaire decided to migrate to Trinidad with his father.

With the expanding population of French planters on the island, the Begorrats saw a future in commerce and trade there. The great explorer, Bougainville, had done for the French islands what Captain Bligh had for the British ones: he introduced breadfruit. But in addition, the great navigator had brought back bamboo from Bourbon Island in the Indian Ocean (now Réunion) and yellow cane from Tahiti (superior in yield to the violet cane then grown on Trinidad). All of these plants would be the stock-in-trade of Begorrats, *père et fils*.

At that time, Trinidad had a population of about six thousand people, a third of whom lived in the new capital, Port-of-Spain; cotton was the major crop alongside cocoa and coffee. The Begorrats operated out of the city, dealing in their imported plants. It is suspected that St. Hilaire was also a smuggler. Most of Trinidad's merchants were contrabandistas: smugglers who supposedly acted with the tacit cooperation of the colony's treasurer, Don Christoval de Robles. Begorrat had a friend whose brother owned sailing vessels involved in the trade with Venezuela; his own brother, Pierre, remained at the helm of the mercantile company in Martinique. This gave him a unique opportunity to smuggle French luxury items to the South American mainland. But if de Robles could be paid off, the Intendant at Caracas on the mainland could not; he established a coast patrol at the end of the 1780s, and smuggling was halted.

St. Hilaire had other interests to occupy him by this time, however. At age twenty-eight, he married Marie Eléonore Catharine Olivier, the daughter of French Creoles from Grenada. With her brother Mathurin, he purchased 128 acres of land in the forest-covered valley of Diego Martin in May 1787. Their estate was called "Mon Désir." Not content with this parcel, Begorrat also petitioned an allotment of 358 acres of land to himself and his family. Begorrat obtained for himself, his father, and his wife a total of 96 acres, with eighteen slaves to work the place.

Leaving Port-of-Spain, the Begorrats prepared the virgin rain forest of Diego Martin for a coffee plantation. Their slaves cleared the land and built an estate house and quarters for themselves. Soon coffee was exchanged for sugarcane, an innovation picked up by St. Hilaire's neighbors. In tribute to the island from which Bougainville had brought it to Martinique, the variety they planted was called "Otaheite" cane, after the old spelling for Tahiti. By the 1790s, sugar became Trinidad's most important crop.

At first imbued with the ideas of the Enlightenment, St. Hilaire tried to be a lenient master, liberating slaves who did especially well. This changed radically when one of his slaves poisoned him, unsuccessfully trying to kill him.

Second only to slave revolts in its ability to inspire fear among slave owners, poisoning was not well regarded by other slaves either. If the act failed, harder work at best and general punishment at worst awaited them; if successful, such poisoning insured that most of the slaves would be sold to new masters, bearing the stigma of being a possible poisoner. Pleasant treatment was unlikely.

The British captured Tinidad in 1797, and St. Hilaire became a capitulant, swearing allegiance to the King of Great Britain; even so, he began to gather republicans around him. These revolutionaries later became involved in the wars of independence against the Spanish Crown on the South American mainland. Sir Thomas Picton, who became the first British governor, became aware of St. Hilaire's activities. Immediately, the planter was brought in for questioning but refuted the accusations upon his dignity as a gentleman and capitulant. He and Sir Thomas became great friends, and St. Hilaire embraced the monarchy.

St. Hilaire became a member of the Illustrious Cabildo, the council of government that had been founded by the Spanish but was retained by the British alongside other institutions, in keeping with the treaty of surrender. Thus, he was able to participate in cases of poisoning with great gusto. It was the policy of the governor to deter future malefactors, and he who had executions carried out as cruelly as possible. St Hilaire, by now one of the biggest of slave owners on the island, was instrumental in drafting at least one series of Codes Noir. These were the laws governing the lives of the slaves; where the Spanish codes had been lenient, St. Hilaire toughened them up considerably.

St. Hilaire's disenchantment with the secularist notions of the Enlightenment brought a rediscovered attachment to Catholicism. In keeping with both their treaty obligations and the precedent they had established in Quebec, the British authorities also kept Catholicism as the established Church on the island; the penal laws that oppressed their co-religionists in most of the Empire would not be applied in Trinidad. This was a policy that would stand them well in other predominantly Catholic areas that they would annex, such as Mauritius. The settlers of the Diego Martin valley turned to St. Hilaire for spiritual aid, and he built a church—the first in the valley—on his estate.

Despite his transformation into a hard master, St. Hilaire preferred the Afro-Caribbean culture, music, and patois of his slaves to the European pastimes of Port-of-Spain, which doubtless reminded him of Martinique. A lavish entertainer, he was able to introduce many of the more prominent Europeans on the island to these things.

One of his favorites was called Gros Jean. Gros Jean had the inborn ability to make up bitingly witty, mocking songs in patois about people he disliked. St Hilaire encouraged this gift, often calling in Gros Jean to sing to one of his less-liked guests. These cruel, pointed remarks, sung *sans humanité*—"without pity"—would be taken up by other slaves on other estates. This was the origin of calypso, or kaiso, as it is more properly called. Beneath St. Hilaire's mansion, there was a cave, where he meted out punishments to those of his slaves who displeased him. But in this somber locale, he would, after Mass on Sundays and feast days, sit as king, *le roi*. There, before his friends and favorite slaves, he would order his "chantwell" or chief calypso singer to sing. They might be songs of praise or insult to individuals, or else they were *mépris*, wars of insults between two or more expert singers. St. Hilaire and Gros Jean became such inseparable friends that the former's wife, Marie Eléonore poisoned the "Mait Caiso" out of jealousy. Gros Jean was buried in the family cemetery.

St. Hilaire died in 1851 at the great age of ninety-two, having known many calypsonians. Buried in the family cemetery alongside his wife, who had died of fever many years before, he nevertheless turned up once more, when his and his wife's remains were disinterred over a century later.

St. Hilaire's Cave remains a popular spot. Not only is it the birthplace of calypso, it was also part of a signaling system with North
Post Station, Fort George, and the Port-of-Spain harbor. It is said
that St. Hilaire used this communication system to outwit the local
authorities with his illicit slave trade and contraband operations.

But the effect of the French planters was greatest in Cuba. Particularly around Santiago de Cuba, their influence was immense—
even today the local Spanish retains a strong French flavor. Sugar
plantations bloomed throughout their range, and the rum distillation began. Cuba eventually became the world's greatest maker of
the liquor until the Cuban Revolution of 1958.

Another blow struck the British and French planters: emancipation of the slaves (1833 for the British, 1848 for the French) meant
that the sugar plantations had to look elsewhere for cheap labor.
Many former slaves simply took up small plots of land and started
farming for themselves. East Indian and Chinese indentured laborers were tried, for the most part unsuccessfully. As soon as their
terms of service were up, these new arrivals settled down as small
shopkeepers and merchants, leaving the cane fields behind forever.
Since slavery was not abolished in the Spanish dominions until
1886, Cuban and Puerto Rican planters continued to benefit from
the institution.

Yet another challenge emerged as the nineteenth century wore
on. As the colonial powers opened up ever more areas of the tropical world to economic exploitation, cheaper and more plentiful
sources of sugar emerged, from Hawaii to Natal. Between
increased competition and labor costs, the British and French
Caribbean sugar industry wilted. Napoléon III gave some relief to
the planters in Guadeloupe and Martinique, however. During the
1850s, centralized distilleries on both islands replaced the unprof-
itable former system, whereby each plantation made its own rum
(which meant that each of the planters had to invest in his own
expensive distilling equipment and act as his own salesman as well).
In contrast, these cooperatives boosted profits, as did a sudden fash-

ion for French West Indian rum in Europe. In 1860, the emperor abolished all trade restrictions on the French West Indies, and six years later gave them permission to regulate their own revenue. Thus, their economies stabilized to a great degree. The British islands, sadly enough, remained in a free fall. As a result, a large number of plantations were broken up among former slaves; others turned to alternative tropical products, such as spices, coffee, bananas, and so forth.

Meanwhile, distilleries in Cuba proliferated. In 1862, perhaps the most famous was founded in Santiago de Cuba by Don Facundo Bacardi Massó. Having emigrated from Valencia, Spain, the wine merchant married the daughter of one of Santiago's most prominent French sugar families: Dona Amalia Luc'a Victoria Moreau.

Don Facundo went to work, experimenting at home with various methods of rum manufacture. He wanted to make rum a civilized drink, the equal of the fine spirits he had sold in Spain. Experimenting with every single step of the manufacturing process, he was successful beyond anyone's wildest dreams, producing both light and dark rums. His personal innovation was a charcoal mellowing process that allowed for a smoothness hitherto impossible with rum. Now Don Facundo was ready to seek a wider public. On February 4, 1862, the Bacardi y Compañia was founded.

Don Facundo bought a small distillery with a corrugated metal roof and distilling flasks made of copper and wrought iron. A colony of fruit bats lived among the rafters of the roof. Dona Amalia, grounded as she was in Cuba's folklore, immediately thought of a use for them. The local peasants believed that the winged rodents brought "good health, fortune, and family unity." She suggested that the animal become the new distillery's logo. The badge caught on and has been Bacardi's trademark ever since.

Although Cuba's loyalty to the Spanish Crown had been proverbial during the wars of independence, which severed most of Latin America from the empire (giving rise to the island's proud title, *Siempre leal Cuba* ["ever loyal Cuba"]), the rising wealth among many of the upper classes led some of their number to agitate for independence. The Bacardis, despite the king of Spain's affection for their product, joined this group.

The family would suffer for their politics during the "Ten Years' War" (1868–1878). Don Facundo's son, Emilio, was exiled to Spanish North Africa because of treasonous activities; his eldest son joined one of the rebel armies. His brothers Facundo and José, along with his stepbrother Henri Schueg, remained in Cuba, running the company during the war years. While the women of the family fled to Kingston, Jamaica.

Time was running out, however, for the remnants of the Spanish Empire. The 1860s and 1870s had seen the overthrow of Queen Isabella II, another in the series of civil wars waged by the Carlists (supporters of the older line of the Spanish Bourbons and restoration of the pre-modern constitution of Spain), and abortive attempts at a republic and at a liberal monarchy with a prince of Italy's house of Savoy on the throne. While Isabella's son, Alphonso XII, was restored at last in 1874, the country had been weakened considerably by all the turmoil.

In the meantime, American supporters of "manifest destiny," which belief had brought the country to the shores of the Pacific by defeating Mexico and pressuring Great Britain out of the Oregon country, had been silenced but were not eliminated by the Civil War. That conflict over, they believed that the renewed nation had a commitment to expand ever further and spread the "blessings of liberty" over the globe, or at least through Latin America. Alaska having been bought from Russia in 1867, their attention turned to the remaining possessions of Spain in the Caribbean and the Pacific. (They also eyed the Polynesian kingdoms of Hawaii and Samoa, but that is another story.) Voices calling for annexation of Cuba were heard as early as 1868.

The resulting Ten Years' War encouraged such voices further, as did subsequent uprisings in 1895 and 1897. The annexationists gathered strength and at last felt that they had triumphed in 1896, when the Republican candidate, William McKinley, was elected with their aid. Ironically, McKinley was one of the few anti-annexationists in his own party. Nevertheless, most of the Republican leadership and such press lords as William Randolph Hearst were convinced that the time had come. The war drums commenced to beat in New York and Washington.

Spain was more discouraged then ever. Alphonso XII had died in 1885, leaving a young and pregnant wife, a Habsburg, former Archduchess Maria Cristina. She gave birth to a son, Alphonso XIII (grandfather of the present king, Juan Carlos), who was literally born king. Although the birth of the "child of the miracle," as he was called, buoyed up the public for a short time, Spain was in a very bad way. Not having recovered from her internal turmoil socially or financially, she was faced with ongoing low-level insurrections in Cuba, Puerto Rico, and the Philippines, the need to protect her position in northern Morocco, and the continuing expense of routine maintenance for her colonies in Guam and the Marianas, Micronesia, and the equatorial coast of Africa. Nevertheless, both the queen regent and her government were grimly determined to face the growing hostility of the United States.

When McKinley was elected, the Spanish were as fearful as the American war hawks were elated. The court of Madrid began trying to garner support from the other European powers. Foreign Minister Carlos O'Donnell made some salient points in his instructions to Spain's ambassador in London:

It is requisite that you stress the effects which the Cuban insurrection may have on the Monarchy in Spain, on the Regency, and on the monarchical principle in general. You should also stress the consequences of a war with the United States, which may be forced upon us in defending our rights and our national honor. . . .

Under the circumstances, the government of Her Majesty would regard themselves as faithless to their duty, if they did not place before the consideration the cabinets of the Great Powers of Europe, the special dangers which they see looming in the near future, and which, though especially affecting Spain, hold also a threat to colonial and maritime nations in general, and may even compromise other very important European interests. . . . There is inherent in the Cuban question a problem supremely European, affecting not only the development of Spain, but also the general interest of Europe, because very grave international consequences may result from the Cuban insurrection, and the daily more absorbent Monroe Doctrine.

The Spanish saw clearly what their defeat at the hands of the Americans would mean for all the European empires—the passing of world power from the old continent to the new. In the ensuing fifty years, O'Donnell's worst fears would be realized.

But the American "New Nationalists," as they were called, were convinced of the same future that the Spanish feared, albeit seeing it in different terms. Flush with victory, Senator Albert J. Beveridge, a Republican from Indiana, rose in the Senate on January 9, 1900, to deliver a speech entitled "In Support of an American Empire." Therein he declared:

It is elemental. It is racial. God has not been preparing the English-speaking and Teutonic peoples for a thousand years for nothing but vain and idle self-contemplation and self-admiration. No! He has made us the master organizers of the world to establish system where chaos reigns. He has given us the spirit of progress to overwhelm the forces of reaction throughout the earth. He has made us adepts in government that we may administer government among savage and senile peoples. Were it not for such a force as this the world would relapse into barbarism and night. And of our entire race He has marked the American people as His chosen nation to finally lead in the regeneration of the world. This is the divine mission of America, and it holds for us all the profit, all the glory, all the happiness possible to man. We are trustees of the world's progress, guardians of its righteous peace.

Stripped of its racial and religious imagery, the same speech might well be given in the Senate today. The war with Spain brought the United States to a definite crossroads in their history.

But what of the opinion of that even then large segment of the

American populace, the Catholics? Spiritually subject to the Pope
of Rome, how would they feel about a war with Spain, with
Austria-Hungary, at that time the two remaining major Catholic
powers (France and Italy then being ruled by anti-clerical governments)? At that time, the hierarchy of the Church in America was
divided between the Ultramontanes, who looked to Rome for leadership, and the Americanists, who wished to remake the national
Church into a new model. Headed by Cardinal Gibbons of Baltimore and Archbishop Ireland of St. Paul, they would become the
dominant force in the American Church, and remain so to the present day. At the outbreak of the war, Bishop O'Connell, rector of the
North American College in Rome, wrote to Archbishop Ireland:

> For me this is not simply a question of Cuba. If it were, it were no
> question or a poor question. Then let the "greasers" eat one another
> up and save the lives of our dear boys. But for me it is a question of
> much more moment:—it is a question of two civilizations. It is the
> question of all that is old and vile and mean and rotten and cruel
> and false in Europe against all that is free and noble and open and
> true and humane in America. When Spain is swept off the seas
> much of the meanness and narrowness of old Europe goes with it to
> be replaced by the freedom and openness of America. This is God's
> way of developing the world. And all continental Europe feels that
> the war is against itself and that is why they are all against us, and
> Rome more than all because when the prestige of Spain and Italy
> will have passed away, and when the pivot of the world's political
> action will no longer be confined within the limits of the continent;
> then the nonsense of trying to govern the universal Church from a
> purely European standpoint—and according to exclusively Span-
> ish and Italian methods, will be glaringly evident even to a child.

Spain was indeed defeated and deprived of her last colonies,
which America gobbled up (save Cuba—it would have been a bit
much to go to war for Cuban freedom, only to annex that country—but we did hold on to the Philippines, Puerto Rico, and

Guam). Nevertheless, her queen regent held on to the throne for her son, and the loss of the aforementioned colonies both saved the treasury a ton of money and allowed the Spanish to concentrate on what became Spanish Morocco. The British, French, Dutch, and Danes (who sold their three sugar islands to the United States in 1916) retained their Caribbean possessions. But the die was cast.

The two world wars exhausted the old continent and put half of it under Soviet domination. In the two and a half decades following 1945, American pressure played a key role in dynamiting our European allies out from their overseas territories (although, ironically, France and the Netherlands retain their colonies in the Caribbean, having transformed them into self-governing entities). With the fall of the Soviet Union, there remained only one empire in the world—the American empire. Interestingly enough, however, old resentments die hard. During the buildup to the Iraq War, the French and Germans refused to go along with American intervention, making warnings somewhat reminiscent of Carlos O'Donnell's. United States Secretary of Defense Donald Rumsfeld replied with language reminding one (in a secular way) of Beveridge and O'Connell—hence the "Old Europe" speech. But of course the playing field had changed tremendously since 1898, and American dominated globalization had completely replaced European colonialism.

Despite all the turmoil that surrounded the Ten Years' War and the American invasion in 1898, Bacardi flourished, spurred on by the American invention in 1870 of artificially produced ice. This development revolutionized alcohol sales, leading to the invention of such rum drinks as the mojito and the daiquiri. Generations of heat-afflicted drinkers have rejoiced ever since. The introduction of Coca-Cola by American forces led to the Rum and Coke, or "Cuba Libre."

In its way, this drink can be seen as a potent symbol of a changing world order—the marriage of rum, lubricant of the old colonial empires, and Coca-Cola, icon of modern American global capitalism. Moreover, despite the difference in their historical origins, both

rum and Coke are made from raw materials originating in the
Third World that required European and American intervention
to be transformed into saleable products. Thus, one drink, the Cuba
Libre, seems to reflect perfectly the historical elements of the
modern world. (That's something to reflect upon the next time you
drink one!)

The Bacardis did well under the new regime. In 1899, American
general Leonard Wood appointed Emilio Bacardi mayor of Santiago de Cuba. Taking his role seriously, Emilio started an institution
that became the Emilio Bacardi Moreau Municipal Museum in
Santiago de Cuba. Even today, despite Fidel Castro's hatred of the
family, the museum continues under its original title, featuring
proudly the mummy Emilio brought back from Egypt in 1912.

During the interwar years, the Bacardi empire steadily grew.
New bottling plants were built in Barcelona, Spain, and New York
City, although the latter had to close, thanks to Prohibition. In
response to this cruel and unusual action by the United States,
Facundito Bacardi invited Americans to "come to Cuba and bathe
in Bacardi rum." Heeding his call, thousands of Americans made
the jaunt, turning Havana into a "sin city" without peer; among
others, this frowsy atmosphere would eventually attract Ernest
Hemingway. "Rum runners" preparing to evade the United States
Coast Guard to bring their illicit yet delicious cargoes into the
United States, used Havana as both a jumping-off point and clear-
ing house for their wares. Of course, since many of these bootleggers were eventually forced to work for American organized crime
syndicates, the organizations also got a foothold in Havana.

Bacardi went from strength to strength. During the 1920s, the
Art Deco Bacardi building was put up in Havana. The first sky-
scraper in the city, it remains a prestigious office address, although
the government now collects the rents.

During World War II, a shortage of whiskey led to a greater
demand for rum, as did the stationing of more American soldiers in
the Caribbean. Bacardi did its best to keep up with the demand,

and it seemed afterward that there was clear sailing ahead for the company. But it was not to be.

When Castro took power in 1959, the Bacardi family fled to the Bahamas and opened a new distillery—the first ever to produce rum commercially there. Meanwhile, the family and company assets in Cuba were taken by the government. The communists continue to produce rum from the Santiago location under the name Havana Club. The Puerto Rico distillery continued to function, and over the following decades Bacardi entered the world of multinational conglomerates, becoming a player in the globalization of the world economy.

Despite these setbacks and an interfamily squabble, the Bacardis continue to own 15 percent of the company, support anticommunist causes, and participate in conservation—most notably for bats.

On a smaller scale, the Bacardi story was repeated several times by other families. In Puerto Rico, for example, Don Juan Serrallés, the son of a Spaniard who had settled in the area, opened a distillery in 1865 on the Hacienda Mercedita sugar plantation near the city of Ponce. There, he produced his first casks of rum using a still imported from France. Today, Félix Juan Serrallés Jr., the great-grandson of Don Juan, runs the company; it now produces and distributes over 60 percent of the rum sold on the island. Like Bacardi, Serrallés, too, has entered the global economy. In 1985, the company acquired the assets of Puerto Rico Distillers, Inc., a subsidiary of the giant Canadian liquor firm Joseph E. Seagram and Sons Ltd. This move allowed Serrallés to more than double its sales volume. In addition, Serrallés acquired the right to manufacture and distribute the Ronrico and Captain Morgan brands in Puerto Rico and several other Caribbean islands, while also producing Ronrico and Captain Morgan for distribution by Seagram's in the United States.

A rum dynasty also flourished in the Dominican Republic, the Hispanic side of the island of Hispaniola, whose sugar industry was ruined in the Haitian slave revolt. Here, too, a family became and maintained its position as the biggest rum producer in the country—

in this case, the Bermúdez family. Claiming descent from Don Diego Bermúdez, a companion of Christopher Columbus, who brought the first sugar cane to Santo Domingo, they claim deep roots in the business.

However that may be, their family company began in 1852, when Bermúdez created the formula for the "Amargo Panacea," a rum to be drunk as an appetizer and that quickly became famous. This was the recovering country's first real industry; until 1927, the company was directed by Don Armando Bermúdez, who transformed it into a nationwide industry. Later, as it became a corporation, its first administrator was Domingo O. Bermúdez, under whose direction the company reached the status of a national institution. Today, Bermúdez is synonymous with Dominican rum.

Across the border, in Haiti, the sugar and rum industry practically collapsed, as almost all the white planters were chased out. A notable exception was the Barbancourt family, originally from Charente, in the Cognac, where they had produced brandy. Arriving in St. Domingue in the eighteenth century, they went to work distilling rum, using the methods they had employed on brandy in France. So great was the result that the local rebels left the family unmolested when the slave revolt took place.

In 1862, Dupré Barbancourt perfected the formula of rum making that the business continues to use; after his death, his childless widow, Nathalie, brought in her nephew, Paul Gardère, to help her run the company. He inherited it when his aunt died, directing the company until 1946. La Maison Barbancourt was incorporated as a limited simple partnership in 1932.

Originally, the Maison Barbancourt did not produce its own cane juice; it distilled its rum from *clairin*—sugar cane juice purchased from a limited number of small-scale suppliers. This was taken to Barbancourt's distillery on Chemin des Dalles in Port au Prince. After Paul's death, his son, Jean, took control, remaining at the helm until his death in 1990. He began a throughgoing modernization. In 1949, Jean relocated the distillery to the Plaine du Cul-de-Sac on l'Habitation Mouline, near Damien, its current location. Work began in 1949 and in 1952 the plant began producing cane juice from the sugar cane grown on its own plantation on the Domaine Barbancourt. Not only did this action turn the enterprise into a real industry, but it also helped insulate Barbancourt from the postwar woes that afflicted Haitian agriculture.

Since the company could always be relied on to turn a profit, Papa Doc Duvalier cast longing eyes on the concern during the 1960s. The Gardères avoided the fate of the Bacardis when Duvalier's advisers suggested "how much damage Haitian civil servants could do to a product that depended on rigorous quality control."

Thierry Gardère, the great-great-nephew of the original Barbancourt, took over the company at his father's death in 1990 and directs it today. Société du Rhum Barbancourt's growing distribution network is now solidly implanted in over twenty countries. Today, over six hundred hectares of land are exclusively dedicated to sugar cane cultivation for Rhum Barbancourt, counting the 20 percent of which are on Domaine Barbancourt's own plantations. Société du Rhum Barbancourt employs 250 persons and its direct and indirect rum production activities are responsible for the livelihood of 20,000 persons. Nevertheless, it remains a partnership with five other family members. Thierry has indicated, however, that if the company is to continue to expand, it will have to invite foreign investment. For now, however, it remains as it has been.

A similar saga took place in Jamaica. In 1825, John Wray, a wheelwright living in the parish of St. Ann on the northern side of the island, opened a tavern in Kingston. Located beside the Theatre Royal, Wray called his establishment the "Shakespeare Tavern." Standing on the Parade (as Kingston's main square is called) across from the parish church, the Shakespeare soon became a center of local social life. It remains there today, still owned by Wray's company.

In 1860, Wray took his twenty-two-year-old nephew, Charles James Ward, into the business, and in 1862 he made him his partner. The business has been known since then as J. Wray and

Nephew. Wray retired in 1862 and died in 1870, leaving Ward as the sole proprietor.

A keen businessman, Ward expanded the company enormously, moving heavily into rum trading and production. At the International Exhibition held in London in 1862, J. Wray and Nephew won three gold medals. The next year, headquarters were moved from the Shakespeare tavern, located as it was in a mainly residential area, to larger premises on Port Royal Street, near the wharves where ships unloaded barrels of rum from the sugar estates. The company continued to win awards and prizes at international exhibitions in Paris (1878), Amsterdam (1883), New Orleans (1885), and Jamaica (1891).

By the time of Ward's death in 1913, the company had acquired three sugar estates and had secured the local distribution rights for a number of well-known brands.

After Ward's death, his estate was administered by trustees; in 1916 the trustees sold the estate to Lindo Brothers & Company Ltd. Shortly after acquiring J. Wray and Nephew, Lindo Brothers & Company purchased the Appleton Estate in St. Elizabeth, and in 1917 it expanded the factory and distillery operations at the estate. J. Wray and Nephew, under the management of Lindo Brothers & Company, also built two additional warehouses to store and age rums, and added an electric bottling line and bottle washing machine to its Kingston operations. Just before World War II, in 1939, Lindo Brothers & Company sold J. Wray and Nephew to Percy Lindo and his family.

As in the rest of the rum trade, the whiskey shortage during World War II helped expand the business enormously. In 1957, Percy Lindo's two sons, who had since taken over the management of the company, sold out to a syndicate that included some of the principal shareholders of the Lascelles deMercado Group. The new owners moved the company's headquarters from Port Royal Street in the center of downtown Kingston to a new complex on Spanish Town Road on the outskirts of the city in 1971. J. Wray and Nephew's offices are still located at this complex. The company was acquired as a wholly owned subsidiary of the Lascelles deMercado Group in 1989. Despite the economic problems Jamaica has suffered since independence, J. Wray and Nephew has managed to continue at a profit. Its Mount Appleton Rum remains extraordinarily popular.

The Lesser Antilles were also affected by the consolidation of plantations into corporations. This process affected even the birthplace of rum in Barbados, what is now the Mount Gay Estate. The estate is located on a ridge in the northernmost parish of Barbados, St. Lucy. In the 1600s, this spot was known as Mount Gilboa and was divided into several small, separately owned sugar plantations. They were named after their respective owners. Tyrell, Jemmott, Jones, Pickering, and Grey. These were consolidated in the early eighteenth century by William Sandiford; he bought most of the land, transformed it into a 280-acre plantation, and renamed it Mount Gilboa. It was passed on to his son, who sold it in 1747 to John Sober.

As absentee landlords, Sober and his son Cumberbatch spent most of their time in England. By 1787, Cumberbatch needed someone to manage the affairs of the flourishing Mount Gilboa estate. He chose his good friend, Sir John Gay Alleyne. In 1801, after Alleyne's death, Cumberbatch honored him, renaming the plantation Mount Gay. The Sober family continued to run the property until 1860.

Then came Aubrey Ward, who bought the estate outright in the early 1900s. He introduced new methods to meet the increasing demand for Mount Gay Rum, while strictly maintaining its traditional character. Ward, along with his business partner and marketing specialist John Hutson, introduced Mount Gay Rum to the international market. These efforts were continued by his son Darnley DaCosta Ward until his own death in 1989.

Although the Ward family continues to be involved with Mount Gay Rum distilleries, majority interest was acquired by the Remy

Cointreau Group in 1989. But despite this globalization, distilling itself remains traditional; while the molasses used at Mount Gay is supplied by Barbados Sugar Factories Ltd., and comes from all over the island, the water that is mixed with it is unique to St. Lucy, coming from a well that has supplied the plantation from its beginning.

In Antigua, the usual pattern of individual plantations producing their own rum prevailed throughout the long sugar decline of the nineteenth century. Antigua rums, despite their lack of off-island distribution, came to have a particular reputation for lightness and smoothness. But in the early twentieth century, the remaining estates gave up distilling. In their place, individual rum shops concocted their own blends, selling them under names like Red Cock, House, and Silver Leaf. In 1932, a number of these rum shop owners joined together to form the Antigua Distillery Ltd.

In 1934, the company purchased a number of estates and a sugar factory and began to produce its own molasses. The factory produced a very high-quality and distinctive grocery sugar known as *muscovado*. The residue of this sugar, known as muscovado molasses, contained a wonderfully pleasant sugar flavor and was used to produce the company's first bottled product in the early 1950s: a unique full-bodied, aged rum called Cavalier Muscovado Rum. In the 1960s, there was a shift in consumer preferences toward lighter-bodied spirits. In recognition of this trend, the company changed its distillation process to produce much lighter-bodied rum. Thus, Cavalier Antigua Rum was born; it has achieved great success internationally.

Rum in Guyana dates back to the early seventeenth century, when Guyana had a large number of sugar estates, with each, in the usual fashion, distilling its own rum. Each rum was given a mark, for example, SWR, AN, ICBU, depending on the estate where it was produced. These rums were shipped to England and thus began worldwide trading under the Demerara rum name, which today can only be applied to rums distilled in Guyana. As we have seen, some found their way into Royal Navy grog.

By the early twentieth century, most of the distilleries were owned by the English companies Booker Bros. McConnel & Company Ltd., trading as Booker Rum Company, and Sandbach Parker Holdings, trading as Diamond Liquors Ltd. These two companies were amalgamated in 1976 as Guyana Liquor Corporation and in 1983 this name was changed to Demerara Distillers Ltd.

By 1960, technological advances and market demands brought about the amalgamation of the many small distilleries into four distilleries, which were further consolidated into Demerara Distillery, with one distillery operation at Plantation Diamond on the east bank of the Demerara River.

The same pattern of consolidation prevailed over a large part of the Caribbean. However, here and there, one finds a single estate (whether revived or in action since its origin) still producing its own; generally, some special ingredient or other will be added to make the product distinctive. Usually, such rums will not travel far beyond that particular island.

But in many places in the region, people with the right equipment, however primitive, will make their own rum as the Appalachian folk make moonshine. Rough stuff to be sure, but much loved by its producers and their friends!

It is hard to overemphasize the part that rum has played and continues to play in everyday life in the West Indies. The popular picture of the sugar planter in his white linen suit, languidly sipping his planter's punch on the verandah of his great house is not only historically accurate, it still has a few real-life prototypes today. Sportsmen and farm laborers alike drink daiquiris to their hearts' content. Rum shops are the gathering places for local communities, and second only to churches for their place in the community. Half a century ago, in bars across the Antilles, rum was served free, but there was a charge for the water that was mixed with it!

In Jamaica, white rum accounts for 90 percent of the rum sold on the island. "Overproof" (what Americans would call 151) white rum is the staff of life for the working class. While it is used in folk medicine as a base for preserving "bush" potions made from herbs and roots, many folk use it like coffee to get started in the morning. Few households are without a bottle for medicinal purposes; it is particularly used for fevers and toothaches. Rubbed hard into the scalp, it is seen as good for headaches; the same effect is sought by placing a rum-soaked cloth over the affected person's eyes while he or she lies down. It is rubbed on the skin for chills or chest pain. Jamaicans claim that a cold can be forestalled by drinking white rum mixed with lime juice and honey. Overproof is also seen as a cure for hangovers; ill Jamaicans will soak a herring in the stuff, set it on fire, and eat it.

Expectant mothers are often asked to bring a bottle of overproof to the hospital. Because of the purity of the white rum, newborn babies are given sponge baths in it to cleanse their skin. At home, new mothers are instructed to rub a bit of overproof on a baby's foot to help it sleep. In some parts of Jamaica, babies are bathed in rum before their christenings.

Bodies of deceased Jamaicans are disinfected with white rum prior to burial. Afterward, family and friends of the departed hold a traditional "Nine Nights" vigil, which requires large amounts of overproof.

Rum plays its part in Jamaican holidays as well. A traditional Christmas drink on the island is made from sorrel, a relative of the hibiscus. The plant's red berries are steeped in boiling water; the resulting liquid is then sweetened with sugar or syrup and flavored with ginger, cloves, and, of course, rum. Even Christmas pudding requires fruits that have been soaked in rum for weeks before the holiday arrives.

Rum is also seen as an aphrodisiac. Not surprisingly, Jamaicans swear that overproof will do the trick. But in Dominica, the island's Macoucherie Rum is seen as *the* magic potion. (The Macoucherie Estate has been in the Shillingford family for several generations and is now the only licensed distillery on the island to produce rum from local cane, which is grown on its own plantation.) On Grenada, the local menfolk put a strip of bark of the Bois Bandé

(Hard Wood) tree in a bottle of rum for a couple of weeks to infuse before drinking it; the combination is supposed to be irresistible.

A more innocent method of attracting feminine attention is the use of Bay Rum, an aftershave made throughout the region (although the Bermudan variety is best known in the United States); it is made of distillate of myrtle leaves mixed with rum.

Both spiritually and economically, rum has repeatedly saved the people of its region of origin from personal, national, and regional ruin. If its origins brought pain, its career has been (at least according to its partakers) a blessing.

Barbados Planter's Punch

1½ ounces gold rum
1 teaspoon sugar syrup or to taste
Dash angostura bitters
Banana slice

Juice of 1 lime
Maraschino cherry
Pinch nutmeg
Orange slices
Water or club soda

Mix all ingredients, except banana, orange slices, cherry, and nutmeg, with cracked ice in a shaker or blender and pour into a large, chilled Collins glass. Garnish with banana, orange slices, and maraschino cherry. Sprinkle ground nutmeg on top.

Banana Bread

2⅔ tablespoons stick margarine, softened
2 tablespoons light cream cheese, softened
1 cup sugar
1 large egg
2 cups all-purpose flour
2 teaspoons baking powder
½ teaspoon baking soda
⅛ teaspoon salt

1 cup mashed ripe banana
½ cup skim milk
2⅔ tablespoons dark rum (or ⅜ teaspoon rum extract)
1 teaspoon vanilla
⅜ cup chopped pecans, toasted
⅜ cup flaked sweetened coconut
¼ cup packed brown sugar
2 teaspoons lime juice

Preheat oven to 375°. Coat an 8 × 4-inch loaf pan with cooking spray; set aside. Beat 2 tablespoons of the margarine and the cheese at medium speed of a mixer; add sugar, beating well. Add egg; beat well. Combine flour, baking powder, baking soda and salt; stir well. Combine banana, skim milk, 2 tablespoons of the rum (or ¼ teaspoon of the rum extract), vanilla, and ¼ cup each of the pecans and coconut; stir well. Add flour mixture to creamed mixture alternately with banana mixture; mix after each addition. Stir in the pecans and coconut.

Pour batter into prepared loaf pan; bake at 375° for 60 minutes. Let cool in pan 10 minutes; remove from pan. Let cool slightly on a wire rack. Combine brown sugar, lime juice, and the remaining margarine and rum in saucepan; bring to a simmer. Cook 1 minute; stir constantly. Remove from heat. Stir in the remaining pecans and coconut; spoon over loaf.

Chapter 6

~~~~~~~~~~~~~~~~~~~~~~~~~~~~~~~

Colonial and Revolutionary America

From France we do get brandy,
From Jamaica comes rum;
Good apples and lemons from Portugal come.
But stout and good cider are England's control—
Give me the punch ladle, I'll fathom the bowl!
—Colonial song

As we have seen, the thirteen colonies benefited enormously from rum. Rum fueled the sailors of the Royal Navy who protected the colonists; rum gave the colonies their place in the Triangle Trade; and rum solidified the connection between the raw settlements and both the older established West Indies and the motherland itself. But great as rum's effect on the external relations of the colonies and the rest of the world was, it was greater still at home.

As early as 1620, the Pilgrims quarreled with the crew of the *Mayflower* as to who would drink the final allotment of beer. In 1630, *Arabella*, the first Puritan ship, carried ten thousand gallons of wine and three times as much beer as water in its hold. Although the Puritans set extremely strict limits on behavior and recreation (outlawing Christmas and Easter), they did allow drinking—as a rare outlet, it was pursued with gusto.

On Richmond's Island, Maine, in 1639, the traveler John Josselyn wrote about Captain Thomas Wannerton, "who drank to me a pint of kill-devil Rhum at a draught." Josselyn wrote of the medical uses for rum, which generally required various herbs to be steeped in the rum and the result to be drunk for relief of an ailment. Poplar root bark, for example, was used in rum for the cure of fever, ague, gout, and rheumatism. Blazing-star or devil's bit was used in the same way against hemorrhoids. Nevertheless, Josselyn also called the drink "cursed liquor rhum, rumbullion or kill-devil."

Despite the Puritans' general tolerance for alcohol, however, rum did not at first find favor with Puritan authorities. In May 1657, the General Court of Massachusetts forbade the sale of strong liquors "whether knowne by the name of rumme, strong water, wine, brandy, etc., etc." This inclusiveness of language was not directed against grape-based liquors; the reasons for the terms used were the fact that in some places in the colonies the stuff was called Barbadoes-liquor or Barbadoes-brandy.

As we shall see, however, this prohibition did not last long. The fledgling colonies soon found that many of the native inhabitants were not pleased at losing their lands. Others had furs to trade, but demanded something of value in return. For both, rum seemed like the perfect solution. It was soon being given in large amounts to the Indians, who, in the Northeast, called it *ocuby*. This was a fateful development.

While various Indian tribes had used different organic hallucinogens in religious ceremonies, none apparently had tried fermented liquids. Although the use of peyote and other such drugs has been jocularly called "the Indian's revenge," their ravages among twentieth-century academics and intellectuals cannot be compared to the wholesale damage done by rum to the North American Indian population.

According to Peter Cooper Mancall in *Deadly Medicine: Indians and Alcohol in Early America*, "Alcohol abuse has killed and impoverished American Indians since the 17th century, when European settlers began trading rum for furs." Despite nascent temperance efforts on the part of various chiefs, the effects of rum on the Indians remind the reader of the damage done by crack cocaine in today's inner cities. Apart from accidents (like falling into campfires), liver disease, and the like, many Indians would do anything for the drink. Squaws were prostituted and children sold into bondage by Indians whose tribal structures had broken down; such folk did not last long.

All was not black, however. Some Indians, such as Powhatan, the great Virginian chief, began to offer alcohol as a hospitality gesture. A colonist wrote that Powhatan "caused to be fetched a great glasse of sacke, some three quarts or better, which Captain Newport had given him five or seaven yeeres since, . . . not much above a pint in all this time spent, and gave each of us in a great oister shell some three spoonefuls" before directing his braves to lodge their visitors.

Mancall relates a 1774 occurrence, whereby the Iroquois sachem Canasatego used the Anglo-French conflict and European toasting customs at a treaty signing. Seeing that the British had offered rum in "French glasses," Canasatego later asked also to be served in English glasses to toast the king of Great Britain. Pennsylvania's lieutenant governor, pleased at this sign of Iroquois dislike for the French, ordered larger glasses, declaring, "They cheat you in your Glasses, as well as in every thing else."

But the English generally used rum as a means of keeping the Indians dependent. Traders found it easy to cheat the Indians out of furs with rum; while they also offered iron axes, knives, hatchets, awls, fish hooks, trade cloth of various types and colors, woolen blankets, linen shirts, brass kettles, jewelry, glass beads, muskets, ammunition, gun powder, and the like, it was rum that the Indians wanted most. In time, use of European products led many of the natives (at least, those whom the rum did not ruin) to adopt

European ways. From this unique synthesis emerged the "Five Civilized Tribes," the Cherokee, Choctaw, Chickasaw, Creek, and Seminole. After the American Revolution, these tribes lived like their fellow southerners, down to owning slave-run plantations (like those of the whites) and maintaining republican governments.

Although the Dutch in New York were not themselves very fond of rum (preferring instead beer, gin, and schnapps), they nevertheless avidly traded it with the Indians. After the Catholic duke of York (later King James II) took over the colony and tried to limit the trade, the Dutch replied, "To prohibit all strong liquor to them [the Indians] seems very hard and very Turkish. Rum doth as little hurt as the Frenchman's Brandie, and in the whole is much more wholesome."

Some of the English and colonial leadership was worried about both damage done to the Indians by liquor and the damage that braves, enraged by drink, were likely to do. So it was that the authorities passed laws restraining the sale of rum to the "bloudy salvages," prosecuting and fining white traders who violated these laws, and punishing Indians who were found drunk. In 1685, Maine taverns were prohibited from selling alcohol to Indians and were held accountable if the Indians drank too much—even if the Indian in question had not entered the tavern, it would still be considered the source of the offense. But this particular law had no more effectiveness than similar legislation passed against bars and their patrons in our own day.

The proprietor of Pennsylvania, William Penn (whose father, as we saw, issued the first rum tot in the Royal Navy), wrote to the earl of Sutherland in 1683, "Ye Dutch, Sweed, and English have by Brandy and Specially Rum, almost Debaucht ye Indians all. When Drunk ye most Wretched of Spectacles. They had been very Tractable but Rum is so dear to them."

It was also very dear, as we have seen, to the white settlers. By 1651, rum, called "kill-devil," was being manufactured in New England. In short order, the colonists were drinking, on average, seven shots a day of 80-proof rum for most people over age fifteen. The prohibition decreed by the General Court of Massachusetts found no more success than later such attempts would. Parents and children drank together; ministers prepared themselves before sermons with rum. Working men were given daily grog breaks, and it was considered part of their pay. For women, tavern keeping was one of the few professions open to them.

As the years passed, the Dutch in New York were less and less able to obtain from the Netherlands the schnapps and gin they loved. Calling rum brandy-wine, they came to love it as much as did their Yankee neighbors to the east. Soon, wherever "strong waters" were named in taverns lists, the liquor was actually neither aqua vitae, gin, nor brandy, but New England rum.

It wasn't long before distilleries all over New England were creating gallons of the stuff. While this alcoholic tide would fuel the Triangle Trade, it also had the result of making rum prices drop at home. Increase Mather, the Puritan divine, wrote in 1686, "It is an unhappy thing that in later years a Kind of Drink called Rum has been common among us. They that are poor and wicked, too, can for a penny make themselves drunk." Despite this rebuke, the good Reverend Mather praised strong drink as "a good creature of God." In 1673, Barbadoes rum was worth 6 shillings a gallon. In 1687, its price had vastly fallen, while New England rum sold for 1 shilling 6 pence a gallon. In 1692, 2 shillings a gallon was the regular price. In 1711, the price was 3 shillings, 3 pence. In 1757, as colonial currency lost value, it was 21 shillings a gallon. In 1783, a gallon cost only a little over a shilling; then it fell to 8 pence a quart. During this time, the average cost of molasses in the West Indies was 12 pence a gallon; so, although a distillery was costly, the profits were huge.

Edmund Burke, the British statesman, said around 1750, "The quantity of spirits which they distill in Boston from the molasses which they import is as surprising as the cheapness at which they sell it, which is under two shillings a gallon; but they are more famous for the quantity and cheapness than for the excellency of their rum." At the same time, an English traveler named Benett wrote of Boston society, "Madeira wine and rum punch are the liquors they drink in common." Major General Friedrich Baron von Riedesel, the Hessian commander during the American Revolution, wrote of New Englanders, "Most of the males have a strong passion for strong drink, especially rum." Future President John Adams declared, "If the ancients drank wine as our people drink rum and cider, it is no wonder we hear of so many possessed with devils." This was an area in which he had some expertise, since, until his death, he always began the day with a tankard of hard cider before breakfast.

Adams was typical of New Englanders of his time and place. Eastern Connecticut was perhaps the most conservative half of a colony that had been founded in response to the perceived laxity of Massachusetts Bay. But Clarence M. Webster tells us in his *Town Meeting Country* (Duell Sloan and Pearce, 1945):

In one store in a small town, twenty-five gallons of West India rum were sold in one week on charge account, and some customers paid cash or bought it by the tumbler for immediate consumption. One of the gallons went to the local dominie. At the raising of the Westford church, the workers were provided with one barrel of rum and one-fourth barrel of sugar. People drank in homes, in taverns, at baptisms, weddings, funerals, and ordinations. As late as 1825, at the installation of a Connecticut minister, free drinks were served at a nearby bar to all clergy and laity, and the church paid the bill.

In Maine, too, rum became a key feature of the local scene. Initially, Maine women made beer at home; the wealthy imported wine from the Portuguese and Spanish islands. By 1700, however, more Maine Yankees drank rum than beer, with cheap New England rum being distilled in Boston (and traded for with lumber) and later Falmouth—now Portland.

Perhaps the best-known town in Massachusetts for rum production was Medford. Early on, its location on the Mystic River made it a prime location for shipbuilding and that is what Medford was best known for—until 1735. In that year, Andrew Hall, a Bostonian, was in the town on business. Tasting water from a local well, he realized that he had found an optimum location for rum manufacture. Hall opened up a distillery and so began an industry that would last until 1905. Interestingly enough, much of the molasses that fed the Medford rum production was brought from the West Indies on Medford-made ships. "Old Medford Rum" became a much sought-after commodity; soon, it was even being exported to the West Indies. Outside the Medford shipyard, on Ship Street, a barrel of rum was placed. Attached to it was a dipper. Shipwrights would serve themselves a ladleful on their way into work and again when their day ended.

When Paul Revere made his famous ride on April 18, 1775, he made only one voluntary stop—at the home of Captain Isaac Hall, Andrew's descendant. There the rebel envoy fortified himself with his host's family beverage. Nor was he the only one to enjoy it that night: Sixty Medford minutemen had gathered at Hall's and were liberally imbibing when Revere arrived. After he told them of the advance by the British regulars, they set off for Lexington; alas, they were too befuddled to find the place, and never did make the battle. Nevertheless, the Gaffey Funeral Home, which the Hall house has since become, annually hosts a gathering of local historians on April 19, who gladly toast Revere in rum. So much a part of New England lore did the local beverage become that Stephen Vincent Benét has Daniel Webster downing a bit of it before arguing a court case with Satan in *The Devil and Daniel Webster*. Medford rum was a name to conjure by until the distillery closed at last in 1905.

Colonial, especially New England, ports boomed with the rum trade. Although, when Roger Williams and his followers first settled the Providence area in the 1630s, their economy was entirely based on farming, by the eve of the American Revolution, the town's income was derived primarily from its port. The Triangle Trade brought great wealth to New England merchants, industrialists, and sea captains. These privileged few and their dependents resented it greatly when Parliament passed the Sugar Act of 1764, levying an import tax on sugar products. Thus, Providence's wealth provided many leaders to the revolutionary movement. Those who survived the break with Britain would, as their counterparts did throughout the smaller New England seaports, replace the former political and clerical leadership as the dominant power. And, since their trade in rum transcended the Triangle Trade to include domestic export, they would play some role in national affairs as well.

Although it had its fans there as elsewhere, rum had not the monopoly of southern livers that it enjoyed in New England. The stills in Virginia and the Carolinas poured out in addition a dizzying variety of alcoholic nectars, made possible by the abundant fruit trees of the sunny South: apple and peach brandy, cherry fling, and even cherry rum. During the two decades of British control in east Florida (1763–1783), planters there mixed orange juice with rum. For that matter, southern scuppernong wine was popular enough to banish rum from a polite local table. Still, it had its uses. Planters would give it to their slaves at Christmas and other holidays, and it was used on them medicinally as well. But if he was not considered a profitable asset, the hapless slave might find himself traded for the liquor that lightened his load. This fate befell Tom, a slave belonging to George Washington. Writing to his agent from his Mount Vernon estate, our first president declared:

> With this letter comes a negro (Tom) which beg the favor of you to sell in any of the Islands you may go to, for whatever he will fetch, and bring me in return for him:
>
> 1 hhd. best molasses
> 1 ditto best rum
> 1 barrel Lymes if good
> 1 pot Tamarind containing about 10 lbs.

Most plantations made their own rum, and doubtless Washington intended to compare the product of his own still with the West Indian product. Certainly, he benefited from it as much as Daniel Webster had in his encounter with the Devil: Washington successfully wooed local voters with seventy-five gallons of rum in his first campaign for election to the colony's House of Burgesses in 1758.

Taverns were scattered up and down the King's Highway, ultimately linking Portland, Maine, with Savannah, Georgia; so, too, on other highways, at ferry crossings, and in cities and towns. The tavern was a vastly important institution in colonial America; here, politics were discussed, plots were formed, and news exchanged. Usually, as the rupture between the Crown and the dominant classes in its colonies loomed, individual taverns came to be known as being either "Tory" (such as the Earl of Halifax in Portsmouth, New Hampshire) or "Whig" (like the Liberty Tree of Boston). Secondary to these improving and civic-minded pursuits, however, there remained the tavern's primary tasks: providing food, serving drinks, and lodging weary travelers.

Then as now, the latter two labors sometimes conflicted. In 1704, a thirty-eight-year-old lady named Sarah Knight set out by "post" (the regular stage coach) on the King's Highway, from Boston to New York. At one tavern where the coach's passengers overnighted, she was kept awake by the topers in the next room, who drank, sang, quarreled, and called for yet more drink. To gain some relief, she said a sort of folk prayer apparently used in such situations:

> I ask thy aid O Potent Rum
> To charm these wrangling topers dum
> Thou hast their Giddy Brains possest
> The Man confounded with the Beast
> And I, poor I, can get no rest
> Intoxicate them with thy fumes
> O still their Tongues till morning comes.

Apparently, the charm worked, for, as she recorded in her diary, "I know not but my wishes took effect for the dispute soon ended with tother dram." It might be worth trying the rhyme today, when stuck in a similar situation.

Rum formed the basis of all popular tavern drinks; many are

still mixed today. Toddy, sling, grog, and flip were all invented in this era, as was the generic term for such drinks: "cocktail." It may well be argued that the cocktail, alongside jazz and the movie musical, constitutes some of America's greatest contributions to world civilization.

One favored drink of the period was black-strap, yet another rum-based drink. A popular parody of the eighteenth-century poem, "I knew by the smoke that so gracefully curled," ran

> I knew by the pole that's so gracefully crown'd
> Beyond the old church, that a tavern was near,
> And I said if there's black-strap on earth to be found,
> A man who had credit might hope for it here.

John Adams's wife's relation, Josiah Quincy, said that black-strap was "a composition of which the secret, he fervently hoped, reposed with the lost arts." Its principal ingredients were rum and molasses, though there were other simples combined with it. He added, "Of all the detestable American drinks on which our inventive genius has exercised itself, this black-strap was truly the most outrageous." Casks of the stuff stood in every country store and tavern. Anticipating the modern-day use of jerky, salmon sharpies (dried fish), peanuts, or popcorn in such places, a salted codfish would be hung alongside to tempt by thirst additional purchasers of black-strap. There were other such concoctions: "Calibogus," or "bogus," was unsweetened rum and beer; and "Mimbo," sometimes abbreviated to "mim," was a drink made of rum and loaf sugar, and occasionally diluted with water.

Taxes on molasses and rum led many Yankees, as an alternative to either paying the imposts or breaking the law, to begin distilling whiskey in home stills. Rye was the favored grain for this enterprise; thus, unwittingly, Parliament's laws led directly to the rise of a drink that would eventually surpass rum in American hearts (and livers): rye. Rye whiskey would remain dominant in the United

States from the early nineteenth century until the 1960s, after which it was rapidly eclipsed. A bit difficult to find today, it nevertheless remains beloved by aficionados, including myself.

But in the meantime, in addition to the smuggling of which we spoke in Chapter 3, some Rhode Islanders, as an open break with the mother country loomed closer, went so far as to attack in 1772 His Majesty's revenue ship *Gaspee*. This hapless craft found itself boarded and burned to the waterline in reprisal for its chasing vessels loaded with contraband rum.

The next year saw an East India ship boarded in Boston Harbor by a group of thugs disguised as Mohawks; prior to their dumping the untaxed tea thereon into the harbor, they had steadied themselves by consuming large quantities of rum at the town's famed Green Dragon Inn. These drinks and monetary inducements were provided to these gentlemen by the archsmuggler John Hancock.

Taverns became the favored meeting places of committees of correspondence, as well as of the provincial congresses (until they were able to evict the various colonial assemblies from their respective state houses—a task rendered easier by the fact that the leaders of the former had generally run the latter as well). When the Continental Congress assembled at Philadelphia, the taverns and rum shops of the town were hard put to keep them supplied, so great was the thirst of the national leadership. Thomas Jefferson himself worked on the Declaration of Independence in Philadelphia's Indian Queen Tavern.

Since the revolution was in fact a civil war, it will come as no surprise that the Loyalists and rebels vied with one another in their consumption of rum, because their tastes were identical. An excess of rum befuddled Colonel Johann Rall's Hessians at Trenton on Christmas, 1776. Not only were the majority killed or captured in the rebel surprise attack, their loss was their opponents' gain: the rum captured by the Continentals was quickly consumed. They could surely have used it at Valley Forge, during the harsh winter of 1777–1778. A sure sign that things were improving for them came in March of 1778, when Washington added a ration of rum for each soldier, in addition to an extra month's pay for having stuck out the winter. Two months later, when news came of the French alliance, there was rejoicing in the camp on May 5: along with prayer, parading, and gun salutes, each man was issued a gill (four ounces) of rum.

Before and after the revolution, rum was an important component of American holiday celebrations, although, as might be expected, more so in New England than elsewhere. Since religious holidays as such were banned there, Yankees made rum flow during civic feasts of their own creation. Thus, Thanksgiving Day saw the stuff consumed by the gallon alongside turkey and pumpkin pie. On election day, drams of rum lent eloquence to campaigners; speakers at town meetings were given wisdom by spirit less than holy; and gills of kill-devil helped militiamen through their drill-paces on muster day.

In the middle colonies and the South, however, rum and allied potations helped out on the Catholic Church's festal days. At Christmas, mummers would go from house to house and be greeted with rum punch; the same drink might be found in New York on New Year's Day, where the old Dutch custom of keeping open house for all was maintained. English, Scots, Welsh, and Irish colonists celebrated respectively the feast days of their patrons: Saints George, Andrew, David, and Patrick.

One of the most commonly celebrated holidays in all the colonies was the king's birthday, which, after the accession of George III in 1760, was celebrated on June 4. Although the intensity of the celebrations of this day varied from year to year (often depending on the feelings for the Sovereign among the prominent at that particular time), many of the festivities later associated with July 4 were indulged in. The Royal governor of a given province would throw a ball or reception, while fireworks were shot off for the amusement of the public. For the poorer sorts, rum and beer were distributed for free. Special church services were offered by the various denominations (although, perhaps, the Anglicans were most fervent). The celebrations for 1766 were extremely lavish, since they followed immediately on the repeal of the Stamp Act, an occasion with which many of the wealthy were particularly happy.

In New York City, Governor Sir Henry Moore had an ox roasted whole, a hogshead of rum and twenty-five barrels of beer opened, and the people invited to join in the feast. His Excellency, the council, military officers, and the clergy dined at the King's Arms, on the west side of Broadway, opposite Bowling Green, where General Thomas Gage had his headquarters. Twenty-five pieces of cannon were ranged in a row and gave a royal salute, and in the evening twenty-five tar barrels, hoisted on poles, were burned and fireworks were exhibited at Bowling Green. Similar festivities took place from Portsmouth, New Hampshire, to Savannah, Georgia. In each place, rum flowed.

On New Year's Day, the Royal governors would receive the leading figures—political, religious, civilian, and military—in each colony. This "levée," as it came to be called, was an important event in the social calendar and was intended to bind the "best people" closer to the Crown. The word levée comes from the French verb lever, "to rise (specifically from one's bed)," and began with the Levée du Soleil or "Rising of the Sun" instituted by King Louis XIV of France at the Palace of Versailles, who received his male subjects in the Royal bedchamber just after rising, a practice that subsequently spread throughout Europe. The levée crossed the English Channel in the eighteenth century, and in Great Britain and Ireland became a formal court assembly (reception) given by the Sovereign or his or her representative in the forenoon or early afternoon, at which only men were received.

In the New World colonies, the levée was held by the governor acting on behalf of the monarch. Because settlers were widely scattered and separated from the seat of government, the annual levée was a very important event and attendance by village leaders and public dignitaries was compulsory.

It was in French Canada that the levée first became associated with New Year's Day. The first recorded levée in Canada was held on January 1, 1646, in the Chateau St. Louis by Charles Huault de Montmagny, the governor of New France (later Québec) from 1636 to 1648. In addition to shaking hands and wishing a happy new year to citizens presenting themselves at the chateau, the governor informed guests of significant events in the mother country, as well as the state of affairs within the colony. (This tradition is carried on today within the commonwealth in the form of the queen's New Year's message. The state of the union address by the president of the United States, as well as the state of the state speeches given by the fifty governors, although not delivered on New Year's Day, has similar origins.) In turn, the settlers were expected to pledge anew their allegiance to the Crown.

The levée was continued by British colonial governors in Canada and adopted by those in the thirteen colonies. Since the provinces of Québec and Nova Scotia remained attached to the empire after 1783, their governors retained the custom. The original two provinces divided eventually into ten; when the oldest of these were grouped into the Dominion of Canada in 1867, a governor-general was appointed to represent the queen on the national level, while the provincial governors were redesignated "lieutenant governors" and continued their viceregal duties within their own spheres. This arrangement continues until today. The governor-general of Canada, the lieutenant governors, and the three territorial commissioners continue to maintain their courts and throw levées on New Year's Day in the name of the queen. The custom has spread throughout Canadian society, so that military establishments, municipalities, and other institutions host similar affairs.

In the newly independent United States, the president also held a New Year's levée at the White House, after that building was occupied by John Adams. This tradition, whereby the executive mansion was opened to the public and the president exposed to the American people, was abolished in 1933; President Herbert Hoover shook six thousand hands that day and swore never to do it again.

All of his successors have followed his example, regardless of party.

In any case, at French colonial levées, guests were treated to wine and cheese from the mother country. Alas, wines did not travel well during the long ocean voyage to Canada; to make the cloudy and somewhat sour wine more palatable, it was doctored with alcohol and spices and heated. The concoction came to be known as *Le Sang du Caribou*, or "Moose Blood."

Under British rule, many of the customs of French Canada were kept, but, in the case of Le Sang du Caribou, rum was substituted as the basic ingredient. It was mixed with goat's milk and flavored with nutmeg and cinnamon to produce an anglicized version called "Moose Milk."

This is still served at the levées held in government houses (as the residences of the viceregal officials are called), courthouses, city halls, and military and naval installations across Canada. It is perhaps the most tangible alcoholic remnant of the grand old colonial revels of the eighteenth century left to us.

Moose Milk

12 egg yolks	40 ounces whole milk
40 ounces rye whiskey	40 ounces heavy whipping
40 ounces dark rum	cream (not canned!)
5 ounces Kahlúa	1 cup sugar
10 ounces maple syrup	

Beat yolks until fluffy and completely mixed. Add the sugar and beat the mixture until thick. Stir in the milk and the liquor. Chill for at least 3 hours (preferably overnight). Whip the cream until good and thick. Don't use canned whipped cream as it will go flat. Fold in whipped cream (it will appear as if it has totally thinned out, don't worry). Add the maple syrup. Chill for another hour. Sprinkle the top with nutmeg and cinnamon to taste (optional). Serve (when serving keep chilled because of the raw eggs). Stir occasionally or the whipped cream will start to separate.

Medford Rum Toddy

2 jiggers dark rum   Dash sugar
Boiling water

Pour rum into drinking cup or mug. Pour boiling water to brim.
Add dash sugar.

Apple Tansy

FOR THE PASTRY: 1 tablespoon raisins
¼ cup vegetable shortening   1 tablespoon dark rum
1¾ cups all-purpose flour   4 teaspoons unsalted butter
½ teaspoon salt
8 tablespoons (1 stick) unsalted   FOR THE SYRUP:
   butter, chilled   1 cup firmly packed dark
4–6 tablespoons ice water   brown sugar
                                      1½ cups water
FOR THE APPLES: 2 tablespoons unsalted butter
4 small tart apples, such as
   Granny Smith

Makes 4 servings.

To make the pastry: Combine the shortening, flour and salt in a food
processor fitted with the steel blade. Using on and off pulsing action,
combine until the mixture resembles fine meal. Cut the chilled
butter into small pieces, add to the mixture and pulse a few times, or
until the mixture resembles coarse meal. Sprinkle with 4 tablespoons of the ice water and pulse a few times. The mixture should
hold together when pinched. Add more water if necessary. (This
can also be done using a pastry blender or two knives.)

   Scrape the pastry onto a floured board, form it into a ball, and
wrap it with plastic wrap. Refrigerate at least 30 minutes.

   To prepare the apples: While the pastry is chilling, peel and core
the apples. Divide the raisins and rum into the core holes, and place
1 teaspoon of butter in each core hole.

To prepare the syrup: Combine the ingredients in a small saucepan, and bring to a boil. Simmer for 3 minutes, and set aside.

To assemble: Preheat the oven to 450°. Divide the pastry into 4 parts. Form one part into a ball and place it between two sheets of plastic wrap or wax paper. Flatten with your hands into a "pancake." Roll the pastry into a circle large enough to cover the apple. Place an apple in the center, and bring up the sides to encase it. Pinch the top together, holding the dough with a little water. If the folds seem thick, trim them off and seal the seams with water. Repeat with the remaining apples.

Place the apples in dough on a baking sheet and brush them with the syrup. Place them in the oven and bake for 10 minutes. Reduce the heat to 330° and brush again with the syrup. Bake an additional 35 minutes, brushing every 10 minutes. Remove from the oven, and allow to cool for 5 minutes. Serve hot or at room temperature.

Note: The pastry and syrup can be prepared up to two days in advance and refrigerated. The apples should be peeled just prior to baking.

Chapter 7

~~~~~~~~~~~~~~~~~~~~~~~~~~~

On the Guinea Coast:
Rum in West Africa

Courtship and Wedding. The routine varies greatly according
to tribe; and in any tribe, according to the man's self-respect
and regard for conventionalities. A proper outline is: First,
the man goes to the father empty-handed to ask his
consent. The second visit he goes with gifts, and the father
calls in the other members of the family to witness the gifts.
On the third visit he goes with liquor (formerly the native
palm wine, now the foreign trade gin or rum), and pays an
installment on the dowry; on the fourth visit with his
parents, and gives presents to the woman herself. On a fifth
occasion the mother of the woman makes a feast for the
mother and friends of the groom. At this feast the host and
hostess do not eat, but they join in the drinking. Finally, the
man goes with gifts and takes the woman. Her father makes
return gifts as a farewell to his daughter.

—Rev. Robert Nassau, *Fetichism in West Africa*

Rum was the lifeblood of the slave trade; in turn, the slave
trade was the soul of West Africa. There were, as we have
seen, important historical reasons for this; but there were geographical ones as well. From Senegal to what is now the northern

Namibian frontier, the coast was broken up by great rivers and deep lagoons. Moreover, from the Sahel southward, the land was covered with deep forests; villages were clearings in a sea of green. In such an environment, kingdoms tended to be small affairs, centering on a few towns, as opposed to the great sultanates further north. Larger entities tended to be confederations, united more by religious or legendary kinship ties than by a European-style centralized government. In some regions, such as the Ibo country of southeastern Nigeria, organization was more primitive still, with small chieftaincies and clan groups taking the place of any larger grouping. Many of these kingdoms had intricate caste systems with rigid distinctions between nobles, commoners, and, in some cases, hereditary slaves. Disunity was aided by successive migrations of various ethnic groups from the north and east, such as the Akan and the Yoruba.

The West African kings, like their counterparts elsewhere in Africa, tended to make up in ceremony what they lacked in resources. As dictated by the particular religion of the place, the king and his court were regulated by a dizzying array of rituals and taboos. This sacral kingship was in many places accompanied by mandatory polygamy, by human sacrifice, and by policies dictated as much by divination as by politics. In such an environment, the gods were often angry. Of course, this pattern was far from restricted to Africa; at various times, the entire human race has lived under such a regime. The patterns of kingship in Africa would have been recognized by the Greeks of the Homeric age, by the Celts of the pre-Christian era, and by the Norse of the sagas. The warlike and ever conquering King Guezo of Dahomey had much in common with King Priam of Troy and Queen Mabh of Ulster; as with them, his martial exploits were the stuff of ballads sung down to our time.

War itself had long been more for purposes of gaining captives than for outright conquest; this, too, is a pattern seen elsewhere, such as in pre-Columbian Mesoamerica. While some of these were utilized for ritual purposes (as witnessed by the skull thrones of the kings of Dahomey and Benin), many more were sold to the Arabs as slaves to be taken north—until, as previously noted, the Tuaregs disrupted the caravan routes and the Portuguese appeared out of the sea.

We have already seen how the Europeans paid for slaves in consumer goods, and particularly in rum. To warehouse the commodities and the human payment they received for them, the Portuguese, British, French, Dutch, and Danes built "factories" and castles on the coast. Even today, many of these remain the centers of modern cities: St.-Louis, Goree, and Dakar in Senegal; St. Mary's in Gambia; Accra, Elmina, and Cape Coast in Ghana; Ouidah and Porto-Novo in Dahomey; and Lagos, Calabar, and Bonny Island in Nigeria, to name a very few.

Western goods soon took their places in royal and temple storehouses alongside native treasures, such as gold and cowrie shells. Even today, the remaining royal courts often count among their precious regalia such items as old morions (crested helmets with curved peaks front and back) and Toledo blades. Rum, in its turn, edged out palm wine as a sacred drink presented to honored guests and used in temple rites to propitiate thirsty deities (when human or animal blood either failed to do so or was not pleasing to a particular god). It would be used in various naming rites for infants, being used to wash the newborns (or, in some places, their umbilical cords or placentae).

The Akan peoples added rum to their rituals by the seventeenth century. The expense and potency of the stuff made it a more valuable offering to the ancestors and gods than native potations.

Beyond its ceremonial role, however, rum made its mark on West African society. Individuals and social groups that profited from the Triangle Trade viewed the drinking of rum as a mark of their social distinction. For young men who had migrated from villages to participate in European coastal commerce, it was the mark of their new independence from the control of rural elders they had left behind in the hinterlands.

European trade extended European influence. Gifts of rum featured prominently in traders' protocol. European merchants used liquor and other European goods to induce some African chiefs to sign treaties of protection. As with the American Indians, rum often lubricated the negotiations, resulting in more favorable terms for the Europeans than they might otherwise have been able to achieve.

Life for the Europeans stationed in the factories was both dangerous and lonely. Dangerous, because the castles were able to survive only with the goodwill of local rulers—a goodwill maintained by monarchs who were mercurial in ways only those held to be related to the gods, or gods themselves, could be. Many a European emissary or factor found his end in some king's palace, his skull and bones being then added to the décor as an especially powerful aid in magical defense.

Disease claimed many of the factory men as well; not for nothing was the Guinea coast called the "white man's graveyard." Yellow fever, cholera, and various other tropical diseases and parasites claimed countless officials, soldiers, and sailors from the various European nations.

Moreover, it was a lonely existence; in a world without telegraph or telephone, a factor might go for months without seeing white men of his own class or news from home. As a rule, European women simply did not make the journey. Rum often provided for such men the only readily available solace. So it was that the Europeans stationed more or less permanently on the West African Coast often took native concubines.

For the locals, this was considered an honor. They did not mind the fact that their new "sons-in-law" often had wives in Bristol, Bahia, or Boston. Polygamy was their own custom and practiced only by those who could afford it. Giving a daughter or wife, even temporarily, to a European was a coveted mark of status.

The result was the growth, around various factories, of a new, mixed society, similar to that which we have already encountered in the West Indies. The mulatto offspring of the traders usually adopted their fathers' names and the trappings of European lifestyle. Speaking their paternal tongues, building churches to their fathers' nominal faiths, and erecting European-style homes, the wealthier among them reveled in imported luxuries and, of course, enjoyed copious quantities of that quintessentially white drink, rum.

They reflected their mother's origins as well. Knowing one or more African language and sometimes clandestinely practicing portions of the local cult, they had a foot in both worlds. This in turn made them excellent middlemen; they were able to mediate between the European merchants and the African kings on the sale of gold, cloth, tobacco, and, above all, slaves. From 1800, many of the most successful slavers were mulattoes; a favored few did well enough to retire to their paternal homelands. Most stayed on, however, providing a unique leaven within the already complex coastal population.

In St.-Louis, the oldest French settlement in Senegal, a uniquely feminist arrangement resulted. For the native mistresses of the French, canny women in their own right, gave birth to daughters cleverer even than themselves. These were the famous *signares*, so called from the Portuguese word for "ladies." When young, such beauties, in similar fashion to the *demoiselles de couleur* of New Orleans's famed "quadroon balls," would make suitable and profitable arrangements for themselves. Adept at both romance and finance, they were renowned both for their skill at love and at speculation. Those among them who did well ended their days as wealthy property owners, possessed of their own estates and slaves, and sending their children to be educated in France. Similar castes grew up in Goree, Dakar, and Rufisque.

So prominent did these *Métis* become that in time they were given full citizenship and a cathedral was founded for them at St.-Louis. This city would serve as the capital of Senegal until 1903. Even now, St.-Louis, with its wrought-iron balconies and its spirited Mardi Gras celebrations, reminds the traveler strongly of New Orleans. This impression is underscored by the Métis themselves, whose saga is so similar to that of the Metoyer clan of the Isle Brevelle in northern Louisiana. Their foundress, Marie-Therese Coin-Coin, who begat a similar clan of *gens de couleur libre*, would have been fit company for the wiliest signare.

Similar groups evolved in Dahomey and Togo, where Brazilian-Portuguese slavers such as Don Francisco Felix da Souza acquired a monopoly of the increasingly furtive slave trade in the early nineteenth century and held it for three decades. In Ouidah, Porto-Novo, and Cotonou, Dahomey, Abeho and Lomé, Togo, and even Lagos, Nigeria, the "Brazilians" erected churches and beautiful mansions. Even today, many of the most prominent (if no longer, as we shall see, wealthiest) families in local society belong to this group.

At Elmina, on the Gold Coast, the De Heer family, descendants of a Dutch trader and his African wives, actually became the local royal family through intermarriage. The De Heers, Ulzens, and other such families dominated the Dutch section of the Gold Coast; over three thousand served in the Dutch East Indies Army in what is now Indonesia. After having been settled there for over a century, most of the African Dutch descendants were forced to leave the country following its independence in 1949, emigrating to the Netherlands. The few who remained behind continued to multiply, thus creating unique communities in both countries. In any case, like their Métis and Brazilian counterparts, they drank rum and built Catholic churches to show their European allegiance.

One of the major changes in the rum trade brought about by the disruption of the Triangle Trade was that slaving was now a purely bilateral thing—in with rum, out with slaves. Despite the decade-long dearth of high-quality New England rum, the African kings and mulatto factors managed to get by, drinking inferior brews. The return of the Yankees in the 1790s was a source of rejoicing from St.-Louis to Benguela. It seemed that all would be well, at least as far as the slavers were concerned.

Two factors would disrupt these arrangements. First, an Islamic revival swept the sultanates of the Sahel, and second, a jihad was declared against the black kingdoms to the south. This first brought trouble to the French in Senegal, where many of the regions were converted to Islam. In a very short time, the local taste for rum was suppressed by the new religionists.

More dangerous to the generality of the coastlands' economies was the concerted effort by the British, French, American, Dutch, and Danish governments to suppress the slave trade. It became a crime under international law, and the fleets of these nations made a concerted effort to suppress it by seizing slave ships on the high seas as well as by pursuing them up rivers and into lagoons. Moreover, the British, French, Dutch, and Danish factories were garrisoned with troops whose aim was partially to break the trade on land.

To this end, the confederate powers agreed to return to their native places, if possible, all liberated slaves. This was easier said then done; hapless slaves who returned to their homes (presuming their native villages survived) were often rejected for a number of reasons: some religious (the slave had already been mourned as dead; it would be taboo to accept him or her back), and some political (if the slavers discovered the return, they might well exact revenge). Many returnees were stoned or even killed.

As an alternative, refuges were established for the rescued slaves. The oldest was Freetown, in what is now Sierra Leone. Initially settled by black Loyalists who had fought for George III in the American Revolution, its early inhabitants were joined by most of the Africans from Great Britain when Parliament ordered all slaves in the mother country freed. Henceforth, Africans liberated from captured slave ships were resettled there, given their choice to emigrate to the West Indies as apprentices, or join the military forces of the Crown. A similar settlement was later established at Bathurst in Gambia.

In 1821, the American Colonization Society obtained land at Cape Mesurado, Africa, using $300 worth of rum, weapons, supplies, and trade goods. The place was renamed Monrovia (after President James Monroe) and was the foundation of the present nation of Liberia.

In 1849, the French settled fifty freed slaves at Libreville in Gabon, to establish a *nouveau village chrétien français*. De Mountier, one of the liberated captives, was made mayor, and the town eventually became the administrative and religious capital of Gabon.

Obviously, the populations of these towns were very mixed; the one thing they shared was the language and culture of the sponsoring country. So it was that the Creoles of Sierra Leone and the Aku of Gambia (by which collective names the settlers were called in those countries) built Anglican churches and schools, spoke English perfectly (as well as their own pidgin, Krio), and in all things conducted themselves as English. They replaced the often sickened whites in the rank and file of the Royal Africa Corps, the body of troops the Crown established to defend its West African outposts.

In Liberia, the American Liberians were devout Methodists and Baptists. They established the only lodges of Prince Hall Masonry (the only such group open to blacks, then as now) outside the United States and dubbed their political formation the "True Whig Party," thus perpetuating the name of the leading American antislavery party for over a century after its merger into the Republican Party. Most telling of all, the flag of their new republic was modeled on the American flag, save with a single star in the corner.

Libreville, as noted, was organized as a regular French town. From that day to this, it has been a center of French influence in Equatorial Africa. In Libreville, as in Monrovia, Freetown, and Bathurst, rum flowed among the inhabitants as a sign of their adopted culture.

There is, alas, in life, a law of unintended consequences. To begin with, the Brazilians, unscrupulous Yankees, and various other folk continued to supply slaves from Dahomey, Togo, and elsewhere to Cuba (which was undergoing the economic expansion—and so needed cheap labor—we saw earlier) and Brazil. While Spain and Portugal had both signed the antislavery convention, both were nonetheless able to evade its provisions. Both nations, having lost their navies during the Napoleonic Wars and being too impoverished to rebuild them, were able to beg off on joining the antislavery fleet. Spanish authorities in Cuba were able to exercise plausible deniability on various pretexts as to where new slaves were coming from. The Portuguese maintained that the slavers were nationals of the newly independent Brazil and so outside their jurisdiction; the Brazilian government asserted that since the slavers trading to Bahia were Portuguese, they had no authority over them.

Thus the trade continued. But it adapted to the changed circumstances. Instead of the large slave ships of the Triangle Trade, new light sloops, capable of evading warships, were favored by the slavers. But since these were so much smaller, the slaves had to be more closely crammed then before. At least one enterprising individual packed each slave into a barrel; that way, if a warship did intercept his craft, he could pitch the barrels overboard and so escape arrest. Since the voyages to Havana and Bahia were so much shorter than trips to Charleston had been, the likelihood of a good part of the human cargo surviving the journey was correspondingly greater.

Even successful liberation by the associated navies had its perils, for the warships were not too well equipped to care for the extra mouths they now had to feed onboard. Since the crews of these ships were sailors in government service, and the new passengers free men rather than potentially profitable trade goods, there could be no question of starving the crew to preserve the liberated captives. If the interception occurred at some great distance from Freetown, Monrovia, or Libreville, mortality among the new arrivals was tremendous.

Nor did their troubles cease after their arrival at their new homes. The local authorities could give them land and rum, but more is required to farm successfully. A few meager implements and a cow were the absolute limit of what could be provided the new settlers.

Nevertheless, despite the discouraging circumstances, in time all four freedmen's settlements prospered. Indeed, the American Liberians did so well that they set to work conquering as much neighboring territory as possible and forcing the locals to labor for them. It was yet another unintended consequence.

More were to follow. By the end of the 1840s, the slave trade had at last been to a great extent choked off. This forced both the Brazilians and the native kings to look for other sources of revenue, if the rum and manufactured goods were to continue to arrive. The Wolof and Serere rulers in Senegal and Gambia, respectively, turned to peanuts in a big way. In various places, ivory, gold, cotton, cocoa, tobacco, and various other commodities began to be harvested for export. But the big item on the agenda was one of the easiest to obtain: palm oil.

In 1853, Dom Francisco Felix da Souza sent some of the stuff to Marseilles, where perfumers immediately saw its utility for soap manufacture. Palm soap soon became the rage throughout Europe, and the oil could not be exported fast enough. The native kings soon transformed large areas into palm groves and set slaves to extracting it, relying on the Brazilians to act as middlemen.

But, again, there were unintended consequences. While slaves were still required to work the new cash crops, and some were sent to the newly emergent Arab slavers in East Africa, the fact remained that the supply of slaves had far outstripped demand. But the traditional endemic warfare between the kings continued, with one difference. Where formerly taking as many captives as possible had been an important goal of these conflicts, the new economic realities inspired the African leaders simply to kill as many of their enemies as they could. Entire villages were wiped out, men, women, and children. Needless to say, this spectacle did not edify the Europeans, nor endear the kings to them.

In addition, the various mercantile companies in France and Great Britain (as well as, after its 1871 unification, Germany) decided that they would do better to directly control the sources of raw materials themselves, rather than work through the kings, Brazilians, and the like. They added their voices to those of the humanitarians demanding outright annexation of West Africa (as well as the rest of the continent).

Missionaries, too, both Catholic and Protestant, who had been restricted to working among Europeans and mulattoes on the Guinea coast by the native rulers, wanted to see their field of endeavor widened to include the natives as well (ever mindful of Christ's mandate to "make disciples of all nations"). They also saw annexation as a way to abolish human sacrifice and polygamy, which heretofore had been sacrosanct under the native laws. Most ironic of all, the Protestants in their number were particularly anxious to suppress the liquor traffic, which they held responsible for exacerbating all of the Africans' worst traits.

Starting, then, in the late 1850s, and using their existing outposts as bases, the French and British began the process of reducing, statelet by statelet, the entire coast to direct obedience. The Spanish, Portuguese, and Germans joined in, and the "Scramble for Africa" was on. The scramble reached its highpoint with the Berlin Conference (1884–1885). Chaired by Otto von Bismarck, this event divided Africa up into zones, and serves as the basis for most of the continent's borders even today. The local kings (at least, those who were not deposed) were incorporated into the colonial structure via a system of indirect rule; this allowed them to maintain their traditional positions (less warfare, power of life and death over their subjects, and the right to command human sacrifice) so long as they kept their people submissive to the new paramount power. The Métis, Aku, Creoles, Brazilians, and the rest of the mulattoes, despised by their employers and hated by the locals, became junior administrators and civil servants under the new regime.

European corporations assumed control of the plantations in most colonies. Backed up by the local government, they were able to impose quotas on the villagers and punish those who fell behind. But between them both, private enterprise and colonial government gradually introduced medical care, universities, railroads, and, as they were invented, telephones, automobiles, modern infrastructure, and all the other things on which modern people pride themselves.

The Protestant missionaries had assumed that colonialism would end liquor traffic. But colonies were designed to turn a profit for their owners, and economic self-sufficiency was the bare minimum requirement for them. Liquor revenues and liquor legislation became crucial to colonial policy. In West Africa, where European settlement was minimal because of the mosquito and tsetse fly, colonial powers exploited the existing demand for liquor as a source of revenue. As a money economy was imposed on the West African coast, opportunities to buy West Indian rum were made ever more widely available.

But some colonies, such as Spanish Equatorial Africa, the Portuguese Cape Verde Islands, the Gold Coast, Sierra Leone, and Gabon, began to grow sugar. As a result, in time they, too, began to manufacture rum. These local brews generally went for ceremonial use or were drunk by the poorer locals and by the native bureaucrats the colonialists trained to work beside the mulattoes.

At length, after World War II Africa underwent another wave of change. Decolonization, sponsored forcefully by the U.S. government, which wished to see American companies replace European ones where possible, saw one country after another turned over to the aforementioned bureaucrats. In most cases, the native kings went along with the change, deferring to the new presidents and generals as they once had to the colonial governors.

For the mulatto population, although some were prominent in various anticolonial movements (Sylvanus Olympio, of an old Portuguese family, is considered the father of Togo), for the most part independence brought social demotion. Often the target of nationalist attacks, many emigrated to their paternal ancestors' nations. Others held on grimly. Their state is tellingly evoked in this passage concerning the fictional da Silvas (based on the real-life da Souzas of Dahomey-Benin) in Bruce Chatwin's masterful novel *The Viceroy of Ouidah*:

> The lives of the older Da Silvas were empty and sad. They mourned the Slave Trade as a lost Golden Age when their family was rich, famous and white. They were worn down by rheumatism and the

burdens of polygamy. Their skin cracked in the harmattan; then the rains came and tambourined on their caladiums and splashed dados of red mud up the walls of their houses.

Yet they clung to their kepis and pith-helmets as they clung to the forms of vanished grandeur. They called themselves "Brazilians," though they had lost their Portuguese. People slightly blacker than themselves they called "Blacks." They called Dahomey "Dahomey" long after the Head of State had changed its name to Benin. Each hung Dom Francisco's picture among their chromo-lithographs of saints and the Virgin: through him they felt linked to eternity.

Whether or not their ancestors' crimes made this a just fate, however, independence benefited few on the Guinea coast. An unintended consequence of colonialism was the creation of a tech-nocratic class in each country, divorced from traditional values, but uninstructed in Western ones. It was to these folk that control over the military, economic, and political infrastructure was given at independence. The result has been an unhappy chronicle of bloody coups, revolutions, and civil wars, and of mismanagement, corrup-tion, and wastage of both agriculture and industry over the past forty-five years. This sad story has been repeated, at one time or another, in virtually every country of the region. What is certain is that the living standard of the average individual in West Africa has fallen drastically since 1960; this cannot have been the intention either of the idealistic poets and writers who lobbied for independ-ence, nor that of the colonial powers who grudgingly gave it.

The rum industry in West Africa today is a perfect barometer of its host economies. Many of the region's countries boast a local brew. In Ghana, it is Gihoc Distilleries; Gabon's product comes from haut-Ogoué, in Padi prefecture; Benin has three different dis-tilleries; even civil war–wracked Sierra Leone manages every year to produce some bottles of its fiery "Man Pickin' Rum." There has been talk in each of these nations of taking steps to promote their rums internationally. It would be a sure sign of their recovery if these rums appeared for sale in the cities that once sent rum over the Middle Passage for slaves.

Kubecake

In her cookbook *A Taste of Africa*, Dorinda Hafner describes kube-cake as a popular sweet sold by street hawkers throughout West Africa. Her recipe inspired this cookie, which combines coconut, rum, peanuts, and cocoa.

14 ounces sweetened flaked
   coconut
3 tablespoons grated fresh
   ginger root, peeled
½ cup dark rum
2 tablespoons natural smooth
   peanut butter

1 tablespoon unsweetened
   cocoa powder
1 pinch salt
½ cup granulated sugar
Confectioners' sugar for
   coating

In double boiler, combine coconut, ginger, rum, peanut butter, cocoa, and salt. Set mixture over simmering water to warm.

Meanwhile, in heavy, medium saucepan, melt sugar over medium heat. When sugar is almost melted, stir constantly with wooden spoon until completely melted and a rich mahogany brown. (Be careful not to let sugar burn.) Add coconut-rum mixture to sugar all at once. (It will sputter, but not splatter.) Stir over medium heat until well blended. Remove from heat and cool to room temperature in bowl of cold water. Cover with plastic wrap and chill for 1 hour.

Put confectioners' sugar into small bowl. Remove mixture from refrigerator and stir to mix. Scoop level tablespoonfuls of dough into one hand. Dip fingers of other hand into cool water and roll mixture into compact ball. Drop ball into confectioners' sugar and toss to coat. Place on wire rack to dry. Repeat with remaining mixture. Allow coconut rum balls to dry for 1 hour. (Store cookies in an airtight container in the refrigerator up to 1 week.)

Makes 42 cookies.

SOURCE: *Vegetarian Times*, December 1997, page 39.

Chapter 8

Batavia's Pride: Rum in the East Indies, Australia, and the Pacific

Officers of the [New South Wales] Corps monopolized all goods coming into the colony. They made first claim and paid only a fraction of what it cost farmers for seed, stock, and farm tools, selling the rest at a profit. Rum became a particularly profitable commodity in a colony where hunger, brutality, drudgery and hopelessness was a common way of life. Groups of officers often put up the money to illegally import shiploads of cheap rum from Bengal, using women convicts as their distributors. Since legal currency was scarce, the officers used rum as the medium of exchange for goods, services, and labor. If an ex-convict or free farmer drank himself into debt, an officer was always willing to settle it—by buying up his land with more rum.

—John Brown, "The Rum Rebellion," from *Military History*

Christopher Columbus had seen his voyages as a way of reaching the Indies, those fabulous lands of spices and gold, whose untold wealth would allow Christendom to jump-start a new crusade and also (with whatever allies the Christians might find there) outflank the Muslims. In actuality, however, the Muslims had reached the Indies first.

South and Southeast Asia had, as had all the rest of the world, seen the rise and fall of kingdoms and empires. Before the birth of Mohammed, the region had been dominated by various monarchies of Hindu-Buddhist inspiration. Of such a background was the fabulous Khmer empire, centered at Angkor Wat in modern Cambodia. Such states dominated what is now Indonesia; it was from these islands that sugar cane (and its sap) first set forth on the path of conquest, centuries before. Chinese traders spread its cultivation to Asia and on to India. By that time, the Muslims had reached the borders of India; in their turn, they brought sugar to the Middle East and North Africa. From there it came to the attention of Europeans during the crusades in the eleventh century.

In the meantime, however, the Muslims came to dominate India and finally the western Indonesian islands. They were expanding eastward, deposing or converting the local rajas and converting them into or replacing them with sultans, when the search for pepper, nutmeg, and other such plants of the Moluccas brought the Portuguese and Spanish into the fray.

At the same time that these powers were first opening up the New World to Europe (and inadvertently letting in the French, English, Dutch, and Danes), they arrived on the other side of the world. Questing for souls and wealth, the initial Portuguese explorers, such as Vasco da Gama and Bartolomeu Dias, pioneered a route around the Cape of Good Hope. Soon, the Indian Ocean was a virtual Portuguese lake. Mozambique, Kenya, the Persian Gulf, Socotra, Pakistan, India, Bangladesh, Sri Lanka, Burma, Thailand, Malaysia, and Indonesia all boasted Portuguese outposts. Just as the Portuguese themselves established Brazil in an otherwise Spanish South America, however, so, too, did Spain colonize the Philippines.

The search for wealth in the East Indies, as this entire vast region came to be called, was quite different from that in the West. While not averse to gold when they could find it, the newcomers were looking more particularly for spices and silks. Moreover, they wanted to trade rather than to settle (with the exception, of course, of the Spanish in the Philippines). This made, on the one hand, the Spice Islands of today's Indonesia all-important prizes; on the other, it required the Portuguese to maintain a vast network of bases stretching virtually all the way back to Portugal (Spain was able to maintain contact with its colony via Acapulco, Mexico).

Both powers, being Catholic, felt obliged to evangelize their new subjects; Spain had particular success with the Philippines, which are now the only majority Catholic nation in the Far East. For Portugal, the question was a bit more complex, since in most places its control was restricted to coastal enclaves; the interiors remained under the sway of local rulers who generally were more or less hostile to Christianity, regardless of whether or not they themselves were Muslim, Hindu, or Buddhist. There were exceptions to this rule, and from time to time one of the native sovereigns would convert. But so engrained was the local religion among the people that this action usually resulted in the monarch's being deposed. Nevertheless, the Portuguese did what they could in this field: St. Francis Xavier personally baptized three million people in the sixteenth century, and even today, many Catholics in these countries bear Portuguese names. Interracial marriage was encouraged by both the Portuguese and the Spanish—this partly made up for the lack of civilian settlers, who were reluctant to leave the good conditions then prevailing at home.

By 1580, the Portuguese viceroy at Goa was the greatest potentate in the Indies. A hundred ports and islands were under his sway, from Amboina to Mombasa. Ships loaded with spices made their way to Lisbon, and money poured into the coffers of the Portuguese Crown from gourmets all over Europe. But this supremacy was to be short lived.

The agency of Portugal's downfall was not any one of the countless sultans and rajas with whom the viceroy's emissaries had to deal; rather, it was the Dutch. Their leadership having turned Protestant, they had thrown off the control of the Catholic king of Spain and were engaged in a revolution against him. As part of this effort, Dutch pirates seized Spanish galleons wherever they could. In 1580, Philip II of Spain inherited Portugal and its empire. As far as the Dutch were concerned, the Portuguese spice trade was the perfect target (although they did manage to take north-eastern Brazil at one point).

From the opening years of the seventeenth century, they expelled the Portuguese from their holdings wherever they could. Thus, they captured Elmina, on the Guinea coast; Cochin in India; Sri Lanka; Malacca; and, at last, Amboina. For good measure, they snatched the Manado peninsula in Celebes from the Spanish, although the latter repulsed them from the Philippines. As a matter of policy, the Dutch forcibly converted as many of the local Catholics to Calvinism as they could, while forbidding any missionary work among non-Christians. Their governor in the Indies, Jan Pieter Coen, ordered the entire population of the Banda Islands murdered or exiled to keep them from trading nutmeg to the English.

The English themselves, starting in the seventeenth century, focused on India. Competing with the already established Dutch and Portuguese, they also faced newcomers: the French and Danes. For a time, the Indian coast resembled the West African, with outposts of competing European powers trying to outtrade each other, against the backdrop of the crumbling Mughal Empire. As the seventeenth and eighteenth centuries wore on, various world wars would turn this rivalry into open conflict, as the different sides fought each other directly and through the medium of native powers.

In order to establish a clear road to their possessions in India, the French in the 1700s colonized Mauritius (which the Dutch had briefly settled, managing during their tenure to wipe out the dodo bird), Reunion, and the Seychelles. From these footholds they began to affect the vast island of Madagascar, with its own competing kingdoms and pirate lairs. In 1788, meanwhile, the British began the settlement of Australia (originally called "New Holland," in token of its discovery by the Dutch), as a penal colony, replacing newly independent Georgia.

As ports changed hands repeatedly, a Eurasian population grew up in each of them, reminiscent of the mulattoes similarly arising on the Guinea coast. Even today, a network of old churches, forts, palaces, and houses in all of these places stands as an enduring reminder of this complex history. So, too, the Eurasians (although many have emigrated to Europe, North America, and Australasia) remain, maintaining the lifestyles of the West to the best of their abilities in their now-independent homelands—and often suffering a certain amount of harassment and even persecution for doing so.

Starting in the eighteenth century, ships of many nations began traversing the Pacific, disrupting to a greater or lesser degree the lives and governments of the primarily Polynesian nations they encountered there. Missionaries of various kinds followed throughout both the East Indies and the Pacific.

All of this activity required shipping. The warships, merchantmen, and pirates plying these vast waters required almost equally vast amounts of the seamen's friend, rum. As in West Africa, the local liquors (in this case, fermented rice wine, generally called arrack, a name also applied to concoctions from palm sap and dates) really could not compete, either in terms of potency or taste. Even some rigidly Muslim sultans acquired a taste for it, claiming that the Koran's prohibition against alcohol only really applied to wine.

The colonial race turned in favor of the British, starting with their victory over the French at Plassey in 1757. Their ever increasing power in the East Indies culminated in their victory in the Napoleonic Wars and their aftermath. By 1830, the British had ejected the Dutch from the Cape, Sri Lanka, India, and Malaysia; the French had similarly been deprived of Mauritius and the Seychelles (although they did manage to hold on to Reunion and began the slow process of annexing Madagascar). India became ever more a British possession, and Australia, New Zealand, and South Africa would be settled in similar fashion to Canada. The Dutch were left in control of Indonesia, and the Spanish of the Philippines; the French would join the British in partitioning the Pacific islands between them.

But by the nineteenth century, the monopoly of the spice trade had been broken; all the colonial nations had access to the seeds and were able to grow spices in any of their colonies that possessed the required climate. Around the world, natives in tropical colonies were forced to grow spices, coffee, and cocoa in lieu of taxes; in partial return, a modern infrastructure was built, fighting between native potentates ended (thus providing a level of physical security hitherto unknown in these regions), and Christianity was introduced. Despite these gifts, from time to time the locals revolted, and in due course were suppressed with the aid of modern warships and weaponry. Nevertheless, officials in each colony were forced to figure out how to turn a profit, in the context of an emerging world economy. Given the breaking of the spice monopoly, many European governors (and the planters who settled in the colonies in increasing numbers) turned to sugar, and thus to rum. In response, a number of West Indian islands, as we have seen, abandoned sugar for spices—thus, for instance, Grenada became known for its nutmeg.

The Dutch in Indonesia were particularly hard pressed. In response, they transformed Javanese agriculture during the nineteenth century. The authorities in Batavia (now Jakarta) created what was called the *Culteur* ("Cultivation") System, by which Javanese farmers were compelled to produce designated crops for sale to the state at fixed prices. The crops—primarily sugar, indigo, coffee, and tea—were then processed for and transported to European markets. By the end of the nineteenth century, Java was the world's largest sugar producer. Sugar mills were built throughout rural Java to process the raw cane and railways and ports were constructed to take the export crops to market. The villages of Java, operating on a subsistence economy before 1830, were transformed. The subsistence economy gave way to a much more diversified arrangement. As a result, the population steadily grew until, by the end of the nineteenth century, there was little uncultivated land left, as towns and cities sprang up to service the burgeoning export trade. From these urban environments would emerge the nationalists who would eventually end Dutch rule in the mid-twentieth century. In any case, as major sugar producer, the Javanese estates would also yield rum.

Despite independence, E&A Scheer Company has remained the biggest dealer in Indonesian rum for centuries. Originally founded in 1712 as a shipowning company, Scheer's fleet plied the Triangle Trade. It conducted a similar trade with the East Indies, bringing return cargoes of the local rum, called "Batavia Arrack" (as distinguished from the rice-based local arracks). The name was justified, despite the drink's molasses base, by the use of some red Javanese rice in the fermentation process. A further distinction is that the liquor is distilled in traditional pot stills, in the ancient Chinese distillers' method. Batavia Arrack is called an "aromatic rum," because of the special treatment given the molasses, the quality of river water used in fermentation, a wild uncultured yeast, and, of course, the rice in the fermenting tubs. Distilled in Jakarta (the postindependence name for Batavia), Batavia Arrack is aged there for three to four years and then sent to the Netherlands by Scheer for an additional four to six years of aging. It is interesting to note that this process has never been interrupted, apart from World War II: not for the 1945–1949 war of independence, not for the crisis in relations between the two countries in 1956 over Sukarno's expulsion of most of the Eurasians, and not for the showdown over Dutch New Guinea in 1963. Profitable trade can be more compelling than questions of national pride or legal ownership.

In any case, Batavia Arrack is extremely popular in northern Europe and serves as the basis for a spiced Scandinavian liqueur called "Swedish Punsch," which is drunk either as an after-dinner drink, with coffee, or as part of a hot toddy; the latter is much called for in those cold climates.

In the nineteenth century, Scheer focused almost exclusively on the shipping and trading of rum and Batavia Arrack. The company blended the original qualities in its warehouse to be able to guarantee consistency in the quality of the product. Stocks were built in Amsterdam to ensure availability at short notice. All rum and Batavia Arrack was shipped from the bonded warehouse in bulk to be sold to customers for industrial use or bottling. As business expanded, an enormous expertise in this particular field of trading and blending of bulk distillates was gained. During the twentieth century, business was stable, despite the crises referred to earlier. Today, the company's activities are still concentrated in the traditional area; recent years have shown rapid expansion in volume and the addition of new markets and customers. Despite this growth, Scheer remains a traditional family-owned company. Twenty years ago, the operating activities were acquired by two family members, who co-own the company with a minority owner who recently was brought in from outside the family. E&A Scheer B.V. is a private company and is still registered and based in Amsterdam. As with the Gardère family of Maison Barbancourt in Haiti, excellence of product has served to insulate the family from revolution and social change.

The Mascarene Islands of the Indian Ocean (Mauritius, Reunion, Rodrigues, and the Seychelles) are reminiscent of the Windward Islands of the Caribbean in many ways. As with those isles, the Mascarenes began with a French-owned, African slave-based, sugar and rum economy (although there were no indigenous inhabitants). Like the Windwards also, they were handed back and forth politically between France and Great Britain in the course of wars fought overseas with little relevance to the immediate area. This had the effect (save in Reunion) of producing a hybrid Anglo-French culture; all three islands also share Afro-French Creole dialects and voodoo-style folk religion (which, of course, uses rum in its

ceremonies), with and under Catholicism. As another similarity
with the Windwards, the abolition of slavery (1835 for the British
possessions, 1848 on Reunion), led to a severe labor shortage and a
resulting importation of Chinese and Indian indentured laborers.
Thus, the stage was set for a social structure (varying in proportion
to each island) beset with African-Indian rivalry and presided over
by a small set of wealthy French-descended aristocrats. So prevalent
were the nobility on Mauritius under French rule that part of the
peace treaty giving the island to Britain required the Crown to recognize the noble titles carried by the locals (probably the best
known of these was Afred, vicomte de Marigny, who was acquitted
in the celebrated 1943 murder of Sir Harry Oakes in the Bahamas).
Above all, on each of the Mascarenes rum was king.

To be sure, Mauritius fits the pattern perfectly. Knowing that
sugar would mean rum, in 1744 the French Crown sent a rum still
to the island, aboard the sailing ship *St. Geran*. The ship was hit by
a storm off the island and went to the bottom, with many of its
modest passengers drowning because of their refusal to undress and
swim to safety. Nevertheless, the sugar and rum industry managed
to get off the ground. Annexation by Britain in 1814, while it con-
served the titles of the Mauricien nobility, also retained the legal
position of the French law and language, as well as the position of
the Catholic Church (emancipation for Catholics would not begin
to reach Britain itself, legally, until 1829). But in addition to these
personal safeguards, planters on Mauritius were given an international market for their sugar. Production jumped, and for the next
150 years, sugar ruled the island.

Its rum was unique. The South African travel writer Lawrence
Green recalled visiting the island in the 1920s and commented on
the "peculiar twang—or as they say in the trade the 'hogo'" of the
local rum. But unlike Mauritian sugar, the local rum was primarily
for use at home, as much for cooking as drinking. Of course, Mau-
ritians prefer to drink their rum neat, rather than in punch or cocktails. This state of affairs was reinforced in 1975 by Mauritius's

accession to the Lomè Agreement. This agreement between the European Economic Community (EEC; now the European Union) and forty-six developing countries allowed the forty-six countries free access to sell their products to the EEC, but only in their raw state. What was a boon to the sugar industry boded poorly for rum.

Nevertheless, "Green Island Rum," the most popular label for locals, has been exported in small quantities to South Africa; it is marketed there by World Wines and Spirits of Johannesburg and is the main rum brand blended on the island by Gilbeys (Mauritius) Ltd. This concern in turn was established by British-based International Distillers and Vintners Ltd., itself established in 1972, along with its export company Rum Distillers (Mauritius) Ltd.

Another company that is attempting to market Mauritian rum is E. C. Oxenham and Company Ltd. In 1932, first-generation Mauritius-born Edward Clark Oxenham founded the company and started producing wine from imported raisins. Despite the small market, the island's plantation economy, and Oxenham's untimely death in 1948, the company was able to survive and then to prosper by hard work and perseverance. In 1987, the company began to distill and bottle rum. It now markets several light and dark rums, under the names "Fregate" and "Bougainville."

Domaine les Pailles, an old sugar estate that has been restored and turned into a tourist center (complete with restaurants, stables, entertainment, and so on), bottles its own label. The Chatel Company from Reunion (of which more, shortly) has set up operations on Mauritius, and three other distilleries also produce the stuff: St. Antoine Distillery, Goodlands; the OK Distillery attached to the Solitude sugar factory, Triolet; and the Medine Distillery, Bambous. We may hope that one day Mauritian rum will come again to the fore.

The Seychelles were settled by order of King Louis XV in 1770. Sent out by the French was a governor, Queau de Quinssy. Over the course of the next several decades, the Anglo-French wars resulted in the colony changing hands a dozen times. On each occasion, de Quinssy cheerfully surrendered and was confirmed in office by the new owners. By dint of this flexibility, he earned the name "Great Capitulator" and died as British governor in 1827.

Sugar was planted, rum duly distilled, and the islands followed the standard pattern. The polyglot Francophone population was much enamored with the rum. As with Mauritius, however, Seychellois rum was made purely for domestic consumption. This may be changing, however. In recent years, foreign businessmen, like the South African D'Offay brothers, whose Trois Frères Distillery produces white and dark rum (the latter spiced and flavored) under the name "Takamaka Bay," and the Italian Renato Longobardi, the owner of "Spirit Artisanal (Seychelles)," who likewise makes two rum varieties, are trying to bring the country's liquor to the wide world.

As already mentioned, Reunion remained in French hands, as it does to this day. Through the nineteenth century, sugar and vanilla vied with each other for the title of main product. In contrast to the other Mascarene Islands, rum in Reunion is big business. In 1815, Charles Desbassyns opened the first distillery, followed a few months later by the first sugar factory. The two industries grew together, and in 1860 Reunion counted 120 sugar factories as against 40 distilleries.

While the majority of these produced their arrack (as distilled rum came to be called on the island), others, such as the Isautier Distillery, continuously producing since 1845, made its rum directly from the cane juice—the old-style tafia. In the first half of the nineteenth century, the rum was all locally consumed; after 1884, it began to be exported to France. In 1921, the French Republic officially regulated rum, both for Reunion, French Guiana, and the French West Indies: "The title of rum or tafia is reserved for brandy coming exclusively from alcoholic fermentation and distillation either from the molasses or syrup coming from the manufacture of the cane sugar, or of the juice of cane with sugar."

During World War I, strong demand for alcohol started a significant race in production for the rum colonies. Unfortunately, in

1920 a slump in prices on the French home market caused a severe crisis for the producing islands. To rescue their economies, a quota system was begun. It established a 160,000-hectoliter limit for pure alcohol (including two-thirds for the French Caribbean), together with a local quota. Reunion escaped this obligation on its territory. As a result, local consumption increased constantly; in 1960, it rose to eleven liters of alcohol per person a year.

In any case, rum so settled into the popular life of the island that virtually every family of settlers—white or black—in the hills has its own recipe for *rhum arrangè*, which is a mix of rum, fruit juice, cane syrup, herbs, and berries. Among the varieties to be found are *rhum faham*, a combination of rum, sugar, and faham orchid flowers; *rhum vanille*, a combination of rum, sugar, and fresh vanilla pods; and *rhum bibasse*, which brings together the usual rum and sugar, together with the *bibasse* (loquat) fruit. The exact recipes are closely guarded secrets and an enormous source of family pride.

The rum produced by various distilleries was sold originally in bulk by central distributors. Retailers and private individuals came to supply themselves at the rum storehouses. At these shops, men met to talk, seated on bags of rice or corn and stoking their thirst by eating salt cod. Rum and its consumption were considered mainstays of sociability. The solitary drinker was seen as cutting himself off from society and to drink like a "pirate" or "savage."

Rum was an essential part of the family dinner, especially drunk in coffee. It was a part of every conceivable party: baptisms, first communions, weddings, and confirmations. Moreover, because of its cheapness, it was the preferred drink for the annual saint's day celebration that each town on Reunion boasts.

It was also a favored drink at wakes, where, mixed with coffee, it helped the mourners stay awake. The assembly was divided into two: women stayed inside the house of the dead person to talk, pray, and continue to keep the coffee flowing. The men would be outside around a fire, telling stories, playing dominoes or cards, and drinking rum. Rum served as a sign of solidarity between the living and the dead.

Lastly, rum played a big part in Reunion's folk medicine. Mixed with healing plants or with salt, it became "herb tea," good for curing the children's worms, fevers, colds, and the flu.

But the tax authorities in Paris looked on this idyllic scene with a typically jaundiced eye. In 1972, to safeguard their earnings from the tax man, the various producers on the island banded together and founded the Compagnie Rhum. This concern produces the most popular brand of rum on the island, "Charrette." But while this label is beloved at home, canny businessmen saw an opportunity to take the island's rum further than it had gone before.

The Isautier family, proprietors of the only distillery on the island unconnected to a sugar plantation, have been in the business since 1845. In 1910, Alfred Isautier, grandson of the founder, took over. He expanded the company's business throughout the French empire, opening facilities in Paris and Madagascar. Although that foundation has been built on to give the company a global reach, its center remains in Reunion, firmly in family control. A similar story might be told about the Chatel family, owners of Distillerie Société J. Châtel & Cie since its founding in 1907.

As already mentioned, Madagascar had long provided a refuge for pirates, refugees, and various other wayward folk since the seventeenth century. The small islands of Nosy Be and Ile Ste. Marie were safe from attack by the various Malagasy tribes. The Malagasy themselves are of extremely mixed origins: Indonesian, African, and Arab influences are detected in their makeup by anthropologists. In any case, many of the great names of piracy made their homes, at least temporarily, in the area. Captain William Kidd's ship, the *Adventure* has recently been found off the Malagasy coast.

As we have seen elsewhere, these European renegades fathered on Malagasy women a new people: the *Zana-Malata* ("Children of Mulattoes"). These would acquire fame under the leadership of Ratsimilaho, the son of a Malagasy princess and Thomas White, an English pirate. He led the Zana-Malata on a number of expeditions against the mainland and carved out a small kingdom for himself. This was doomed, however, by the rise of the Merina tribe in the center of the island, who would, over the course of the nineteenth century, conquer most of the island.

The Zana-Malata ended up with little to fear, however. Ile Ste. Marie was annexed by France in 1818, and Nosy Be in 1841. From these two bases, the French gradually took control of all Madagascar, annexing the whole country in 1890. Over this period, the Zana-Malata, who had accepted French citizenship, took on all the ways of civilized behavior. In recognition of their progress, Empress Eugenie endowed a Catholic church on Ile Ste. Marie in 1857.

Among other elements of European ways, first the Zana-Malata and then the Malagasy as a whole took quickly to rum. With sugar planting having been introduced to the country on a wide scale by the French from Reunion, many Réunionnais rum customs came with it. *Rhum arrange* (rum flavored with ingredients like vanilla, aniseseed, cinnamon, and orchid) made its appearance; along with the ingredients added in Reunion, Malagasies might also add honey or lemon grass. Another favorite was *punch coco*, made with coconut milk. Rum even penetrated the nation's folklore, giving rise to a whole school of rum magic.

Commercially made rum, *roma*, must be distinguished from home brews, like *toaka gasy*, made from distilled rice and sugar cane, and *betsa-betsa*, tafia-like fermented cane juice. Not surprisingly, the two major Malagasy rums are distilled in areas of Zana-Malata influence: St.-Claude comes from Brickaville near the east coast, and Djamandjary comes from the Sirama Distillery on Nosy Be. Madagascar is yet another country that claims rum as its national drink.

While the planters of Reunion were looking for fresh territory to plant sugar cane, their former fellow citizens in Mauritius were not idle. At the same time that their island had fallen to Britain, the Dutch had lost the Cape to the British. While Cape Province itself was not humid enough for sugar, the Crown inadvertently paved the way for what is now Natal to be settled. Many of the Boers, restive under British rule and annoyed by the ending of slavery throughout the empire in 1835, fled with their families and property and slaved north and east of the Cape Colony's border. This was the famous "Great Trek." As it so happened, their reports of the humid area they had discovered reached Mauritius; as a result, the depressed years of the 1840s attracted many planters to the new land. The British promptly declared Natal a colony; much as this annoyed the Boers, it pleased the Franco-Mauritians, whose security needs were thus met. The sugar planters called in workers from India to cultivate the cane, thus adding another element to South Africa's volatile racial mix (and, eventually, giving Mahatma Gandhi his start; as a lawyer he defended the Indians in Natal before returning to India to lead the anticolonial movement).

As it happened, Catholics had been few in South Africa. But the new arrivals from Mauritius set about building churches. To this day, many of the oldest churches in the province are named after French saints. For that matter, it is no surprise either that South Africa's leading distiller of rum, Edward Snell and Company (founded in 1848), is headquartered in Durban, Natal. As with Mauritius, however, the Lomé Convention hampers the country's rum export business.

In India itself, the British encouraged large-scale cultivation of sugar throughout the nineteenth century. Vast irrigation projects in north India and what is now Pakistan allowed more acreage to be turned over to sugar cane. While sugar was not new, entrance into the world economy was, and many Indian peasants were impoverished in the attempt to keep up.

Rum was distilled and was (and is) particularly popular among the Anglo-Indians and Goans (Indo-Portuguese), who drink it almost as much for its ties to their background as for its taste. The so-called Brown Sahibs, the ethnic Indian elite, have also taken to rum. Fittingly, McDowell and Company, yet another colonial-era company, is the foremost distiller in the country. It, too, however, is hobbled in exporting its wares.

The Spanish in the Philippines also found themselves, by the mid-nineteenth century, in need of a cash crop. For a long time, there had been sugar plantations on the western half of the island of Negros. But the easygoing mestizo (Spanish Filipino) *hacenderos* were more interested in having a good time than making a living. This changed when new immigrants from Spain came to the area, looking to enrich themselves and revolutionize the economy. This revolution affected rum as well as sugar.

Typical of the new breed was Don Joaquin Elizalde, who, together with his uncle, Juan Bautista Yrissary, and the Manila-based Spanish businessman and financier Joaquin Ynchausti, established a trading partnership in 1854. They acquired the Manila Steamship Company, renaming it Ynchausti Y Cia. Later, Valentin Teus, a cousin of the Elizaldes, joined the partnership. Teus bought a distillery in Hagonoy, Bulacan, from Elias Menchatorre and merged it with Ynchausti Y Cia. Six years afterward, a rectifying plant of this distillery was constructed in San Miguel District, Manila. This small distillery was transformed by four generations of the Elizaldes into the modern Tanduay Distillery, considered one of the largest in the Philippines.

The Elizalde family invested and developed agricultural properties in the western Visayas, particularly in Panay and Negros Occidental, where they grew sugar cane. Ynchausti Y Cia used its steamboats to transfer the raw materials to the Tanduay compound where it produced rum.

In 1893, Don Joaquin Elizalde became the majority stockholder in Ynchausti Y Cia, and the company was renamed Elizalde & Company, Inc. This paved the way for further diversification of its business interests. Slowly but surely, Tanduay was transformed into a successful industry, producing quality rum and other distilled spirits for both the domestic and international markets.

In May 10, 1988, Twin Ace Holdings Corporation, owned and managed by the Lucio Tan Group of Companies, acquired Tanduay Distillery from the Elizalde family. The new management launched a plant modernization and expansion program that increased the distillery's production capacity by almost fifty times. Through various mergers and acquisitions, Tanduay has become a billion-dollar business. But the Filipino thirst for rum is far from quenched.

Rum is a key part of Australian history and was a catalyst for several key occurrences there. In 1786, Britain's Parliament ordained that New South Wales should be organized as a colony and appointed Captain Arthur Phillip as the first governor. He arrived at Botany Bay in January 1788, with the celebrated "First Fleet"—11 ships carrying 1,030 people (hundreds of convicts of both sexes and four companies of Royal Marines) and livestock and supplies intended to last two years. This is generally regarded as the beginning of the Australian nation.

While the new settlers became accustomed to the strange land they found themselves in, a body of soldiers was being raised in England to provide permanent security, the New South Wales Corps. It arrived with the Second Fleet in 1790. Immediately, it assumed the defense of the new colony. Governor Phillip believed that the future of New South Wales depended on the arrival of free settlers and favored granting lands to soldiers and "emancipists," prisoners who had served their time.

With regular shipments of convicts, the population of Sydney Cove, as the new town was called, soon swelled to four thousand. Ships began arriving there regularly, and by the time Phillip left, the future looked bright. His second-in-command, Major Francis Grose, took over, however, and all power in the colony descended on the officers of the New South Wales Corps. With one of their own as acting governor, they had a near monopoly of the land grants and used convicts as labor on their farms.

They also had a monopoly on commerce in the settlement and controlled the supply of rum bought from passing ships. This they used to pay the convicts' wages. More than this, under their tutelage rum became the actual money of New South Wales: items were bought and sold with the stuff and contracts were discharged. For this reason, the settlers called the corps the "Rum Corps." One of its officers, John Macarthur, became its acknowledged leader.

So things passed until the Crown sent a new governor: our old friend, Admiral William Bligh. His instructions were to assist the independent small holders who had settled the Hawkesbury valley and to break the power of the rum traffickers. Alas, rum was to prove less an ally to him on this occasion than when he had used it to keep his men alive on his epic cruise in the open boat after the mutiny on the HMS *Bounty*.

After his arrival in August 1810, Bligh went to work by eroding the power of Macarthur and his associates. For two years they bided their time. Then, on January 26, 1808, the officers of the corps led their rum-emboldened men in a march on Bligh's residence, Government House. Armed with loaded guns and fixed bayonets, they arrested and imprisoned the governor. This occurrence is, to date, Australia's only military coup. For the next two years, until the arrival of a new governor, officers of the corps took the role of governor on themselves. The arrival of Governor Lachlan Macquarie with his own regiment in 1810 restored the power of the governor and saw the New South Wales Corps disbanded. Bligh was released and Macarthur was exiled to England for a decade. The "Rum Rebellion" was over.

But rum was also to play a happier role in the life of the colony. The new governor soon discovered that the town hospital was an affair of tents and temporary buildings established in the notorious "Rocks" area when the First Fleet arrived in 1788. Macquarie set aside land for a new hospital on the western edge of the government domain and a new road for it, Macquarie Street. Although the plans were drawn up, the British government refused to fund the project.

Undaunted, the doughty Macquarie contracted Garnham Blaxcell, Alexander Riley, and Darcy Wentworth, a consortium of businessmen, to erect the new hospital. In exchange, they were to receive a monopoly on rum imports, convict labor, and supplies; from this bounty, they were expected to recover the cost of the building as well as a considerable profit. Their contract permitted them to import forty-five thousand (later increased to sixty thousand) gallons of rum to sell to the thirsty colonists. While the hospital did not turn out to be very profitable for the contractors, it was a boon to the colonists. Among them, the "Rum Hospital" became a very popular institution, indeed.

On completion of the hospital, Francis Greenway, the now famous convict architect, was asked to report on the quality of the work. He condemned it, claiming that it "must soon fall into ruin." Greenway found that there were weak joints in the structural beams, feeble foundations, shortcuts taken with the construction, rotting stonework, and dry rot in the timbers. Even though Macquarie had ordered the contractors to remedy these defects, many remained hidden until the 1980s, when extensive restoration work was undertaken.

A large central building that served as the main hospital and two smaller wings (quarters for the surgeons) made up the hospital. In 1894, the present buildings in Macquarie Street that form Sydney Hospital replaced the central building. The smaller wings remained intact. The Sydney Mint occupied the southern section and recently became a museum. The northern wing, built as quarters for the principal surgeon, remains today as the Macquarie Street colonnaded facade of the much-enlarged Parliament House. Sydney Hospital continues its work, and has been the scene of many medical "firsts."

But if rum ultimately worked to the benefit of Sydney's colonists, it did real damage to Australia's Aborigines. As with so many indigenous peoples around the globe, they had no resistance to it. "Grog," as they called it (and all liquor, in time), made them more pliable, more dependent on the colonists, and disrupted their social systems. In the latter half of the nineteenth century, the government outlawed alcohol on the Aborigines' reserves; but this made many of them all the more eager to get it. In 1970, it was legalized on the reserves, an act that did little to help. Aborigines now have a lifespan twenty years shorter than the general population and are twenty times more likely to be homeless. Of course, grog is not the only reason for these problems: poverty, lack of clean water, and poor healthcare all play their roles.

Nor was this the only unfortunate result to stem from rum. Up to the mid-nineteenth century, Australia was dependent on rum imports. But exploration revealed that what is now the state of Queensland was ideal for sugar cane. Soon, plantations were being opened in that new colony's tropical north; sugar was building fortunes, and rum distilling followed "as the night the day."

But there was a labor problem. The Aborigines would not serve as cane workers; what to do? Chinese indentured laborers were a partial solution, but they were relatively expensive. Kanakas, the natives of various South Pacific Islands (particularly the Solomons), were quite cheap however. In 1863, the first of them were brought over to work for Robert Towns (founder of the great modern center of Townsville). From this time on, professional kidnappers— "blackbirders," as they were called—stole no less than sixty thousand Kanakas to work the fields of Queensland. One of the first acts of the new Australian Federal Parliament (created through the federation of the six Australian colonies in 1901) was the Pacific Island Laborers Act, which forbade the practice. Almost all of the Kanakas were sent home after that, but about sixteen hundred remained; their descendants live near Rockhampton.

Despite the lack of Kanaka labor, the Queensland plantations and distilleries continued to flourish. Rum is the second most popular alcoholic beverage in the country after beer. Perhaps the most popular Australian brand is Bundaberg, or "Bundy," as it is called in true Australian slang.

By 1880, the town of Bundaberg, Queensland, made its name as Australia's sugar cane capital. Eight years later, a consortium of local sugar millers calling themselves the "Bundaberg Company" started producing rum. So popular did Bundaberg rum become—even though it did not carry its own label—that in 1939 the Australian government requisitioned all rum stocks for its own armed forces, the Royal Navy, and the U.S. military. In 1974, the Bundaberg

Company began bottling its own product. At present, more than twenty-five thousand Bundaberg rum drinks are consumed every hour of every day in Australia. Whatever the past difficulties, the successors of the First Fleet still like guzzling rum as much as their predecessors.

As the Europeans explored other island groups in the Pacific and added them to their empires, they generally looked to copra (dried coconut) as a cash crop. The drink of choice for the residents was usually made from fermented coconut milk and passed under the flexible name of "arrack."

A few places were found to be suitable for sugar cultivation. One of these was Fiji. Since the native Fijians would not work the cane fields, Indians were brought in. Now just comprising over half of the population, the Indians' enmity with the natives has kept the country somewhat unstable since independence. A calming factor, surely, is South Pacific Distilleries Ltd., which produces both white and dark rums under the name "Bounty." Extremely popular in Fiji, the label is exported solely to Australia, New Zealand, and Vanuatu.

The French in Polynesia also found places to grow sugar, and rums, particularly dark rums, are distilled in Tahiti to this day. But the island chain where sugar's (and thus rum's) supremacy was most remarkable was Hawaii.

As noticed earlier, Hawaii was united at the end of the eighteenth century by King Kamehameha I. Although the French and Russians contested for the position, the British were the most influential power in Hawaii, until the advent of New England Congregationalist missionaries. Once they settled down, their sons took up as much land as they could and opened sugar plantations. Rum had the effect it normally had on native peoples; in 1791, it was first tasted by Kamehameha I, having been brought in by Captain James Maxwell. The wise king saw the dangers of local production of alcohol and took steps to control it. Several of his successors became alcoholics. At last, the wily Yankees deposed the country's last queen, Liliukolani, in 1893. A few years later, they were able to press for annexation. But despite the great power for so many years of the sugar interests in Hawaii, rum has been commercially distilled there only at intervals.

At the beginning of the colonial era, the nations we have surveyed were connected by the most delicate thread of wooden ships. Each had existed more or less in isolation. But the coming of the Europeans meant more than mere subjugation, it meant entry into a world economy, a world civilization. For better or worse, the empires of the British, French, Spanish, Portuguese, Dutch, and Danes were the foundation stones of the global village in which we all now live. Though the world has changed, and messages can be sent round the world via the Internet in seconds, rather than waiting months for them to arrive by ship, we are united to that earlier world by the liquor that fueled it.

Mauritius Rum Punch (Cold)

¼ cup lime juice   1 cup water
½ cup sugar   Dash of bitters or nutmeg
¾ cup rum

Dissolve sugar in water, add rum and lime juice. Blend well. Chill and serve with a dash of bitters or nutmeg.

Makes 4 servings.

Mauritius Rum Punch (Hot)

2 cups hot strong tea   2 tablespoons brandy
Rind of ½ lime   1 teaspoon bitters
Juice of 2 lemons   6 ounces caster (superfine)
2 cups rum   sugar

Mix sugar, lemon juice and lime rind in bowl. Add hot strained tea and leave to draw. When cold, add rum and brandy. Add bitters, serve warm, keeping it over a mild heat.

Makes about 16 cocktail glass servings.

Poudine du Pain (Bread Pudding)

1½ pounds (24 ounces) stale
   bread (pain baguette is
   ideal)
3½ ounces melted butter
½ cup milk
½ cup water (room
   temperature)
½ cup dried raisins

½ cup rum
4 tablespoons white sugar
2 tablespoons orange rind
   grated
2 eggs
3 tablespoons natural vanilla
   essence

Soak the raisins in the rum.

Soak the bread in the milk and water for 30 minutes. Break the bread in small pieces. Add the butter, orange rind, eggs, and 2½ tablespoons of natural vanilla essence. Hand work the mixture and add more water if necessary to form a firm and smooth dough, but not watery.

Add the raisins and rum (or whisky) and work into the mixture until well distributed.

Heat up the oven to 400°.

Place an oven earthenware or oven glass dish (of a suitable size) on the kitchen table ready to receive the prepared pudding dough. Do not put the dough into the oven dish yet.

Place 4 tablespoons sugar into a medium saucepan, add 2 table-spoons water and ½ tablespoon of the natural vanilla essence.

Place the saucepan pan over low heat and slowly stir the mixture until the sugar dissolves completely and the mixture starts to bubble. Continue to stir until the hot caramel turns golden brown. Quickly remove saucepan and pour the caramel into the oven dish. With a suitable heat-resistant spatula, spread the caramel all over the oven dish bottom and half way up the sides.

Place the bread pudding dough into the oven dish and distribute evenly until surface is level all round.

Put dish in oven (middle position) and allow to cook until the bread pudding reaches a golden brown color on top. Reduce oven temperature to 320°. Test the pudding mixture at intervals with a cake skewer. When the skewer comes out clean, your pudding is cooked.

Remove from oven and allow to cool in the oven dish.

When the oven dish and pudding are thoroughly cold, carefully detach pudding from around the sides of the oven dish with a flat knife to stop the pudding from sticking to the sides.

Place an upside-down serving plate on top of the oven dish. Invert the oven dish and the serving plate together in one go.

Carefully remove the oven dish from the top of the bread pudding. Cut into slices with a sharp knife. Enjoy and think of the times when Grand Mere used to prepare this poudine for you.

Chapter 9

Rum as Sacrament: Voodoo and Obeah

Strictly speaking, what I had been watching was not really the practice of Obeah but rather the making of a protective fetish or good luck charm; our friend was working in the role of Myal man and cared nothing if he was observed. Had he been really making Obi, he would have been surer of his privacy and would have squatted on the ground surrounded by his paraphernalia and this would have been the scene with little variation:

Most of the ingredients to be used are concealed in a bag from which he draws them as he needs them. The special offering of his patron, which must include a white fowl, two bottles of rum, and a silver offering, are on the ground beside him. Before him is the inevitable empty bottle to receive the ingredients. The incantation opens with a prolonged mumbling which is supposed to be "an unknown tongue." This is accompanied by a swaying of the body.

Gradually ingredients are placed in the bottle and a little rum is poured over them. The throat of the fowl is deftly slit and drops of blood are allowed to fall first on the silver offering and then on the contents of the bottle to which is finally added a few feathers plucked from various parts of

the fowl with a last libation of rum. During all this process
the Obeah man has been drawing inspiration from frequent
draughts of rum, reserving a substantial portion to be
consumed later when he makes a meal off the flesh of
the fowl.

When the bottle concoction has been completed and
the last incantation has been said over it, the Obeah man
entrusts it to his patron with minute instructions how it
is to be buried on some path where the intended victim is
sure to pass or as near his dwelling as possible.

—Joseph J. Williams, S.J., *Voodoos and Obeahs*

I magine a hot, tropical night. A band of islanders are swaying to
the throbbing beat of drums. A priestess sprinkles the drums
with white, overproof rum, fills her mouth with it, and then
sways, spitting it out over the participants. She starts chanting in a
corrupted version of Yoruba. A goat is brought forward, which she
first pets; the priestess then decapitates the animal. Its blood pours
out and is captured in half-filled glasses of the rum. The participants drink the mixture down and begin to dance. This is kumina,
an African-based folk religion found on the island of Jamaica.

Alcohol has always played a part in religion; as far as we can
tell, humans have poured out libations to the gods. Creation myths
of various kinds see wine or whatever fermented fluid the given
culture imbibes as a gift of the deity and a remembrance of whatever paradise from which humanity was expelled. A lot of booze, as
anyone who likes the stuff will tell you, can induce an otherworldly
feeling; until the next morning, paradise can feel very near.

There is, of course, a greater significance, for in many cultures
wine and other drinks have been closely associated with the blood of
gods and men. This is certainly true of traditional Christianity,
whether Catholic or Orthodox. In these churches, it is believed that
wine is actually and physically transformed into the blood of Jesus.
Comparative religionists will say that this simply shows that Chris-

tianity partakes of an almost universal motif. Believers will reply with Tertullian, the Church father, that "the soul is naturally Christian," a sort of early anticipation of Carl Jung's collective unconscious.

Certainly, the symbol of the Holy Grail is very powerful; in Christian minds, with its graphic combination of the Chalice used at Mass (the Last Supper having been the first of these ceremonies) and a repository of Christ's blood shed on Calvary, it is a very powerful symbol. Such occurrences as the miracle of Lanciano, where, in 800, the wine used by a priest who doubted the Real Presence turned to actual blood (which survives today and, oddly, it is of the same blood type as that on the Shroud of Turin) have reinforced this belief. Regardless of the explanation one gives the fact, it remains: alcohol has always had a sacred character.

When the Europeans began to bring rum to the colonial world, it had an enormous effect on local religiosity. In Africa and Madagascar, local priests soon discovered that it carried a much bigger punch than did the palm wine they were used to. Many of the native cults specialized in using dancing and alcohol to induce a state whereby the believer would be possessed by one or another of the gods. For this purpose, rum had it all over palm wine.

On the West African coast, the faiths of the Dahomey and the Yoruba featured a pantheon of gods not unlike those of the Greeks, Norse, and others. There was a god of war, a god of agriculture, a god of death, and so on. Beyond these lesser deities, of course, there was a creator. But he was seen as being remote and unconcerned with the affairs of men. For those who wished to prosper in this life, it was the lesser divine folk, the *orishas*, who had to be dealt with; they were the ones who must be propitiated for success in this life.

Moreover, like the gods of other peoples, the orishas were seen to be enormously petty and jealous. They fought with one another, played favorites with humanity, and were not above playing tricks on each other and hapless mortals—they had no moral sense. Above all, they craved the food and drink of this world, only available through the votaries who sought their aid. Curses and defense against those curses were also a large part of this worship.

When the slaves were brought from the Guinea coast to the Americas and elsewhere, they came into contact with the religion of their masters: Christianity. Among the French, Spanish, and Portuguese, this meant Catholicism. With the Dutch and English, it was various sects of Protestantism they encountered. In either case, they did not lose their own religious notions overnight. Of course, these had been weakened somewhat by the very fact of the Africans' captivity. The gods of their homeland had not shown the same power as the God of their captors. Thus, the less well instructed among them regarded the Christian God with a wary respect. They might cling to their own deities, but they were careful not to directly offend a spirit who had given His own devotees such power over them. By the same token, however, the old gods were seen as still retaining some ability to help or to harm, even in the new land. Some went so far as to think that their captivity was a punishment by the orishas, who would eventually take them back to Africa, if they showed themselves worthy enough.

In Protestant colonies, the slaves discovered hymn singing; in the Catholic ones, they encountered the saints. Now, it must be understood that while not possessing those who pray to them, various Catholic saints are prayed to for particular things—their specialties, so to speak. Thus, St. Anthony is invoked to find lost objects, St. Lazarus when the believer is in danger of death, and so on. In certain ways, some of the saints resemble some of the orishas. It was easy to identify one with the other. Did a particular saint remind the African exiles of a particular orisha? It made sense to transfer the rituals associated with the one to the other. Having identified, say, St. John the Baptist with Ghede, the god of death, the dances traditionally done in Ghede's name might be performed on St. John's Day.

To be sure, a certain amount of this sort of adaptation has a long history in Christianity. Since various hilltops in pagan Europe had been sacred to the gods of that region, it made sense to dedicate them to St. Michael; while the reverence given that spot would continue, it would, as the Church fathers laid down, be offered to someone worthy of it. Moreover, since St. Michael was Heaven's warrior, and "the gods of the gentiles are demons," as Isaias tells us, the archangel would keep the site free of Satanic influence. So, too, the evergreen tree and the mistletoe, sacred plants in various European cults, were brought in and rededicated to Christ.

But how far could this process be allowed to continue? It was and is a question with which theologians have wrestled, and over which slave masters differed severely. For some, the sort of "communion" we saw in the opening paragraph was a blasphemous burlesque of the Mass, the reception of the blood of the Lamb of God. Identifying saints with orishas was similarly an assault on the saints themselves. Others, particularly the less devout, were blasé about the whole affair; they were quite happy to let the slaves do what they liked, so long as they showed due respect to them and did not revolt.

In any case, a whole family of hybrid religions grew up: kumina in Jamaica, Santeria in Cuba, voodoo in Jamaica and Louisiana (with its lighter "hoodoo" version among blacks in the Anglophone United States), and macumba, umbanda, and candomble in Brazil. While there are regional differences among them, they share a worship of the orishas: the "Seven African Powers," a concern with luck in this life, a fear of witchcraft, and the ritual use of rum.

Due to the Protestant lack of reverence for the saints and eschewing of ritual, kumina is the most African of the cults to be found in Jamaica, with negligible European or Christian influence. The one exception is the use of Christian hymns (often barely recognizable) in their worship. Male and female leaders must exhibit a great deal of strength in their control of zombies or spirits and assume their positions of leadership after careful training in the feeding habits, ritual procedures, dances, rhythms, and songs of a variety of spirits by a previous king or "Captain" and queen, or "Mother."

In kumina, one is said to catch "Myal" when being possessed by one of the three classes of gods—sky, earthbound, and ancestral zombies—this last is the most common form of possession. Each god can be recognized by the particular dance style exhibited by the possessed and by the songs and drum rhythms to which it responds. Once called by music and other ritual items, especially with rum mixed with blood, the spirits take control of their chosen hosts. The possessed dance in the given style proper to the spirit "riding" them.

Santeria, voodoo, and the rest are very similar in belief, but their ritual is eked out with Catholic trappings; each of the orishas is depicted by a cognate saint. Also, while kumina folk generally do not consider themselves Christians, most Santeros (as the priests or practitioners of Santeria are called—believers are called Santeristas), as well as pratitioners of voodoo, etc., would claim to be devout Catholics.

As frightening as the world of Yoruba-based religions might be to more conventional Christians, there is a flip side that frightens even the most dedicated orisha worshipper. This is the practice of curses and black magic. Many Santeros, traiteurs, and other such practitioners make a good bit of money providing protection against these evils (called obeah in the Anglophone West Indies). Some will, if the price is right, also furnish the requisite curses and so on against the consulter's enemies. In all of these endeavors, rum plays its part.

The colonial authorities reacted to this latter practice with great severity. A 1760 Jamaican law prescribed "death or transport for any Negro or slave who shall pretend to any supernatural Power and be detected in making use of any Blood, Feathers, Parrot Beaks, Dogs Teeth, Alligators Teeth, broken Bottles, Grave Dirt, Rum, Eggshell, or any other Materials relative to the practice of Obeah or Witchcraft, in order to delude and impose upon the Minds of others." Nevertheless, this sort of thing goes on to this day. Traditionally, part of the fee given the obi-man, as a black magic practitioner is called, is a quart of white overproof rum.

Some, but not all, of the orishas love rum themselves. Eleggua, for example, is the messenger between human beings and the other orishas, and the keeper of the gates between our world and theirs. He must be honored first during any ceremony; without his approval, nothing will happen. Generous and cruel, he is regarded as a demonic figure in Brazil, but as a benevolent guardian figure in Cuba. Seeing him as a childlike trickster figure, the Santeristas give him candies, candles, toys, rum, and cigars. They sprinkle his image with rum to keep him pacified. As Exú in Brazil, however, he is treated completely differently. There, too, he also lives behind the door or (preferably) outside at the front gate. He is also propitiated first, but only to send him away so that he will not ruin rituals and festas. In Haiti, he is Papa Legba, but in all three countries, he is depicted as either St. Peter, St. Anthony, or St. Lazarus.

Ogoun is the god of war. In Grenada, he has an appetite for sheep and white cocks; he relishes a shot of strong rum with his meals. The Haitians honor him not just as a general (he is often depicted as a colonial-era general in cocked hat), but also as a politician. He likes to be saluted with dark rum. Often, this rum is poured on the ground and then lit. He is identified with St. James the Great, *Matamoros* (the "Moor Killer"). Ogoun is said to have incited the slaves to the great revolt in Haiti in the 1790s.

Those possessed by Ogoun sometimes wash their hands in flaming rum without suffering any burns. They may dress up in red, wave a machete, chew a cigar, and demand rum in the old Creole phrase, *Gren mwe fret* ("my testicles are cold").

Ghede is the god of the dead, called "Baron Samedi" in Haiti. He is seen either as a white man or a skeleton with a top hat on his head, a cigar in his mouth, a bottle of rum in one hand, and very often a walking stick in the other. He is the most common voodoo spirit to be possessed by; those so possessed dance and drink a lot. Without him, it is impossible to reach the spirit world, for he guides one past Ellegua/Legba/Exú, who guards the crossroads. He also watches over the spirits of the dead. Perhaps because of his doleful job, he loves a party: nothing pleases him more than rum, women, and dancing. To represent him at soirees in his honor, a raccoon skull wearing a top hat is placed inside a log with a cane and a small bottle of red rum. The base is then decorated with bones and alligator teeth; the top is ringed with purple and black glass nuggets. The saint identified with him is St. John the Baptist.

Ghede/Baron Samedi had a younger brother, Zaka or Azaca, who is the god of farming. While protecting the crops, he wears (at least in Haiti) a blue denim shirt, a straw hat, and rolled-up pants. Always barefoot, Zaka carries a pickax and straps a straw "macoute" sack across his back. Much is made of the fact that he plays the country bumpkin to his brother's urban sophisticate: where the baron smokes a fine cigar, Zaka puffs on a clay pipe; the death god relishes aged dark rum, but Zaka prefers clear and coarse *clairin*. Zaka protects work, renews hope, and brings prosperity. He is given corn cakes and cornmeal as offerings; of a wily nature, he takes his food into a corner to eat in secret.

Fans of the old *I Love Lucy* show will remember that Cuban club owner and performer Rickie Ricardo often beat a drum and sang "Babalu." This was a reference to the orisha of health, called in Cuba "Babaluaye." Miraculous but severe, he is represented by St. Lazarus, who came back to life—the epitome of a cure. The foods associated with Babaluaye are tobacco, rum, doves, and hens. His emblem is crutches, reeds, and cowries and his dance posture is infirm or lame. Santeros honor him by drinking rum and smoking cigars in front of images of St. Lazarus.

As might be thought from its use in placating the gods directly, rum plays a signal role in making good luck charms and in working curses. One popular New Orleans charm required the maker to say, before starting to work, "God before me, God behind me, God be with me." Then he or she must gather the materials: a small amount of allspice, a white bean, black pepper seeds, a medal or statue of St. Benedict, rosemary, chamomile, calamus root, a small lodestone, a few strands of hair, and breadcrumbs. The blessing of God duly invoked, all the materials are wrapped in red cloth or a red bag. All these are sewn up tightly so that nothing can escape.

Every Friday (save Good Friday), the charm is moistened with a small amount of rum. Then it is kept in some safe secret place. Some folk will make charms for each room of their home.

Such protection may be necessary. *Gurunfindas* are the talismans made by Santeria's black witches, *mayomberos*, to ward off evil from themselves; the theory is that such evil will then be directed toward others. To make a gurunfinda, the mayombero must first hollow out a *guiro*—a hard, inedible plant found in the tropics—and fill it with the heads and hearts of a turtle and different kinds of parrots; the tongue and eyes of a rooster; and seven live ants. Next, he adds seven teeth, the jawbone, and some hair of a cadaver, the cadaver's name written on a piece of paper, and seven coins to pay the dead spirit for his or her services. Then he pours rum over the mixture and leaves it buried beneath the ceiba tree for twenty-one days. When he disinters the guiro, the mayombero marks the outside of the fruit with chalk and then hangs the charm near his home.

The mayombero has equally colorful means at his disposal to kill an enemy outright. One means of doing so is to gather nine clay pots, dirt from nine tombs, nine coins, ashes, Guinea pepper, Chinese pepper, black pepper, white rum, cooking oil, and nine wicks. These ingredients obtained, he next writes the name of his victim on the bottom of each pot. The mayombero next fills each of the pots with a handful of dirt from one of the tombs, after leaving a coin at each tomb as payment for the dirt. He then mixes ashes in with the dirt and adds the pepper. To this mixture he then pours in nine spoonfuls of the rum in each pot. He must now fill the nine pots with cooking oil and insert a wick in each pot. These makeshift lamps are then taken to the cemetery at midnight. Next, the nine lamps are lit and the mayombero asks the souls of the dead to kill his enemy.

Mayomberos revel in such work. Depending on whether they wish to cause illness, send bad luck, or break up marriages, they will create such makeshift lamps. The ingredients differ considerably, however—one such recipe requires the frying of a scorpion in oil until the scorpion dissolves, and the addition of said oil to the pot. But most of these spells require rum.

It should not be thought that such things take place only in the West Indies, Miami, or Louisiana. Throughout the American South, hoodoo or conjure is practiced. One of the most common ingredients in spells in the South is graveyard dust. A popular method for getting it is for the conjure doctor to take the dirt from the seventh grave from the cemetery gate; failing that, the third grave on the left will do. But depending on the spell, he may ignore the position and take the dirt from the grave of a murderer, a baby, or one of the doctor's own loved ones. The doctor collects it from the head and foot of the grave and from over the corpse's heart In any case, the dirt should be dug only by hand and with a silver spoon. In hoodoo, however, nothing is free. So, once the dirt has been taken, the doctor must pay for it. He will leave on the ground a dime and three pennies, a shot of rum, and a shot of whiskey.

Even outside of such obviously magical procedures, rum has worked its way into everyday rituals in the Creole Zone. Among the Garifuna (black Caribs) of Belize, rum plays a big part in mourning. At the moment of death, a glass of water with a cross and a burning candle are placed beside the body. These symbolize that the soul is still alive. To avoid disturbing the soul, no one cries or speaks loudly. The old people clean the body in a bath of strong rum and then dress it for viewing. Later, they embalm the body with rum-soaked rags. After a nine-day period of prayer (a novena), a party called a *beluria* is thrown. In addition to eating vast quantities of conch soup, chicken soup, and sweet rice, huge amounts of rum are drunk and spilled about in honor of the deceased.

Similar activities take place on Carriacou in the Grenadines. When anyone opens a bottle of rum, the first drink is poured onto the ground, along with water or a soft drink as an offering to dead loved ones. This "ground wetting" is performed to give thanks to God and to invite the dead to join the festivities at homecomings, birthdays, weddings, and so on.

In Jamaica, it is common to pour the ever popular overproof rum around the foundations of a new house as an offering to the spirits. A traditional cake at a Jamaican wedding feast often includes a tot of rum and leftover slices being mailed to those who couldn't attend (taking home a piece of cake and placing it under a pillow is said to hasten marriage). Still practiced on the island is the Christmas dance/parade called *Jonkanoo*. In this event, several masked figures, reminiscent of mummers, dance to the beat of Gombay drums. Surviving also in the Bahamas (as Junkanoo), Belize (John Canoe), and Bermuda (with "Gombey dancers"), it also graced the Carolinas (as Johnkankus), until Emancipation in 1865. Featuring set characters such as the cow head, the horse head, the devil, the different categories of warriors and Indians, as well as a character known as Pitchy-Patchy (a strange sort of vegetable character), it is said to be a tribute to an African slave trader from Axim in Ghana, called "John Conny," who died about 1720.

Today, it is considered a secular festivity, connected with Christmas. But there is good evidence that in early days it was bound up with obeah and that the dancers were dancing to be possessed by the orishas. A favored accompanying dish at that time was a goat's head boiled in rum and served out to onlookers and participants. Accounts of Jonkanoo in the nineteenth century tell us that at the end of the dance, the devil figure would be offered rice, rum, and nuts.

But that is all long ago. Today, the obeah connections to Junkanoo have almost entirely evaporated, much like the pagan connections have to the Christmas tree. Before Vatican II, in many areas where Santeria, voodoo, and the like were rampant, the orishas were slowly being superseded by the saints whose images they bore. The downgrading of reverence to the saints in many Catholic clerical circles since the 1960s has led to a "repaganization" of these hybrid religions and an assertion of independence from Catholicism on the part of many of its practitioners.

In my opinion, the likelihood is that whenever the Catholic Church's priests once again encourage devotion to the saints, the same process will recommence. For the simple fact is that, whatever its faults, Catholicism, with its unbloody rituals, its worldwide reach, and its appeal to look beyond this world of pain and suffering, offers escape from the fear-haunted region of the orishas. Despite the Yoruba-based religions seeing spirits in everything, they remain primarily concerned with "luck" in this life. But what will in all probability remain (as it has with Junkanoo) is the lavish use of rum to celebrate life and death, Christmas and Easter.

Alcohol is, in western magic, symbolic of the element of water. Because of its ecstatic possibilities, alcohol is seen as being more powerful than ordinary water, in a sense more "real." A near universal motif in the world's folklores is that of the "water of life," a special sort of water which will revive the dead, cure all disease, or bestow immortality. Many a folktale tells of a hero sent to get the water of life from some far-off spring, lake, or river. Often, he will be assisted by magical helpers, one of whom can see things from afar, and another who can walk many miles in minutes (another wide-ranging motif). Upon arrival at the miraculous body of water, the far-seeing helper announces that the king, princess, or family member the hero is trying to save is dying; the long stepper then brings the precious liquid back in the nick of time.

Not surprisingly, "water of life" is a common name for hard spirits—*aqua vitae* in Latin, of course. The French "water of life" is *eau de vie*, a clear fruit brandy that was originally invented in the seventeenth century as a hopeful cure for plagues like cholera, but quickly found more effective and upbeat uses. In Swedish, *akavit* is vodka, and the Gaelic *uisquebagh* (a cognate of *vodka* from whence comes our "whiskey") means the same thing. In classical and Hindu mythology, the gods themselves had such potations—ambrosia and soma (the latter giving its name to the all-purpose drug in Aldous Huxley's *Brave New World*). The idea of the "Fountain of Youth" stems from such ideas, and wine always represents elemental water in the ritual of the nineteenth century "Order of the Golden Dawn" and its more contemporary spin-offs.

In Christianity, of course, the Blood of Christ is embodied in wine, literally so for Catholics and Orthodox Christians, and symbolically for Protestants. The presence of this Blood in the Holy Grail transformed that vessel into a means of healing and even of achieving immortality, and the language of prayer addressing the Precious Blood is filled with alcoholic imagery: "Blood of Christ inebriate me," as St. Ignatius says in his prayer, "Anima Christi."

The sacredness of alcohol in general and the specific place of wine in Catholic liturgy in particular doubtless turned rum into a sacred vessel for the devotees of African-derived religions. The frequent use of white rum in Voodoo ritual certainly takes us back to the "water of life" and makes clear the reasons for its use as a purifier (especially of the newborn) and so forth.

Even in cultures where a clear distinction was made between sacramental wine and other spirits, the latter nevertheless conferred a sort of makeshift sacredness on business and personal transactions. Blood-brotherhood in Europe, for example, often required that the putative brothers jointly shed their blood into a goblet of wine, after which they both drank of the same cup. In pre-Reformation England, after a wedding, a bit of bread was placed into a large goblet. The priest then blessed the cup according to a set liturgical formula. The bride and groom would drink from it and then the whole company present; this ceremony was considered to seal the marriage, and the modern bride and groom's feeding each other a slice of wedding cake at their reception is a survival of this custom.

So liquor of all sorts has a place at every important celebration, conferring—whether those celebrating the occasion are conscious of it or not—a sort of solemnity upon the proceedings. As we shall see in the next chapter, rum has continued to benefit from this.

Doodoo Love Potion Cocktail

1 ounce vodka
1 ounce crème de cacao

1 ounce gin
1 ounce dark rum

Mix all ingredients and pour over ice with several fresh mint leaves in a tall glass. Burn a pink and red candle anointed with mint oil.

Recipe courtesy of Erzulie's Authentic Voudou, 510 Rue Dumaine, New Orleans, Louisiana.

Mannish Water
(Goat Head Soup)

As an example of the decay of magic, this Jamaican recipe is still considered an aphrodisiac, even if it is no longer dispensed by obi-men!

Goat head
Water
3 green bananas
2 potatoes
1 yam
1 chopped carrot
1 chopped chocho

12 pimento seeds
5 stalks escallion
8 sprigs thyme
1 scotch bonnet pepper
5 cloves garlic
1 cup white rum
Salt and pepper to taste

Clean goat head very well. Place meat in a large pot and cover with water. Add garlic and bring to a boil. Simmer for 2 hours and add spices. Add remaining ingredients except rum and simmer for another hour. Add rum, additional spices to taste, and simmer for 30 minutes. Then serve warm.

Chapter 10

~~~~~~~~~~~~~~~~~~~~~~~~~~

The Festal Board:
Rum and Holidays

The Hollanders, in those early days of the settlement of the valley of the Hudson, did not have so many enjoyments. Christmas was a day of rest, as well of some hilarity. It was the custom of the country for some one of the neighbors to make pitchers of hot rum (in the later days called spiced rum), of which the visitors partook freely. The well-to-do families in those days had pitchers that would hold three gallons, which were used to hold milk, used with mush, for the evening meal called supper. Sometimes they used cracked corn called "samp" and milk, and cold meats and vegetables. Cabbage was used to a very great extent. New Year's was very similar, roast goose then being the universal dish, accompanied with the neighborly drink of hot rum. "Paas" was a day celebrated by eating hard eggs and drinking egg cider. The latter was made of sugar, eggs and cider, thoroughly beaten up together. At "Pingster," the young people met together and gathered large quantities of a delicious fruit called "Pingster" apples, also squawberries and wintergreen berries with the young growing wintergreens. These, with egg-nog, made an enjoyable feast. The "Pingster" apple

is a succulent, soft pulpy fruit, growing on a bush similar
in size and appearance to the lilac.

—John Fitch, quoted in *Schermerhorn Genealogy
and Family Chronicles* (1888)

R eligion, of whatever variety, tends to commemorate its mysteries and doctrines, its anniversaries and holy men, on
particular days. Outside of alcohol-condemning Islam,
celebration of these feast days (as well as of civil holidays) tends to
include imbibing of specific drinks. As Europeans and their descendants spread their forms of Christianity across the globe and
brought their drinks with them, the festivals of Christmas, Easter,
and the rest took root in virtually every nation. Not surprisingly,
rum, associated as it has been with this movement, has found its
way into the calendar of Christian celebration.

The traffic was not one way, however. Rum also came back to
Europe. As might be expected, it has sown deep roots in the festive
activities of the major imperial nations: France, Spain, Portugal,
Great Britain, and the Netherlands. But through the mediation of
the Danes (and to a degree the Swedes), whose lesser successes in
the colonial competition belie their status as great seafarers, rum
made its way into central Europe via the Baltic trade. As a result,
the festive pastries and drinks of the Germans, Poles, Czechs, Russians, and Italians often use rum. The Danes themselves invented
rum pudding, a concoction that is appropriate at any time.

Colonial trade brought tropical fruits and sugar to these areas as
well as rum. These products were particularly welcome on the
holiday menus of various cold-weather festivals. Rum, with its
vaguely sweet and extremely warming taste, served as the perfect
compliment.

But it was in Canada that rum, as we saw at the various levées,
came truly into its own. Nor is it just at official functions that rum
has come into its own in the Dominion of the North. Demerara

rum, stored in cod barrels, has become the primary drink in New-foundland. Since World War II, "Skreech," as this liquid is called (from its purported results on the drinker), has become synony-mous with Newfie culture. But the island province's love of the stuff dates back at least to the eighteenth century. Thus, Captain George Cartwright described Christmas among his Newfoundland crew in Labrador back in 1770:

> At sunset the people ushered in Christmas, according to the New-foundland custom. In the first place, they built up a prodigious large fire in their house; all hands then assembled before the door, and one of them fired a gun, loaded with powder; afterwards each of them drank a dram of rum; concluding the ceremony with three cheers. These formalities being performed with great solemnity, they retired into their house, got drunk as fast as they could, and spent the whole night in drinking, quarreling, and fighting. . . . This is an intolerable custom; but as it has prevailed from time imme-morial, it must be submitted to.

Even today, rum plays its role in the celebrative life of the fishing industry. Whenever a fishing boat passes to a new owner, it must be "denamed" before it can be renamed. The crew sneaks on board the boat the night before a christening and pours rum on the bow and decks of the boat. This washes away the old luck. The next day, the rechristening is done with champagne.

Similar practices dominated all the Maritime Provinces. In nineteenth-century Yarmouth County, Nova Scotia, according to Jackson Ricker in his *Historical Sketches of Glenwood and the Argyles*, the rum jug took its place at all gatherings. "It was present," he wrote, "on holydays such as Christmas, Easter, etc.; on militia train-ing grounds; at launchings, and house raisings; and no election could be held without grog." Ricker claimed that "the decanter of rum on a table [could be seen] where any certain candidate enter-tained the men who voted for him. The custom then observed at elections required each candidate to have what was termed an 'open house' where a barrel of pilot bread, a ham, a cheese, with coffee and tea and a decanter of liquor constituted 'the feed.'"

The rest of Canada shared this love. At Hudson's Bay Company posts throughout the west of Canada, rum was used not only to trade with the Indians and to please the company's French Canadian employees, but also in the ceremonial life of the organization. Each new post was "christened" with a bottle of rum. This custom was duly carried out at the March 19, 1825, opening of Fort Vancouver (now Vancouver, Washington). Supervised by Governor George Simpson and Chief Factor John McLoughlin, the French voyageurs in the company's employ broke a bottle of rum on a flagstaff and hoisted the Union Jack.

In his official report to the Hudson Bay Company's London headquarters, Governor Simpson said, "At sunrise I mustered all the people to place the flagstaff of the new establishment and in the presence of the gentlemen, servants, chiefs, and Indians, I baptized it, by breaking a bottle of rum on the flag-staff and repeating the following words in a loud voice:—'on behalf of the Honorable Hudson's Bay Company, I hereby name this establishment Fort Vancouver! God Save King George the Fourth!' The object of naming it after that distinguished navigator, Captain Vancouver, is to identify our claim to the soil and trade with his discovery of the river and coast on behalf of Great Britain."

Although McLoughlin generally required sobriety at this faraway outpost, on Christmas Eve in the large banquet hall he would treat his guests to the famous Hudson's Bay rum, probably some of the same beverage with which the post was christened.

Nor ought this be much of a surprise: even then, rum had come into its own at Christmas, both in Europe and overseas. At Yuletide, its dominion remains unbroken. In Puerto Rico, there exists an age-old custom known as *la parranda*. Musicians stroll from house to house in the streets of Old San Juan, expecting to find hospitality in food and *ron cañita*—rum flavored with sugar cane. Although home preparation of the cañita rum was prohibited many years ago in order to protect the monopoly of the island's major commercial companies, everyone knows someone who can provide the home-made stuff. As with moonshining in the American South, however, this activity is frowned on by the authorities and severely punished when detected.

But eggnog is the ultimate Christmas drink in North America. Theories on its origin are legion. It doubtless came to America from Europe, since it resembles innumerable milk and wine punches concocted long ago in the mother continent. But in America, rum replaced wine, as it had in Moose Milk. Many claim that the name "eggnog" was originally "egg-and-grog." This became "egg'n'grog" and thus "eggnog." So it is said.

But other commentators claim that the "nog" of eggnog derives from the word "noggin," a small, wooden, carved mug used to serve drinks at tables in taverns ("tankards" were reserved for drinks beside the fire). This school asserts that eggnog started out as a mixture of Spanish sherry and milk, a mixture called by the English "Dry Sack Posset." It would be natural to call such an egg drink in a noggin eggnog.

Yet another school maintains that in the seventeenth century, Europeans consumed a very strong ale that they called "nog"; it was especially popular in Britain. The Germans had their own *Biersuppe* ("Beer Soup"), an egg-based ale. During the same period, the French consumed *Lait de Poule*, a mixture of egg yolks, milk, sugar, and spirits, such as sherry, rum, or brandy. Supposedly, in America the German ale's name and the Lait de Poule's ingredients combined to make our eggnog. George Washington created his own recipe that included rye whiskey, rum, and sherry. Given its strength, only the bravest would try the president's brew.

Whatever the case, the drink's utility as a wintertime drink caused it to spread throughout North America. Its potency and taste served well against the winter cold. But one improvement would certainly make it unbeatable: the addition of heat. According to British tipplers, in the 1820s Pierce Egan wrote a book called

Life of London: or Days and Nights of Jerry Hawthorne and His Elegant Friend Corinthian Tom. To publicize this work, Egan created a hot variation of eggnog he called "Tom and Jerry." This mixture added a half-ounce of brandy to the basic recipe (fortifying it considerably and adding further to its popularity). So renowned was this drink that pubs were even called "Tom and Jerries" for a while during this period. But the American version claims that Professor Jerry Thomas, a bartender at San Francisco's Occidental Hotel in the 1860s, is Tom and Jerry's creator. He traveled and put on exhibitions throughout the major cities in the United States and Europe, performing on stage and as a celebrity bartender. These activities helped popularize his 1862 book *The Bartender's Companion and the Bon Vivant's Companion.* It is considered the first standard guide to mixing cocktails and helped relieve a great deal of stress during the War between the States.

Whatever the case, the Tom and Jerry's popularity grew through the nineteenth century and remained strong through the first half of the twentieth. Specially labeled Tom and Jerry mugs and bowls were created, and the libation became a New Year's favorite (the creation of the famous animated cat-and-mouse team in 1942 didn't hurt either). But it is an elaborate drink to make, requiring the making of a stiff batter and so on—an effort that the lazier post–World War II generations were reluctant to make. In the 1960s, liquor manufacturers attempted to rescue the beverage with premade Tom and Jerry batter mixes, but to no avail. Having become rarer than steak Diane, the remaining places that serve it are very few indeed. I have only encountered it in recent decades at Lexington Restaurant, St. Paul, Minnesota, and the Pied Piper Bar at San Francisco's Palace Hotel. Oddly enough, however (or perhaps not so oddly considering the region's weather), it has begun, since the fall of the Soviet Union, to make a small comeback in Russia and the Baltic states.

In any case, eggnog itself, in the 1800s, was nearly always made in large quantities as a social drink. An English visitor to America wrote in 1866, "Christmas is not properly observed unless you brew egg nogg for all comers; everybody calls on everybody else; and each call is celebrated by a solemn egg-nogging. . . . It is made cold and is drunk cold and is to be commended."

New Year's in Baltimore, when young men traditionally called on all of their friends, was another eggnog day. At each of many homes, the visitors were offered a cup of eggnog, becoming drunker and drunker as they made their rounds.

Eggnog remains an indispensable part of American Christmas. But in Puerto Rico, *Coquito* is the traditional Christmas drink, using coconut milk and rum. On December 24 in Mexico, *Noche Buena*, a special meatless feast is served, alongside of Mexican rum *ponche*. This drink consists of rum, sugar cane, and various fruits and flowers (depending on the state) mixed with boiling water.

In Costa Rica, the Christmas drink is *Rompope*, consisting of a liter of whole milk, a quarter-liter of rum, a stick of cinnamon, five berries of pepper from Jamaica, a hundred whole grams of sugar, and three eggs. The milk is warmed up with the cinnamon, the pepper, and the sugar. When it arrives at the boiling point, the mixture is passed through a strainer that resists the heat, the rum and eggs are added, and then the whole is mixed with an iron rod.

For the Anglo-Indians, the use of rum is a strong connection to the European half of their ancestry, as is celebrating such festivals as Christmas. A month before the day itself, preparations for the feast begin. A special plum cake is begun by soaking its ingredients—raisins, nuts, and an orange peel—in rum. Plum rum is also made by soaking the fruit in the liquor, and then drawing off the beverage. These creations and other Christmas foods are sent, when ready, to family and friends with other goodies on beautifully decorated trays. The custom is called concata, a word of Portuguese origin. After Midnight Mass, families return to their homes to enjoy a glass of plum rum together before bed.

As mentioned in Chapter 5, the drink of choice for Jamaicans during the Christmas season is sorrel. Made from dried sorrel sepals (a meadow plant), cinnamon, cloves, sugar, an orange peel, and rum, it is usually served over ice. Every Jamaican household has its own recipe.

Starting in November, the search for guavaberries begins in the British Virgin Islands. These wild cherry-looking berries are picked, washed, and then soaked in a demijohn or in one-gallon glass bottles containing dark Meyers Rum and an assortment of spices. This mixture sits fermenting from three to six weeks; syrup is then added to make the guavaberry liqueur. Visiting carolers finish their Christmas carols by asking for guavaberry, in a melodious ditty:

> Good mornin', good mornin', an how are you dis mornin'?
>   [Repeat]
> Good mornin', good mornin', ah come fo' mi Guavaberry
>   [Repeat]
> Good mornin', good mornin', put it on de table
>   [Repeat]

St. John's in the neighboring U.S. Virgin Islands (until 1917 the Danish West Indies) also boasts Christmas guavaberry liqueur. Although now commercially made, many families continue to make their own.

In the French Antilles, one serves various liquors at Christmas. Shrubb is extremely popular, consisting of dried orange peels that are marinated in white rum for three days to a week, after which the mixture is combined with sugar, poured into water, and brought to boiling. The concoction is then allowed to stand and cool, turning into syrup. Said syrup is then further mixed with a lot more rum and then filtered. Thus is Shrubb born, and thirstily quaffed by Christmas merrymakers. So it is with Ti-punch, which sees white rum mixed with cane syrup and a slice of green lemon.

But rum affects solid Christmas food as well, most notably the Christmas pudding made famous by Charles Dickens. Pudding's story goes back to the fourteenth century. In those days, a porridge called frumenty was made by stewing beef and lamb with dried fruit such as raisins, currants, prunes, wines, and spices. Typical of the medieval habit of combining sweet and savory tastes, this stew was served as a fasting dish in preparation for Christmas.

By the seventeenth century, frumenty was making the transition to plum pudding by being thickened with eggs and breadcrumbs. At about this time, rum began to be added to the mix. A setback was suffered during the Puritan oppression of the 1649–1660 Commonwealth. In keeping with their dark creed, the murderers of Charles I banned Christmas and with it any food whose preparation might indicate Yule festivities on the sly. So it was that Oliver Cromwell banned not only mincemeat but Christmas pudding as well. This was described as being a lewd custom; its rich ingredients were dismissed as "unfit for God fearing people."

Although Cromwell's politics were somewhat echoed by the overthrow of Charles I's son James II, and by the latter's son's (also called James) exclusion from the throne in favor of the German George I, it was nevertheless the latter who resurrected Christmas pudding. The new king did this despite some objections by the Quakers.

It was in the time of George's great-great-great-granddaughter, Queen Victoria, however, that steamed Christmas pudding came into the splendor described by Dickens in *A Christmas Carol*. By that time, all sorts of customs had grown up around the dish. It was to be made by the twenty-fifth Sunday after Trinity and prepared with thirteen ingredients (representing Jesus and his disciples). Every member of the family took turns to stir the pudding from east to west with a wooden spoon, in honor of the three kings. A silver coin was put into the pudding mixture before steaming. Whoever found the coin was ensured health, wealth, and happiness for the coming year.

As their empire expanded throughout the nineteenth century, wherever the British went, they brought their customs (and their Christmas pudding) with them. In the "settler colonies" of Canada,

Australia, New Zealand, South Africa, and southern Rhodesia, the new arrivals made a point (even south of the equator, where December is in summer) of preserving these customs—and recipes—unchanged; their descendants do so today, and Christmas pudding, rum, and all remain as they are in England.

But in colonies like India and the West Indies, the locals took up cooking for their masters and changed Christmas pudding in accord with their own ideas and materials. So it was that the Christmas pudding that was brought to the Antilles by English settlers in the mid-seventeenth century was modified by the Africans who arrived in the area as slaves. Thus, English pudding gradually evolved into Caribbean Rum Cake. At some point, steaming changed to baking and the ingredients used were slightly altered. Rum cake is very popular in the Caribbean at Christmas and is always served at weddings and christenings. The Caribbean Rum Cake is also known as Caribbean Fruitcake or, by the addition of burnt sugar, Black Cake. Whatever the name given this treat, it requires not merely rum being added to the batter or employed in a covering sauce, but that the constituent ground raisins, prunes, and cherries be steeped for months in rum and wine. In the Virgin Islands, a local variant, Vienna Cake, is made. This is a plain cake layered with various fruit mixtures and mint jelly, flavored with rum, and frosted.

As already mentioned, rum made the trip throughout the Baltic in Scandinavian ships. Up the rivers it traveled and eventually it ensconced itself in holiday cooking even as far as the Alps. There, the dessert symbol of Tyrol is the *Zelten*. Although once exclusively a Christmas cake, it is now produced year round by bakeries and pastry shops. A sort of refined version of a fruit loaf, there are a number of versions, each one linked to generations-old recipes. Added to the basic mixture of yeast, flour, and milk are sugar, butter, walnuts, dried figs, raisins, pine nuts, candied fruit, and, of course, rum. At the end of the complex preparation process, it is decorated with walnuts and almonds and then placed in the oven. Heart-shaped, rectangular, or circular, Zelten remains the chief emblem of Christmas in Tyrol. It is prepared two to three weeks before Christmas, as it improves with time.

In Germany, the best-known Christmas cake is *Stollen*. Not surprisingly, Luebeck, the once-great Hanseatic port, is renowned for its Stollen as once it was famous for the rum imported there. Stollen dough is the heaviest of all yeast-raised doughs. The cake boasts raisins, almonds, citrus fruit soaked in rum, and marzipan, is flavored with vanilla, almond, and yet more rum, and lastly is covered with powdered sugar. In the version produced in the Saxon capital of Dresden, rum-flavored raisins and kirsch take the place of the citrus fruit. The elector of Saxony (and king of Poland), Augustus the Strong, ordered the biggest Stollen of all time in 1730. It weighed 1.8 tons and was made by the bakers' guild on the occasion of the Zeithainer Lustlager attended by twenty-four thousand guests.

But pastries are not the only Christmas foods flavored by rum. As might be expected, in rum-loving Brazil, the beverage makes its way into main courses. *Ceia de Natal* is the typical Brazilian Christmas turkey. It is marinated in Cachaça, or light rum, with onions, garlic, tomatoes, lime juice, and other spices.

Rum has affected other holidays as well. The pre-Lenten season of carnival or Mardi Gras has been a major observance in all traditionally Catholic and Orthodox nations. Such of these as are located in the tropics and love rum are awash in it in the period before Lent's rigors move in. In the United States, the center of Mardi Gras is New Orleans, Louisiana. There, the semiofficial drink of Mardi Gras is the Hurricane, made from rum and fruit juices.

Halfway through Lent is Laetare Sunday, a day whose joyful nature is symbolized by the rose-colored vestments priests wear at the Mass that day, replacing the purple mourning of Lent. The three days preceding are called mid-Lent, or *Mi-Carême*. Since the Middle Ages, Mi-Carême in France has been an occasion of parades, dancing, and feasting. The custom spread to the West Indian colonies of Guadeloupe and Martinique, where Mi-Carême is a day filled with drinking wine and rum, eating, and dancing, in order to forget the sacrifices of Lent.

Once Lent ends, Easter and its rejoice arrives, and with it another set of rum-flavored pastries and cakes. Baba is called "Babka" in Poland and "Baba" in France, the latter after the French word *baba* ("dizzy"). These are small cakes made from yeast dough containing raisins or currants. They are baked in cylindrical molds and then soaked with sugar syrup flavored with rum (originally they were soaked in a sweet fortified wine). After these cakes are soaked in the wine sauce for a day, the dried fruits fall out of them.

Baba is claimed to be a version of a *kugelhopf*, which was invented in Lemberg (modern-day L'viv) in the 1600s. As a result of the War of Polish Succession, King Stanislas Leszcynski, the sovereign of Poland and father-in-law of King Louis XV of France, was deposed and exiled to Lorraine and became its duke. With him came his Polish chef, Sthorer, to prepare kugelhopf for the exiled king. While the chef added raisins to the recipe, the king found the bread too dry, so he dipped it in rum. So enchanted was Stanislas with his new creation that he named it after his favorite hero from *A Thousand and One Nights*, Ali Baba. Later, the chef refined the sweet bread by using brioche dough. In the eighteenth century, Jean Anthelme Brillat-Savarin, a celebrated French chef and a writer on gastronomy, added to the cake a special rum sauce; he called the new recipe *Baba au Savarin*. The dessert became very popular in France, but the people called it Baba au Rhum and soon dropped the name Savarin. In other parts of the world, the cake is known as simply Savarin.

Via the Baltic seaport of St. Petersburg, the country's "window on the West," rum came to Russia. *Kulich* is a traditional Russian Easter cake, flavored with rum and saffron, prepared like bread, and formed into the shape of a hat. Only consumed during the forty days after Easter, Kulich is not baked any other time of the year. The Russian Orthodox Lenten fast is very strict. It is a complete fish and vegetarian diet, without any animal products. The Kulich is very rich in butter and eggs and is used to break the fast.

Easter and Pentecost are major feasts in Guadeloupe and Martinique and bring the natives out in the morning to the beaches and river banks. Families get up very early to pitch tents at their chosen locations. Around ten o'clock, they eat a traditional cucumber and crab salad, and wash it down with a *dékolaj*, the first glass of rum.

In Catholic countries, All Saints' Day (November 1) and All Souls' Day (November 2) are great days, indeed. For during this time, apart from honoring the saints whose names do not appear on the calendar, they also reverence the memories of their dead loved ones. Often, depending on the country or region, families will descend on the family plot and clean it. They might light candles in honor of the dead, thus turning cemeteries in such areas into fairy-lands. Picnics are often held there, so that the living and the dead can be reunited, not only in prayer, but also in festivity.

In Catholic Germany, after paying visits to relatives' graves, god-parents stop by their godchildren's homes with gifts of braided sweet bread called *Strietzel* or *Spitz'l* in Bavaria, and *Hefezopf* else-where in Germany. The Strietzel comes in varying lengths and can be more than three feet long. One of the major ingredients is dried currants, which have been soaked in rum.

In the Philippines, the two days feature the sort of picnics to which we earlier referred, with the men in particular enjoying themselves gossiping, singing, and generally relaxing. Key to this activity, however, is the ever present rum bottle, which plays as much a part in the Filipino All Souls' celebrations as it does in carnival. During this period, Italians delightedly consume *Fave dei morti* ("dead men's beans"). These are butter cookies flavored with rum.

In some places, rum plays a part in the veneration given partic-ular saints, like an unconscious echo of voodoo. San Juan Bautista (St. John the Baptist) is particularly revered along the central Caribbean coast of Venezuela, where the feast day is observed from June 23 to 25. The celebrations in the state of Barlovento are well known, in particular in the former slave trade center of Curiepe. There, the statue of the saint is paraded through the streets and periodically sprinkled with rum, leading to his reputation as San

Juan *Borrachero* (St. John the Drunkard). San Benito el Moro (St. Benedict the Moor) is the patron saint of the people around Lake Maracaibo. He, too, is associated with drinking rum and accordingly gets his statue sprinkled with the stuff.

Rum has found its way not only into calendar festivals, but also into celebrations of the stages of life. As mentioned in Chapter 5, in remote parts of Jamaica, infants are bathed in rum before they are christened. But similar customs may be found on all the shores of the Irish sea. In Cumberland, England, rum butter and oatcakes were given to friends who called at the house to see a new baby. In turn, they would leave "a silver coin, and on the day of the christening, when the butter bowl was empty, the coins were placed in it. A sticky bowl, with plenty of coins sticking to it, meant that the child would never be wanting." A special bowl for this purpose was often passed down in families; there are a few still around.

In the southern Italian region of Molise, *Pizza Dolce* in Gambatesa is served at weddings. The outside of the cake is covered with whipped cream and then the sides are dusted with very thinly sliced almonds. Inside, from top to bottom, there is a layer of moist white cake, a layer of Italian pastry cream flavored with rum, another layer of moist white cake, a layer of chocolate-flavored Italian pastry cream, and finally a layer of moist white cake.

Scotland is renowned today for its whisky. But in the nineteenth century, rum maintained its place beside the local product. This is borne out by a passage in the 1847 *History of the Town and Castle of Dumbarton*, describing funerals at that time, "In these early days, and even at a later period, when the family could afford it, there were three services of bread, wine, and spirits at funerals, or what was called three rounds, one of rum, one of whisky, and one of wine. But now, in modern times, it is judged more genteel to give only one service of wine; and, within these few years, the teetotalers aver that it is most genteel to offer no wine at all." Although this gloomy prediction has not as yet afflicted the Scots, it was later fulfilled in the United States, as we shall see in the next chapter.

In keeping with its great influence on seamen, rum continues to play a part in ceremonial life aboard ship. At various "crossing the line" ceremonies, those who have never before crossed the equator are initiated with satirical rituals requiring much rum.

A more accessible tradition is Auckland's rum race. This is a weekly fixture on the calendar of the true-blue Kiwi yachtsman. Hundreds of people skip off work an hour or so early on a Thursday or Friday afternoon to crew on keelboats for the Royal New Zealand Yacht Squadron's rum race. The prize remains what it always has been: a bottle of rum.

But perhaps the most spectacular use of rum for festive purposes is the German *Feuerzangenbowle*. It is a sort of hot punch, which requires a pot, a spoon, and a fireproof metal framework or grating to prepare. Lemons and oranges are cut up in thin slices and placed in the pot with various spices. Then four bottles of dry red wine are poured in while a bottleful of rum is heated separately. Then comes the exciting part! In Germany, *Zuckerhut* ("Sugar Hat"), a specially made sugar cone, is soaked with the rum, placed on the framework, and set aflame. Little by little, the rum-soaked and burning sugar drops into the wine, until at last it is completely consumed. With the spices removed and a bit more warm rum added, the bowl is ready to be portioned out into cups and drunk.

Originally, the Feuerzangenbowle might be drunk any time in cold weather, although it was particularly popular on New Year's. But that began to change in 1944, with the release of a gentle fantasy film, *Die Feuerzangenbowle*, starring Heinz Ruehmann. Ruehmann played the youngest of a party of five arrayed around a steaming Feuerzangenbowle. The four old men fondly recall their days in high school. Ruehmann's character cannot share his feelings because he had been tutored privately. Shortly after this, a new student shows up at a high school; it is Ruehmann, who begins to enjoy (or otherwise) everything he missed.

Given the horrific events playing out in Germany and the world, the film took on a tremendous poignancy after 1945. As a paean to innocence and nostalgia, it became an enduring hit with German college students and is shown around many campuses in that country in November, usually the evening before a holiday. After the film is finished, students depart to their own Feuerzangenbowle parties. In the icy German night, the blue flame of the burning rum and sugar casts a mellow glow and playful shadows over the proceedings, while participants dream of the past and hope for the future—a future free of the war and injustice that claimed so many at the time of the film's appearance. If there is indeed magic in rum, this surely is it.

Irish Christmas Rum Punch

¼ cup sugar	4 cloves
1⅓ cup water	Pinch of nutmeg
1 lemon	1 cup rum

Place the sugar and water in a saucepan. Cut the lemon into thin slices, and add it along with the cloves and nutmeg. Bring to a simmer and stir until sugar is dissolved. Add the rum and heat until the mixture is piping hot. Serve immediately in heated mugs.

Makes 6 servings.

Tom and Jerry

6 eggs	1½ ounces Jamaica rum
6 teaspoons powdered sugar	Hot milk (or boiling water)
1 teaspoon allspice	Grated nutmeg
¾ ounce brandy	

Separate the eggs and beat the whites into a very stiff froth. Beat the yolks until very thin and fold the whites into the yolks. Add the sugar and allspice. Mix thoroughly. Pour 2 tablespoons of the mixture into each mug. Add the brandy and rum, fill up with hot milk or boiling water, stirring gently. Sprinkle with nutmeg.

Christmas Eggnog

6 eggs   ½ cup rum
2 cups heavy cream   ½ cup brandy
1 cup milk   ½ cup whiskey
¾ cup sugar   1 tablespoon nutmeg

Separate the eggs and set the whites aside. Mix yolks well, gradually adding the cream, milk, and sugar. Whip the egg whites until soft peaks form. Fold the whites into the yolk mixture. Gradually add the rum, brandy and whiskey. Let the eggnog sit uncovered in the fridge for at least 2 hours. Sprinkle nutmeg over the top right before serving.

Puerto Rican Coconut Milk-Rum Christmas Drink (Coquito)

1 12-ounce can evaporated   ¼ teaspoon true Ceylon
   milk   cinnamon (sold as
1 14-ounce can condensed   "Mexican cinnamon" or
   milk   "canela" in Hispanic
2 egg yolks   markets)
2 cups fresh coconut milk or 1   1 cup Puerto Rican white rum
   15-ounce can coconut milk   Ground domestic cinnamon,
Pinch salt   as garnish

Place all the ingredients in a blender and process for 3 minutes at high speed until frothy. Store in a glass container in the refrigerator and serve chilled, dusted with a little cinnamon.

Makes 6 cups.

Hot Buttered Rum

1 cup butter   2 cups vanilla ice cream,
1 cup brown sugar   softened
½ cup sifted fruit sugar   Rum
1 teaspoon ground nutmeg   Boiling water
1 teaspoon ground cinnamon

In a small mixing bowl, beat together butter, both sugars, and spices until well combined. Beat in the ice cream. Turn into a 4-cup freezer container. Seal and freeze. To serve, spoon about ⅓ cup of the mixture into a mug, and add one jigger of rum and ½ cup boiling water. Stir well.

Makes 4 cups.

Black Bean Soup with Rum

2 cups dried black beans,
  soaked overnight
2 cups onion, chopped
1 cup celery, chopped
6 sprigs parsley, chopped
2 tablespoons fresh thyme
  leaves, chopped
1 bay leaf
3 tablespoons unsalted butter
1 large ham hock

6 cups beef broth
4–6 cups water
Salt and pepper, to taste
⅓ cup dark rum
Lemon juice to taste
Eggs, hardboiled, chopped;
  fresh parsley, chopped;
  and lemon slices, as
  garnishes

The night before, soak beans in cold water to cover by 2 inches. Change water at least once. Drain and rinse. In a heavy kettle, cook onion, celery, parsley, thyme, and bay leaf in the butter over moderate-low heat, stirring, for 10 minutes. Add ham hock, beans, broth, 4 cups water, salt and pepper to taste. Bring the mixture to a boil, reduce heat, and simmer, uncovered, for 3 hours, adding more water as necessary to keep beans covered. Discard ham hock and bay leaf. Put the mixture through the medium disk of a food processor into a large bowl and then return it to the kettle. Stir in rum, lemon juice, and more salt and pepper to taste. Adjust the consistency with hot water and garnish for serving with the eggs, parsley, and lemon slices.

Makes 7 servings.

Ceia de Natal
(Brazilian Christmas Turkey)

The marinade suggested in this recipe is indigenous to Brazil in that it utilizes one of Brazil's great ingredients, Cachaça, made famous around the world in the sweet taste of the Caipirinha, one of Latin America's most popular alcoholic beverages. Balanced with the tart taste of lime juice and zest, this marinade is versatile and is the first step to making your holiday turkey. Note: This recipe requires advance preparation.

One 12-pound turkey

MARINADE:
2 cups cachaça or light rum
2 medium onions, diced
6 cloves garlic, chopped
4 ripe tomatoes, diced
1 cup olive oil

2 bay leaves
1 cup fresh lime juice
¼ cup grated lime zest
2 cups of water
½ cup chopped scallions
1 cup chopped parsley

In a large bowl, combine all the marinade ingredients and mix well.
     Place the 12-pound turkey in a roasting bag and cover it with the marinade. Close the bag so that it has no air pockets and let the turkey marinate overnight in the refrigerator.

Ginger Rum-Glazed Ham

1 7- to 8-pound half of a fully
     cooked cured ham (shank
     end)
⅓ cup chopped preserved
     ginger in syrup

3 tablespoons firmly packed
     brown sugar
3 tablespoons dark rum
Parsley sprigs for garnish
     (optional)

Preheat oven to 350°. If the ham comes with the skin still attached, remove most of it with a sharp knife, leaving a layer of fat and a collar of skin around the shank bone. Trim the fat, leaving a layer about ⅓-inch thick, and score the layer remaining into diamonds. Bake the ham on a rack in a roasting pan in a 350° oven for

55 minutes. In a blender, blend together the ginger, the brown sugar, and the rum. Then spoon the glaze over the ham, spreading it, and bake the ham for 30–35 minutes more, or until the glaze is brown and bubbly. Transfer the ham to a platter, garnish the platter with the parsley, if desired, and let the ham stand for 15 minutes before carving.

Jamaican Dark Rum Christmas Fruitcake

1 pound currants
1 pound raisins
1 pound prunes
1 pound dried figs
1 16-ounce jar maraschino cherries, drained
½ pound mixed candied fruit peel
¼ pound almonds, chopped
1 tablespoon angostura bitters
2½ cups dark Jamaica rum

FOR THE CARAMELIZED SUGAR:
¾ pound brown sugar
½ cup boiling water

FOR THE FINAL COOKING:
2 teaspoons grated lime peel
2 teaspoons vanilla
4 cups flour
4 teaspoons baking powder
1 teaspoon ground cloves
1 pound butter (4 sticks) softened
2¼ cups sugar
9 large eggs

Step 1: Preparation Day. Chop currants, raisins, prunes, figs, and cherries. Put in large bowl with the mixed fruit peel and chopped almonds. Stir to combine. Sprinkle on bitters and pour rum over mixture. Soak for a minimum of 24 hours, and as long as one month.

Step 2: Caramelizing the Sugar. Put brown sugar in heavy pot. Stir, letting sugar liquefy. Cook over low heat until dark, stirring constantly, so sugar does not burn. When almost burnt, remove from heat and stir in hot water gradually. Mix well, let cool, and set aside for use in next step.

Step 3: The Final Cooking. Preheat oven to 250°. Bring fruit from its resting place. Stir lime peel, vanilla, and the caramelized sugar into fruit. Mix well. Set aside. Sift together flour, baking powder, and ground cloves. Set aside. In a mixing bowl, cream together butter and sugar until mixture is light. Add the eggs, one at a time, until blended. Stir in dry ingredients gradually. When mixed, stir in fruit mixture. Divide evenly into 9 × 5 × 3-inch loaf pans lined with buttered parchment paper or waxed paper; or use 1 10-inch tube pan, lined. Place pan(s) in large shallow pan of hot water. Cook in 250° oven for 2½–3 hours, or until a knife inserted in center of cake comes out clean. Cake should have shrunk from sides of pan.

Cool for 24 hours in pans. When cool, moisten with rum, remove from pans, and wrap in aluminum foil or a rum drenched cloth. Cakes may be stored to ripen. If keeping for any length of time, check occasionally to add more rum.

Makes 1 large or 2 medium-size cakes.

Ukrainian Rum Baba

FOR THE DOUGH:
1 packet active dry yeast
   (¼ ounce)
1 cup lukewarm milk
1 teaspoon sugar
4–4½ cups flour
6 eggs separated
1 cup sugar
½ teaspoon salt

1 teaspoon vanilla
1½ sticks soft butter
1 cup warm milk

FOR THE RUM SYRUP:
1 cup water
1 cup sugar
⅓ cup dark rum
1 teaspoon lemon juice

Proof the yeast in 1 cup of lukewarm milk and the teaspoon of sugar. After you have a good yeast sponge, beat in half the flour until smooth. Place in a large buttered bowl, cover with a towel, and let rise about 1 hour until doubled in bulk.

Meanwhile, separate the eggs and beat the whites until they are rather stiff. Set aside in a draft-free place. Beat the yolks with the sugar, salt, and vanilla until pale, and set aside. Now beat the butter until well creamed. Add the yeast mixture, and stir well. Then stir in the egg-yolk mixture, the cup of warm milk, and the rest of the flour. Fold in the egg whites.

You now have a very soft dough. Place in a large buttered bowl, cover with a towel and let rise until doubled in bulk, about 45 minutes to 1 hour. Butter a very large tube pan, or use 2 medium-size tall pans or fancy baba molds, and sprinkle with fine breadcrumbs. Fill the pan(s) one-third full. Cover and let the dough rise in a warm place. Preheat oven to 375°. When dough is more than doubled in bulk, bake in a 375° oven for 10 minutes, then lower the temperature to 325° and continue baking for 30–40 minutes.

While the baba is baking, make the rum syrup. Heat the water with the sugar, stirring to dissolve the sugar. Turn off the heat and add the rum and lemon juice.

After you remove the baba(s) from the oven, unmold them onto plates and baste with the rum syrup. Continue to baste until all the rum syrup is used and the babas are soaked.

Serve with berries and cream. Do not freeze.

Makes 2 cakes.

Christmas Rum Balls

6 ounces semisweet chocolate morsels	2½ cups vanilla wafer crumbs
½ cup rum	½ cup powdered sugar, sifted
3 tablespoons corn syrup	1 cup pecans, chopped fine
	Powdered sugar

Melt chocolate morsels in top of double boiler or in microwave. When smoothly melted, remove from heat and stir in rum and corn syrup. Set aside. Combine crumbs, powdered sugar, and pecans. Mix well. Stir into chocolate mixture; let stand 30 minutes. Shape into 1-inch balls. Roll in sugar. Store in an airtight container in refrigerator.

Makes about 5 dozen.

𝕶ulich

⅓ cup golden raisins
3 tablespoons rum
½ cup sugar
1 packet active dry yeast
    (¼ ounce)
½ cup warm water (105–115°)
6 tablespoons butter, softened
3 eggs
2 tablespoons vanilla
3 tablespoons powdered milk
¾ teaspoon salt
⅛ teaspoon saffron, ground
    (optional)

4¾ cups all-purpose flour
¼ cup almonds, slivered
¼ cup candied orange peel,
    chopped
2 empty coffee cans (1-pound
    size)
Wax paper

FOR THE SUGAR GLAZE:
1 cup confectioner's sugar
Reserved soaking rum
2 teaspoons lemon juice
1 teaspoon water

Soak raisins in rum for at least 30 minutes or overnight.

Combine ½ teaspoon sugar along with yeast and water in small bowl. Let stand until foamy, about 5 minutes.

In a large bowl, beat together with an electric mixer the remaining sugar, butter, eggs, vanilla, powdered milk, salt, the saffron (if desired), and the yeast mixture until blended. Add 2 cups of the flour and 1 tablespoon of soaking rum, beating for 2 minutes at high speed.

Drain raisins and reserve rum for glaze. Stir raisins, almonds, and orange peel into dough with wooden spoon. Stir in enough of remaining flour to form a soft dough. Turn out onto floured surface and knead until smooth and elastic, about 5 minutes.

Place dough in greased bowl, turning to coat. Cover; let rise in warm spot for 1½–2 hours, until doubled in bulk. Grease well two 1-pound coffee cans. Line bottoms with rounds of waxed paper.

Turn dough out onto floured surface. Punch down; knead a few turns. Divide in half and place in prepared cans. (They should each be about two-thirds full.) Let rise, covered, for about 1½ hours, or until dough has risen to top of can.

Preheat oven to 350°. Brush tops of breads lightly with water.

Bake in lower third of 350° oven for 35–40 minutes or until golden brown on top and a long skewer inserted in center comes out clean. Check after 25 minutes and tent with foil if browning too quickly.

Using oven mitts, carefully remove bread from each can by turning the cans upside down, and while supporting the top of the bread, gently twisting off the can. Cool upright on wire rack to room temperature.

To make sugar glaze: Stir together confectioner's sugar, reserved soaking rum, lemon juice, and the water as needed in small bowl, until good drizzling consistency.

Drizzle glaze over the breads. Garnish with candied orange peel and slivered almonds, if desired.

Traditional Christmas Pudding

4 ounces shredded suet (from butcher)

2 ounces self-rising flour, sifted

4 ounces white breadcrumbs

1 level teaspoon ground pumpkin pie spice

1 pinch ground cinnamon

8 ounces soft dark brown sugar

4 ounces sultanas (golden raisins)

4 ounces black raisins

10 ounces currants

1 ounce mixed candied fruit peel, chopped fine

1 ounce almonds, skinned and chopped

1 small cooking apple, peeled, cored, and chopped fine

Grated zest of ½ large orange

Grated zest of ½ large lemon

2 tablespoons dark rum

5 ounces stout (e.g., Guinness stout or porter)

2 large eggs

1 ladle brandy, for flaming

Begin the day before you want to steam the pudding. In a very large mixing bowl, add the suet, sifted flour, breadcrumbs, spices, and sugar. Mix together very thoroughly, then gradually mix in all the dried fruit, mixed fruit peel, and nuts followed by the apple and the grated orange and lemon zests. In a smaller bowl, pour the rum and stout, then add the eggs and beat together thoroughly. Pour the liquid mixture over all the other ingredients, and mix very thoroughly. The mixture should have a fairly sloppy consistency—that is, it should fall instantly from the spoon when it is tapped on the side of the bowl. If you think it needs to be looser, add more stout. Cover the bowl and leave overnight.

The next day, pack the mixture into a lightly greased 2-pint pudding basin, cover it with a double sheet of baking parchment and a sheet of foil, and tie it securely with string. It's also a good idea to tie a piece of string across the top to make a handle. Place the pudding in a steamer set over a saucepan of simmering water and steam the pudding for 8 hours. Keep an eye on the water underneath to make sure it doesn't boil away; add boiling water to the saucepan from time to time. When the pudding is steamed, let it cool completely, then remove the steam papers and foil and replace them with some fresh ones, again making a string handle for easier handling. Keep in a cool place away from the light.

To complete the cooking, place a steamer on top of a saucepan filled with boiling water, and turn down the heat till the water is simmering gently. Place the Christmas pudding in the steamer, cover and leave to steam away for 2¼ hours. You'll again need to check the water from time to time and maybe add boiling water.

To serve, remove the pudding from the steamer and take off the wrapping. Slide a palette knife all around the pudding, then turn it out onto a warmed plate. Place a suitably sized sprig of holly on top. Now warm a ladleful of brandy over direct heat, and as soon as the brandy is hot, light it. Place the ladle, now gently flaming, on top of the pudding, but don't pour it over until you reach the table. When you do, pour it slowly over the pudding, sides and all, and watch it flame to the cheers of the assembled company! When both flames and cheers have died down, serve the pudding with brandy butter, Cumberland Rum Butter (see below), or cream.

Makes 8–10 servings.

Cumberland Rum Butter

4 ounces butter
8 tablespoons rum
8 ounces brown sugar

Nutmeg, cinnamon, or
  pumpkin pie spice to taste

In a warm bowl, use a wooden spoon or electric beater to cream butter and sugar until very soft. Add spices, being careful not to put in too much. Gradually beat in the rum and then when smooth press into an attractive dish and put in fridge. Serve with Christmas pudding or mince pies.

Plum Rum Cake

2 cups flour
2 cups sugar
1 teaspoon ground cinnamon
1 teaspoon ground cloves
1 teaspoon baking powder
1 teaspoon salt
3 eggs
1 cup oil

2 4½-ounce jars plum baby
  food
3 tablespoons dark rum

FOR THE GLAZE:
1 cup icing sugar
2–3 tablespoons lemon juice
2 teaspoons dark rum

Preheat oven to 350°. Grease and flour a 10-inch bundt pan. Sift together dry ingredients. Add eggs and oil, and beat at slow speed. Add baby food and rum. Mix well. Bake for 40 minutes. Cool 10 minutes and remove from pan. Mix glaze and pour over cake while still warm.

Chapter 11

"Rum, by Gum":
Prohibition Triumphant

We're coming, we're coming,
Our brave little band.
Against Demon Rum
We all take our Stand

We don't use tobacco because we do think
That the people that use it are likely to drink!
Away, away, with Rum, by gum!
Rum, by gum, rum, by gum!
Away, away, with Rum, by gum!
The song of the Temperance Union!

Oh, we don't eat cookies,
Because they have yeast.
And one little bite
Turns a man to a beast.
Can you imagine a sadder disgrace
Than a man in the gutter
With crumbs on his face?

Away, away, with Rum, by gum!
Rum, by gum, rum, by gum!

Away, away, with Rum, by gum!
The song of the Temperance Union!

Oh, we don't eat fruitcake
Because it has rum
And one little bite
Turns a man to a bum.
Can you imagine a sorrier sight
Than a man eating fruitcake
Until he gets tight?

Away, away, with Rum, by gum!
Rum, by gum, rum, by gum!
Away, away, with Rum, by gum!
The song of the Temperance Union!
—Nineteenth-century Temperance song

The end of British rule in the United States found a country in some ways changed, in others much the same. While the wreckage of the war would take some time to repair, and over a hundred thousand Americans were forced into exile because of their loyalty to the Crown, by the same token the former colonial elite were now completely in charge. This made for a stability found in few postrevolutionary societies. As we have seen, the Triangle Trade had made fortunes for much of the New England elite. Despite the initial British ban on trading with Unites States, there were plenty of other markets for American rum. So it was that by the early nineteenth century, there were forty rum distilleries in Boston, twenty-one in Hartford, and eight in Newport. Because of its continuing importance in the social and economic life of the new country, "rum" came to be a generic word in the United States for all hard liquor, as seen in such phrases as "demon rum," "rum pot" (for a drunk), and "rum row" (for a barroom brawl). Commenting on this situation in his 1921 book *The American Language*,

H. L. Mencken declared that "an Englishman never uses rum in the generic sense that it has acquired in the United States, and knows nothing of rum-hounds . . . the rum-trade, and the rum-evil, or of the Demon Rum." John Russell Bartlett's 1848 *Dictionary of Americanisms* contains this definition of "rum bud":

> A grog blossom; the popular name of a redness occasioned by the detestable practice of excessive drinking. Rum-buds usually appear first on the nose, and gradually extend over the face. This term seems to have reference to the disease technically defined to be unsuppurative papule, stationary, confluent, red, mottled with purple, chiefly affecting the face, sometimes produced and always aggravated by the use of alcoholic liquors, by exposure to heat, &c.

But the days of rum's supremacy in the world of American liquor were approaching their end. President Thomas Jefferson, annoyed at the British and French for their treatment of American shipping, was able to push through Congress the Embargo Act of 1807. This measure banned the importing of anything from Great Britain, France, or their colonies. As might be expected, this stimulated the growth of a flourishing illegal trade from British Canada and Spanish Florida—a precedent that would be repeated in the 1920s.

By the time the restriction on West Indian molasses was lifted after the War of 1812, bourbon and rye whiskeys had replaced rum to a great degree as America's libation of choice. But America's thirst had not been replaced. As the frontier expanded and Americans moved ever further westward, the boredom of rural life and the strain of unrelenting toil found release in the bottle. Moreover, the millions of acres of farmland that were opening up were planted with grains—wheat, barley, corn, and rye—that were all key ingredients for whiskies of various kinds. The difficulties of transporting grain prior to the coming of the railroad meant that most of the crops would spoil before they could reach any market. Turning them to whiskey was a cheap, profitable way of dealing with grain. So important did this sideline become that the Federal government's attempt to tax whiskey in 1798 led to the Pennsylvania Whiskey Rebellion. As a result, by 1815, the country was awash in the beverage.

According to Abraham Lincoln, describing the rural Midwest of his time, "we found intoxicating liquor . . . used by everybody, repudiated by nobody. It commonly entered into the first drought of the infant, and the last drought of the dying man. From the side board of the parson, down to the ragged pocket of the homeless loafer, it was constantly found. . . . To have a rolling or raising, a husking or hoe-down, anywhere without it, was positively insufferable." He added further that, at that time, alcohol had come forth across the land, "Like the Egyptian angel of death, commissioned to slay if not the first, the fairest born of every family." Henry Adams said of that era that nearly every American family, regardless of their social position, had an alcoholic member.

Bad as this situation was, the War between the States would make it worse; moreover, the emergence of the noted drunk Ulysses S. Grant on the national scene (eventually as president) led the antidrinking forces to declare open war at last on demon rum. Reformist ferment was in the air. With slavery vanquished, the fervor of the abolitionists found outlets in many other fields, of which temperance was only one. America of the "Gilded Age" (as Mark Twain slyly called it, differentiating it from one of gold) was a nation filled with vices of all kinds. Unscrupulous robber barons kept whole families working in sweatshops from before daybreak till after sundown, with no regard to health or on-the-job safety. Civil service positions were appointed under the "spoils system," whereby new political electees would replace existing bureaucrats with their friends and supporters. In many places, all political offices were up for sale.

Nor was the realm of personal morality much better. Abortions and contraception were rife, and prostitution was endemic to larger cities (it was in fact Protestants of various types who would successfully crusade to have the first two things outlawed). Women could not vote, and patent medicines and narcotics were freely available. Standards of cleanliness in restaurants were also very low. It was in this atmosphere that armies of reformers emerged to combat each and all of these perceived evils. Of them all, however, the most obvious was the widespread abuse of alcohol.

While temperance folk could be found in all churches, the Methodists and Quakers led the attack. Although such Catholic figures as Father Theobald Mathew, the Paulist fathers, and Archbishop John Ireland of St. Paul, Minnesota, beat the temperance drum and called for total abstinence, the majority of Catholics (particularly those of French, German, Italian, and Polish descent, who did not face the same drinking problems as their Irish coreligionists) considered the temperance movement to be pure killjoyism. Hence, in the 1876 presidential election, the then heavily Catholic and southern Democratic Party was castigated by its Republican opponents as favoring "rum, Romanism, and rebellion." By the end of the nineteenth century, Americans had spent over a billion dollars on alcoholic beverages each year, compared to $900 million on meat, and less than $200 million on public education.

The political struggle against demon rum had already begun. Believing that neither the Grant-loving Republicans nor the three R–pushing Democrats would ever rally to their cause, temperance folk founded the Prohibition Party in 1869 to offer candidates committed to the prohibition cause to American voters. The party maintained that neither the Republicans nor Democrats would bring about Prohibition, nor, once achieved, would they enforce it.

The Prohibition Party offered candidates for offices at national, state, and local levels, and reached its peak in 1884, when in New York State the party's presidential candidate polled enough votes to ensure that the Democrat, Grover Cleveland, carried the state and the electoral college. The party reached the peak of its vote in 1888 and 1892 at just over 2 percent of the popular vote total. Divisions soon emerged, with one group calling for a "narrow-gauge" approach, whereby the party would focus on the liquor issue to the exclusion of all others. A second group put forward a "broad-gauge" approach. These folk offered positions on a full range of national issues in an attempt to build a larger coalition in support of dry candidates. The party, despite small numbers and vicious internal conflicts, still exists today.

But other temperance folk urged apolitical solutions. In the fall of 1873, in towns across Ohio and New York, groups of women worried about the damage caused by booze met in churches to pray and then marched on saloons to ask the owners to close them. Known as the Women's Temperance Crusade, this movement swept across twenty-three states and led to the closing of thousands of establishments that sold liquor. In Fredonia, New York, on December 22, 1873, the local ladies group formed the first local Woman's Christian Temperance Union (WCTU). The very next night, Dr. Dio Lewis gave a lecture on temperance at the Hillsboro, Ohio, Music Hall. The following day, under the leadership of Eliza Thompson, the daughter of a former governor and wife of a highly respected judge, seventy ladies concluded their devotions and started from the Presbyterian Church to the saloons.

According to Helen Tyler, in her history of the movement, *Where Prayer and Purpose Meet*, "Walking two by two, the smaller ones in the front and the taller coming after, they sang more or less confidently, 'Give to the Winds Thy Fears,' that heartening reassurance of Divine protection now known to every WCTU member as the Crusade Hymn. Every day they visited the saloons and the drug stores where liquor was sold. They prayed on sawdust floors or, being denied entrance, knelt on snowy pavements before the doorways, until almost all the sellers capitulated." In three months, the women had driven liquor out of 250 communities.

To give permanent status to this work, a preorganizational discussion was held in the summer of 1874 at Chautauqua, New York, a locale already synonymous with moral uplift. It was decided to hold a national convention that autumn in Cleveland; the WCTU was officially launched. Its first president was Annie Wittenmyer and the second was the noted educator and reformer Frances E. Willard.

Behind the WCTU's temperance reform was "protection of the home." The ladies adopted the motto "For God and Home and Native Land." Using the weapons of education and example, the WCTU hoped to obtain pledges of total abstinence from alcohol. Their enemies list would not stop with demon rum: later on, it included tobacco and narcotics (such as the then-available over-the-counter morphine and cocaine). The white ribbon bows the membership wore symbolized purity and their watchwords were "Agitate, Educate, Legislate." To promote its causes, the WCTU was among the first organizations maintaining a professional lobbyist in Washington, D.C., thus establishing a custom perhaps more pernicious than the one they wished to root out.

In any case, the success of the WCTU and the desire both for greater male involvement in the cause and unity among its diverse membership led to the formation of a new temperance umbrella organization at Oberlin, Ohio, on May 24, 1893. This organization would campaign for unification of public antialcohol sentiment, enforcement of existing temperance laws, and enactment of further antialcohol legislation. The Reverend Howard Hyde Russell was elected state superintendent of what was officially named the Ohio Anti-Saloon League. That same year, a similar organization was founded in Washington. These bodies merged into the National Anti-Saloon League on December 18, 1895, in Washington, D.C. The name of this national organization eventually became the Anti-Saloon League of America, with Russell being named the first superintendent of the national league.

A league ringleader said of the group, "It has not come . . . simply to build a little local sentiment or to secure the passage of a few laws, or yet to vote the saloons from a few hundred towns. These are mere incidents in its progress. It has come to solve the liquor problem." The slogan was "The saloon must go." Protestant (particularly Methodist) churches lent themselves to the fight, which was carried on politically via a nonpartisan method. Individual politicians who supported the league's platform would be supported, regardless of party. Thus, if one candidate was dry and the other wet, the league would throw itself into defeating the wet candidate. If both candidates for public office supported the dry cause, the league would not get involved in the race. If both candidates were wet, it would attempt to find its own dry candidate for the primary. Initially, the league chose to use the local option as the tool to make the country dry, rather than pushing for national prohibition. It would thus sway the country precinct by precinct.

It is perhaps hard for us today to understand just why this movement was so successful. Beyond the earlier mentioned reformist mood in the country, there was perhaps a deeper underlying cause. The United States is in its origins a Puritan nation. Of course, many other ingredients have been added to the mix since the Pilgrims came to Plymouth Rock, but the fact remains that Puritanism remains an important substratum in the mental bedrock of America. An examination of the national history shows that as a result the culture has regularly swung between periods of libertinism and repression. After the weakening of the Puritan influence in New England subsequent to the witch trials of 1692, there was the Great Awakening, the religious revival of the mid-eighteenth century stirred by the sermons of Jonathan Edwards. This in turn gave way to the social and political ferment attendant upon the Revolution. This, too, made way for the Great Revival of the early nineteenth century. The Civil War era was notable for its loose morals; shortly afterward the growth of Darwinism and robber baron fortunes had their effect: In time-honored fashion, the country was ready once again for a bout of the Puritanical. Surely the Temperance movement benefited from this.

The league grew rapidly. By 1908, only four states did not have state leagues. In the ten years between 1905 and 1915, the number of churches cooperating with the league more than doubled. The league's power was made manifest in the Ohio gubernatorial election of 1905, when the wet Republican incumbent was ousted by a Democratic dry in a major upset.

None of this is to say that Prohibition was unopposed. Catholics, for all of their voluntary temperance societies, were overwhelmingly opposed to prohibition. Of course, the transubstantiation of wine into the Blood of Christ lies at the heart of their religion. The question had been hashed out in Catholic circles centuries before the New World was discovered; the majority view among them (and the Eastern Orthodox) was expressed by St. John Chrysostom in a homily delivered in A.D. 388: "If you say, 'Would there were no wine' because of the drunkards, then you must say, going on by degrees, 'Would there were no steel,' because of the murderers, 'Would there were no night,' because of the thieves, 'Would there were no light,' because of the informers, and 'Would there were no women' because of adultery." Lutherans and Anglicans saw things in much the same light.

But most of these groups (save the last) were recent immigrants. There was also a homegrown opposition without religious reasons for their stand. Mark Twain, then on his way to becoming an icon of American letters, wrote from New York to the San Francisco paper *Alta California* on May 28, 1867 (as Prohibition first began to be noised about in the wake of the Civil War): "Prohibition only drives drunkenness behind doors and into dark places, and does not cure it, or even diminish it." This would remain his frequently repeated view until his death in 1910.

Despite such religious and literary allies, the liquor industry's response was ineffective. Brewers, who thought that they would not be targeted, refused to get involved in fighting the league; many distillers simply buried their heads in the sand. Still others gave up without a fight, as when the last of the Medford rum distilleries closed in 1905. A minority of distillers attempted to counter the league's ever increasing output of propaganda; but disunited as they were, and with morality apparently on the side of their opponents in an America whose Puritan spirit was easily evoked, the picture looked bleak. Big Tobacco today doubtless understands the feeling.

Flushed with innumerable local victories, in 1913, with the

Reverend Woodrow Wilson ensconced in the White House, the league switched its target to national prohibition. On December 10, 1913, a parade of over four thousand leaguers marched down Washington's Pennsylvania Avenue singing temperance songs. Awaiting them on the Capitol steps were Alabama congressman Richard Hobson and Texas senator Morris Sheppard. Superintendent Purley Baker gave the two legislators copies of the proposed Eighteenth Amendment to the Constitution. Subsequently, Hobson and Sheppard introduced it to their respective legislative bodies. There it stalled.

Antibooze forces, such as the Anti-Saloon League of America, the WCTU, and the Prohibition Party, rallied to try to win dry seats on Capitol Hill. Wayne Wheeler, later the head lobbyist for the league, described his work:

> Word went out from Washington and state headquarters to send letters, telegrams, and petitions to Congressmen and Senators in Washington. They rolled in by tens of thousands, burying Congress like an avalanche. . . . We started off, early in 1914, with about 20,000 speakers, mostly volunteers all over the United States. They spoke at every opportunity to every sort of gathering. . . . As the climax approached we doubled our forces. Even that wasn't enough, so for a time the world's largest prohibition printing establishment ran three shifts a day, every hour of the twenty four, grinding out dry literature.

The election of 1914 saw a growth in dry congressional seats.

In the new Congress, the Hobson-Sheppard bill came up for a vote, but fell short of the two-thirds majority it needed. But the league and its allies felt sure their time would come. It did, and sooner than anyone thought.

One of the many strange historical phenomena in American life is that every war of modern times has caused a diminution of liberty. The increasingly complex nature of conflict, the fear that the enemy may have some secret weapon or intelligence device, and, of course, the unspoken conviction that the enemies of the United States are the enemies of God, combine to form a brew headier than any rum. Most recently, we saw this in the buildup toward the 2003 Iraq conflict, when annoyance with the French over their refusal to support an American invasion of Iraq was responded to by renaming french fries "freedom fries," by pouring French wine in gutters, and by boycotting French goods. When Wilson was at last able to get the country into the war in Europe, a similar hysteria hit the United States. Sauerkraut was renamed "Liberty Cabbage," dachshunds were kicked in the street, and German speakers were harassed. The league had found its opportunity.

The league decided to latch on to the rush of patriotism and anti-German fervor, an easy task as most of the brewers were German Americans. Wheeler declared that "Kaiserism abroad and booze at home must go." In supporting Wilson's war food control bill, Wheeler pointed out that resources used for alcohol production were being diverted from the war effort. The Eighteenth (Prohibition) Amendment to the Constitution was reintroduced amid a flurry of flag-waving and singing.

The wets attempted to stymie the amendment by adding a provision that would cause it to lapse should seven years pass by without the sufficient number of states to ratify it. In this form, both drys and wets voted for the amendment, the latter never realizing the power that their opponents held on the state level. On January 16, 1919, Nebraska became the thirty-sixth state to ratify the Eighteenth Amendment. It became law on January 17, 1920. Celebrations were held by drys all over the country, commemorating the death of John Barleycorn.

The Volstead Act was enacted, which both defined alcoholic beverages (so strictly as to doom the brewers) and made the Treasury Department responsible for enforcement of the amendment. The league cooperated by launching a public relations campaign in favor of the new law.

What had been left out of everyone's calculations was the response of regular people. Demon rum had true allies, even if it was "the drink that dare not speak its name." The first (and legal) reaction was to vastly expand the tourist trade. Americans flocked to Canada, Mexico, and Cuba—anywhere they could have a drink in peace. As we have seen, the House of Bacardi and many other rum distillers owe their modern growth to Prohibition.

But many Americans could not afford to travel, and still others felt that, regardless of what the law might say, the right to drink was God-given. This was an intoxicating thought indeed in a culture where morality and legality are synonymous. Soon, illegal clubs—"speakeasies," which were secret watering holes where topers could find refuge—opened up in every major town. (The term goes back to the 1800s, when to gain entrance to such an establishment, you had to "speak easy" and name the person who referred you.) They were, of course, the inspiration for the modern "smokeasies" in antitobacco states like California and New York.

A probable candidate for Twain's place in the world of American letters was H. L. Mencken, who, like Twain, was both an unbeliever and a compulsive critic. He shared with Twain a hatred of pretense and prohibition. Unlike the Missourian, he lived through the actual experience. Writing about the "noble experiment" in an editorial for the *Baltimore Evening Sun* in 1925, he declared:

> The real victim of moral legislation is almost always the honest, law-abiding, well-meaning citizen, what the late William Graham Summer called the Forgotten Man. Prohibition makes it impossible for him to take a harmless drink, cheaply and in a decent manner. In the same way the Harrison Act puts heavy burdens upon the physician who has need of prescribing narcotic drugs for a patient, honestly and for good ends. But the drunkard still gets all the alcohol that he can hold, and the drug addict is still full of morphine and cocaine.

But whether out on the town or in the privacy of their homes, Americans were faced with a major problem by the closing of breweries and distilleries. Where would they get their favorite drinks? A class of gentlemen arose to help in their hour of need: the bootleggers. These were a colorful cast of criminals, boasting such names as Al Capone of Chicago, Frank Costello of New York, and the latter's Boston-based partner, Joseph P. Kennedy (later ambassador to Great Britain and father of a future U.S. president).

Where would they get their wares? Home brew and bathtub gin could be drunk, of course, but the former suffered in taste, and the latter could be dangerous. Nevertheless, the United States was surrounded by wet countries and wetter oceans. An opportunity opened up for smugglers unequalled by any other, perhaps, save the Embargo of 1807 and the Union blockade of the South during the Civil War. Bermuda, the Bahamas, and Cuba had all enjoyed booming economies during that conflict due to their location close to the blockaded coast of the Confederacy. In those safe havens, large European deep-draft oceangoing freighters were able to land their cargoes, which were then reloaded onto fast and maneuverable shallow-draft blockade runners. The latter craft then attempted to slip past the Union blockade into Southern ports. Successful missions brought immense profits, as much as $425,000 for one round trip. Officers and crews of the runners as well as the islands' merchants and tradesmen became quite wealthy, as exemplified by the fictional Rhett Butler in *Gone with the Wind*.

The trade was two-way, of course. The runners would travel the 560 miles from Charleston, South Carolina, to Nassau in the Bahamas, with loads of cotton. There they would meet up with British vessels and would trade their cotton for goods the British carried. Returning to Charleston, the blockade runners would sell their shipments for huge profits. As an example, salt that cost $6.50 in the Bahamas sold for $1,700 in the South.

When Morris Island fell to Union forces in 1863, Charleston, whose harbor the island guarded, became a bad risk for the runners. Attention shifted to Wilmington, North Carolina, the last major port in Confederate hands. Bermuda's St. George Harbor lay 674 miles away and soon was filled with sleek low-profile blockade runners. The wharves were laden with bales of cotton, and the brothels and bars were full of free-spending and raucous profiteers. One Confederate midshipman said of this company:

> They were a reckless lot and believed in eating, drinking and being merry for fear that they would die on the morrow. Their orgies reminded me of the stories of the pirates in the West Indies. They seemed to suffer from a chronic thirst that could only be assuaged by champagne, and one of their favorite amusements was to sit in the windows with bags of shillings and throw handfuls of the coins to a crowd of loafers in the street to see them scramble.

Bermudans were far from neutral in the conflict, despite the reluctance of the British government to get involved. Their sympathies were entirely in favor of the South, and the Union consul in St. George was once mobbed in the street by Confederate sympathizers. A toast heard in that town went: "Here's to the Confederates that produce the cotton; to the Yankees that maintain the blockade and keep up the price of cotton; and to the Britishers who buy the cotton and pay the high price for it. So three cheers to a long continuance of the War, and success to blockade runners." St. George's Harbor was the site of the only formal salute the Confederacy ever received from a foreign government.

Halifax and certain other ports in the Canadian Maritime Provinces also boomed, not, to be sure, as trading ports, but as refuges for the runners, places where they could rest their crews, repair their ships, and take on coal. Moreover, the Confederate privateers also operated out of these places at times. In any case, the Southerners brought much needed business to a moribund economy.

Given that Canada, Bermuda, and the Bahamas had benefited from those episodes, it was widely supposed in these countries that history would repeat itself. So it did. The fact that these three areas remained under the British Crown, from which the supposedly free United States had been liberated, was not lost on the legions of the thirsty. Hence rose this popular Prohibition-era rhyme:

Sing a song of sixpence,
   A case full of rye.

Four-and-twenty Yankees
   Started going dry.

When the case was opened,
   The Yanks began to sing,

"To hell with the stars and stripes,
   and God Save the King!"

One particularly clever way of bringing in the booze was detected by authorities in Bridgewater, Massachusetts. According to the *Bridgewater Bulletin* for December 25, 1923, "Police officials report they have just unearthed the most unusual way of selling liquor that has come to their notice. Foreigners have been coming in to the city of late selling overalls to workmen. Police officials were puzzled to know why the demand was so great. Investigation developed that a pint of liquor was concealed in the back pocket of each pair of overalls."

If demon rum was banned, it could nevertheless conjure a navy to bring it ashore to the waiting bootleggers. Thus rose the "rumrunners," daring and adventurous men (and sometimes women) who used fast launches to evade the authorities and bring their illicit if delicious cargoes ashore. For years, Al Capone, for example, ran Cuban rum from the Mississippi beaches up to Chicago by way of Memphis and St. Louis. But from 1920 on, the U.S. Coast Guard became their chief foes at sea. Agents from the U.S. Treasury Department's Prohibition Bureau, such as Elliot Ness, were left to fight the land war.

The rumrunners were a motley crew who met a fleet of tramp steamers, New England and Canadian fishing schooners, steam yachts, and even tugboats, that sailed from St.-Pierre and Miquelon off Newfoundland, from Bermuda, and from the West Indies. At first, the heavily laden vessels dropped anchor just outside the three-mile territorial limit and later, after the United States worked out international agreements, outside the twelve-mile limit. A group of these ships, awaiting the rumrunners to relieve them of their cargoes, was called a "rum row." The principal rum row was off the New York–New Jersey coast, but others were established in New England waters, off the Virginia Capes, and in Florida. At the commencement of Prohibition, federal authority ended three miles off the beaches. Thus, almost anything that floated sufficed to transfer cargoes from the rum row to hiding places ashore. Even rowboats were used at times. When the territorial boundaries were pushed out to twelve miles, more seaworthy craft were needed to be able to carry several hundred cases of contraband at high speeds and in all weather. Moreover, such craft would have to be swift enough to evade the Coast Guard cutters.

At first, the Coast Guard had few vessels capable of capturing the quickest rumrunners. They patrolled the rum rows, but could do nothing since they lay outside of territorial waters. But as time went on, eventually through luck or otherwise, they were able to seize some of the rumrunning craft and set them to work hunting down others. Eventually, money was found by Congress to give them swifter vessels.

American rumrunning soon became a mob franchise, even as bootlegging had. But stories abound of a curious chivalry among them. In Narragansett Bay, rumrunners sometimes would employ a beachfront summer estate in the owner's absence as a transfer point. One absentee owner found an envelope stuffed with hundred-dollar bills in his mailbox. He tucked it in his pocket and went back to the city. A month later he found another. Month after month, he went down to the shore to collect his "rent," but never saw his tenants.

Shortly after the United States established Prohibition, most of the Canadian provinces followed suit (the lone holdout was then-staunchly Catholic Québec, which instituted prohibition in 1919, but scrapped it within two years). But while the provincial laws made it illegal to sell liquor within the specific province, it was not illegal to manufacture and export the stuff. In the 1920s, Nova Scotia fishermen began using their vessels to transport alcohol to both the United States and eastern Canada. The main places to pick up the liquor were at St.-Pierre and Miquelon, two small French-owned islands in the Gulf of St. Lawrence, just off the coast of Newfoundland. Most of the liquor they transported was produced in Montreal and Toronto, Canada. St.-Pierre became a huge off-shore base, where the Canadian distillers warehoused vast stocks of Canadian-distilled whiskies; these were legally exported to St.-Pierre. The American rumrunners purchased up to three hundred thousand cases a month from the St.-Pierre facility. But the locals were hard at work as well. According to Harry Bruce in "An Illustrated History of Nova Scotia," at least half of the Lunenburg schooners in 1925 were rumrunners.

It was not only the Maritimers who played the rumrunner role. All along the Canadian border similar activity occurred, the nature of which was determined by local geography. A major source of bootleg liquor for the eastern American cities was Montreal, Quebec, from which it was transported by motor car (the minions of the Treasury Department having supervision of the railroads), down the Hudson and Connecticut River valleys to the New York and Boston markets. Nor were scotch and gin the only beneficiaries. Rum itself underwent a small revival in Canada. Sugar from the Caribbean was brought by ship to Montreal, where it was turned into rum. A $10 case of rum sold for $80 in New York or Boston. At least one Canadian fortune remains from those days: Sam Bronfman, patriarch of the family owners of Seagrams, made his fortune running booze to the States.

Thus, Lake Champlain, the centerpiece of the old "Conqueror's Road" in the French and Indian War, found itself in the middle of another conflict. Abercorn, Québec, on the American line near the lake, had always featured a collection of "line houses," not quite respectable establishments, a little higher than bordellos in public estimation. Even in the nineteenth century the place was known as a hotbed of illicit fun. But Prohibition put the tiny place on the map.

Its most prominent businesswoman was "Queen Lill," Lillian Miner. When Franklin County, Vermont, became dry, far in advance of the rest of the country, Queen Lill began making large annual contributions to the local WCTU chapter, because dry laws were good for business. Her establishment was actually half in Canada, half in the United States. She bought liquor legally at one door, and sold it illegally at another, until the provincial law came in 1919. Then she had a pipe laid under the river that separates Québec and Vermont, so that rum could be pumped to and bottled at a house on the Vermont side. Despite raids and other problems, she was able to make quite a large fortune. Only the repeal of Prohibition drove her out of business.

Toronto, Ontario, was also a center for distilling. That being the case, the Great Lakes between Canada and the United States, with their innumerable islands and sheltered inlets, became a hotbed of rumrunning. Canadian lake ports brimmed with illegal liquors.

Typical of these outposts was Kingston, whose waterfront provided a convenient port for bootleggers to run booze across the water to the United States. These were halcyon years for Kingston's rumrunners and a single night's work provided the means to spend freely on fast women and slow horses. A favorite hangout was the Prince George Hotel, where rumrunners and bootleggers threw lavish parties.

Hamilton, Ontario, boasted a sort of Scarlet Pimpernel rumrunner, Ben Kerr. As a descendant of a prominent Hamilton family, he owned one of the city's largest marinas. He also sponsored the championship Pal's hockey team. But by night, Kerr led a double life. He ran three fast motor boats from distilleries in Toronto and eastern Ontario to numerous harbors in New York. Acquitted of manslaughter in Canada, he was charged with murder in the United States. He promptly jumped bail and managed to elude

American authorities for several years. After evading rival gangs for some time, he disappeared one dark night in Lake Ontario.

Demon rum also came to Detroit from Toronto, via the tiny village of Lasalle, the oldest French settlement in southwestern Ontario. Despite (or because of) its seclusion, it hosted such rumrunners as Al Capone.

Prince Edward County, Ontario, is virtually a large island. Main Duck Island, twelve miles from the shore of Prince Edward, was a convenient staging point for rumrunners smuggling liquor into the United States during Prohibition. Although it was obvious where the booze was headed, there was no law against stockpiling the stuff. But when the provincial government bowed to the temperance lobby and banned the sale and consumption of alcohol, it allowed its manufacture for export to remain legal. Boatload after boatload of export whiskey left the Ontario distilleries, only to be smuggled back into the province and bootlegged to local consumers. While this was far easier than slipping past the U.S. authorities, eventually the province cracked down, and rumrunning for domestic use came to an end.

Western Canada also joined in the fun, particularly on the unpatrolled border between Manitoba and Saskatchewan and the United States. Bootleggers had actually blazed numerous trails along back roads to avoid what little law enforcement there was. The only problem with these roads was their turning to mud in the rain. In addition, the winter snows blocked the roads, so the criminals operated in these areas for only a few months out of the year. In this part of the country, the bootleggers faced not the "Untouchables," but the Royal Canadian Mounted Police, with whom they had some remarkable shootouts.

The waters between Vancouver Island and southwestern British Columbia were also very active with rumrunners during Prohibition. "Mother ships" would offload cargo worth millions of dollars to high-speed rumrunning yachts; many of these were built in Victoria and were outfitted with World War I–surplus Liberty engines. One of these mother ships was the former lumber carrier *Malahat*, later converted into the world's first self-propelled log barge. The rumrunning days were a colorful but brief epoch in Victoria's history that ended with the tragedy of hijacking and the conviction of two rumrunners: Cannonball Baker and Harry Sowash. A famous trial took place in the court house in Bastion Square and the men were hanged in 1926.

During Prohibition, Bermuda again profited from the situation in the United States, as we saw it had during the Civil War. The distance from the island to the East Coast was too great for quick crossings in small booze-laden boats, which worked well from the Bahamas and Cuba. Even so, Bermuda accounted for a good part of the alcoholic beverages transported illegally to the United States before the repeal of Prohibition in 1933.

The Prohibition years were also good to the Bahamas; rumrunners from New Providence, Grand Bahama Island, and Bimini slipped into Biscayne Bay, Florida, to supply bootleggers. Rumrunners flooded Bimini with cases and barrels of liquor to be smuggled to the United States. The island's six hundred people were joined by hundreds of rumrunners and liquor agents, who were making scores of dollars by smuggling booze into America. Bimini was awash not only with booze, but also with money. The liquor came from Cuba, the Caribbean, and especially from Europe. Each bottle imported into the colony was taxed, thus even the colony's government profited from Prohibition.

New arrivals also poured into Bermuda, Grand Bahama (where they laid the foundations of the Freeport resort area), and Nassau. But many of the most colorful gravitated to Bimini. One of the most remarkable was the American aviator Arthur Pappy Chalk, who began his airline service to the island in 1919. Flying rumrunners and U.S. undercover revenue agents alike, he brought out Al Capone. Big Al came to work out liquor deals with Bahamian liquor merchants. Another such character was Bimini Bill McCoy. A skilled rumrunner, he never watered down his liquor—his shipments were called the "real McCoy." (Whether or not this is the origin of the term is debatable, but even if it was not, its use in this case was undeniably appropriate.) Representing the females was Gloria Lithgoe. A veritable seagoing Kate "Ma" Barker, she feared neither rival gangs nor the U.S. Coast Guard.

Of course, the onrush of American funds and bootleggers, followed by American organized crime, had a tremendous effect on all these countries. Ever since World War I, cultural dominance over the English-speaking world was slowly but inexorably following military, social and economic dominance from London to New York and Washington. Gradually, Bermuda, the Bahamas, and Anglo-Canada turned from following British trends to more or less aping American ones. The power of the local oligarchies, largely based upon traditional patterns, was being eroded in favor of new ones, based upon media and banking—in imitation of the American elites. In Canada, it gave rise to "Maple Leaf nationalism," an attempt to build a synthetic nationality that would owe little to either the British or the French, in the same way that American nationalism does. By the twenty-first century, this process was nearly complete. Paradoxically, this development bred in each of the three places a determined resistance, centered on remaining at least nominally under the Crown. Bermuda was the only British colony in history whose people were actually allowed to vote on independence from Great Britain—a measure they rejected. Nevertheless, the new political classes in each of these three countries kept up a continual low-level erosion of the Crown, in Canada removing its symbols from such things as post office and mail boxes, and in general minimizing the monarchy in the life of the nation whenever possible.

World War II, which saw the entire tottering British Empire propped up by American intervention, both quickened the process and extended it over virtually the entirety of what became known as the Commonwealth. In the nonwhite colonies, independence was hastened through both indirect pressure and occasionally direct intervention by the United States—often with disastrous results for the newly "freed" peoples. In the case of the other "old dominions" apart from Canada—Australia, New Zealand, and South Africa— ties to Britain were loosened considerably, a loosening greatly aided by Britain's entrance into the European Union. The apartheid government in the Union of South Africa swept into power in 1948 avowedly imitating the American revolutionaries. Emphasizing the fact that both nations shared the initials "U.S.A.," their republic was finally created through a paper-thin majority in a 1960 referendum. But shortly after becoming a republic the following year, they found that their racialist policies made them a pariah in the view of successive American administrations (who were dismantling legal segregation in the South during that period).

It took a while longer in Australia and New Zealand. But American aid during World War II and the service of their armies alongside that of the United States during the Vietnam War tightened their ties to what was fast becoming the new mother country. Like their Canadian colleagues, the new elites in Australia and New Zealand attempted to create new nationalisms based upon recent immigrants and the pre-European inhabitants of their countries. Eventually, knighthoods, various other civic customs, and the queen of England herself came under attack as "foreign"—as though either country had known anything else during their corporate existences. In 1999, the Australian republicans managed to bring abolition of the monarchy to a referendum. Although the attempt was defeated, 55 to 45 percent, republicans in government continued to attack the monarchy quietly. What was most telling about the referendum, however, was that the Australian Republican Movement was led by Malcolm Turnbull, at the time Australian head of the great New York banking firm of Goldman-Sachs. Its major funding came from Australian-born American multibillionaire Rupert Murdoch; a typical specimen of the new face of power in the twenty-first century, Murdoch possessed a media empire controlling at least half the press in his native country, many outlets in the United States, and even a goodly portion of the media in Great Britain itself, including the renowned *Times* of London. Indicative of Murdoch's true interests, perhaps, was his ownership of the Los Angeles Dodgers and his stated intention of being buried in the new Catholic cathedral of that city, despite his being a Presbyterian. His Catholic ex-wife and the millions he donated to the archdiocese were sufficient to gain him entry into that prestigious spot.

Nor was the growth of American influence unfelt in Great Britain itself. After the Suez incident of 1956, in which the British and French regained control of the canal only to lamely withdraw when the Soviets threatened war (promised American support being withheld at that juncture), the United Kingdom abandoned any pretense of an independent foreign policy. (It should be noted that the same event had the opposite effect upon the French; the affair helped mightily to launch General de Gaulle into power two years later and to keep the Gaullists there for over two decades—even now the French tend to be unhelpful toward American foreign and military initiatives.) Under Margaret Thatcher's prime ministry (1978–91), the Conservative party became much like the American Republicans; Tony Blair would later accomplish a similar miracle with the Labour party, now curiously resembling the Democrats. In getting rid of the hereditary House of Lords and various other measures, Blair boasted that he had brought American-style politics to Britain; so he had, if the lowest voter turnouts since 1918 are any indication, conforming as they do to U.S. voting patterns.

Even Ireland, confirmed by her tragic history of hating all things British, followed suit. Although American-born Eamon de Valera made Ireland a republic, even his brand of nationalism in the end was too Irish to survive. In 1976, citing American Church and State separation, Ireland dropped the religious articles from her consti-tution. Despite several referenda defeating the proposal, divorce was at last legalized in 1995. Once again, American precedents were cited. American pop music reigns supreme over the Emerald Isle, and few are the young Irish, in the cities anyway, who know any of their own nation's songs.

So it is throughout the non-Muslim world, to a greater or lesser degree. American music is everywhere, as are our television and films. Few countries are without McDonald's and KFC, and fewer still lack that basic symbol of American empire: Coca-Cola. All of this lay in the far future, of course, during Prohibition. But in the Bahamas and Bermuda, gallons of Coke were mixing with gallons of rum, as Americans drank and locals profited. At Nassau, the colonial government greatly expanded Prince George Wharf to accommodate the huge flow of alcohol.

Nor was this the only effect the Bahamas would see. The influx of thirsty American tourists increased the demand for food, lodging, and other items. The local banking industry boomed as new hotels, warehouses, bars, distilleries, and wharves were built to accommodate the increased traffic. Similar prosperity hit Bermuda.

Even though the Coast Guard was becoming more adept at its job (the development of Coast Guard aviation was a by-product of the struggle against the rumrunners), both government will and the popular desire to continue the "noble experiment" was waning. The widespread corruption of law enforcement and government officials, the rise in power of organized crime, and the general decay in manners (prior to Prohibition, public drunkenness was frowned on; during and after, it became a symbol of freedom), all combined to heighten public disgust.

Alcohol was glamorized to an incredible degree. Where Mencken poured contempt on the "noble experiment," a new generation of writers like Thorne Smith, Charles MacArthur, Alexander Woollcott, Dorothy Parker, and Robert Benchley offered in their novels and essays descriptions of cocktails that made them seem laced with ambrosia. This was not surprising, as many literati turned the "speaks" into second homes; out of such environments were distilled the wit of the "Algonquin Round Table," which came to a head with *The New Yorker*. Such still-thriving Manhattan drinkeries as "21" and Chumley's began then and have been pouring ever since. Jazz music had flourished in the speakeasies, and it triumphantly emerged to conquer a country, and then the western world. By the middle of the 1920s, there were an estimated thirty thousand speakeasies in New York City alone. It was maintained by such as frequented them that you could get booze at any building on 52nd Street between Fifth and Sixth Avenues, provided you knew where the speakeasies were and what the password was.

Nor was the action confined to Manhattan; every town of any size (and many without) possessed some. Out in Chicago, such establishments as Durkin's and Lottie Zagorski's kept the thirsty supplied, and down in New Orleans, even staid Antoine's, founded in 1840 and run by the same family ever since, got into the act. One tendency in movie-haunted Los Angeles was for speaks to give themselves high-sounding names like the Hollywood Arts Council or to masquerade as other kinds of businesses, such as the Tikla Tile Company. The Masquers' Club, an actors' organization founded in 1925, kept the likes of Errol Flynn, W. C. Fields, and the Barrymore brothers in their favorite beverages. Not surprisingly, until the imposition of the Hayes Code in 1934, movies frequently offered "bright young things" drinking impressive amounts—something not missed by young things who wanted to be bright.

Even in the leadership of the Anti-Saloon League of America a fissure was developing, with one faction wanting to focus on rigorous enforcement of the law, and the other desiring to educate the public. Meanwhile, the wets formed the Association against the Prohibition Amendment. Using the same tactics the drys had used so successfully, they began to find cracks in the armor of Prohibition and the league. Suddenly, the league was on the defensive posture. Seeing the Prohibition battle as won, churches and wealthy donors alike stopped contributing. Still, uniting with anti-Catholic sentiment, the league contributed mightily to the defeat of the rabidly wet Al Smith in 1928. But it was to be its last victory.

The Great Depression gave everyone a lot more to worry about besides Prohibition. Economic experts of all parties complained about the loss of tax revenues on alcohol, and ordinary people craved a drink in the midst of their financial woes. By 1932, both political parties had a repeal plank in their platforms and the end of the dry era in America was at hand.

One month after Franklin Delano Roosevelt's election as president of the United States, the Twenty-first Amendment to the Constitution to repeal Prohibition was introduced in Congress. Only a year passed before the required thirty-six states ratified the repeal amendment. On December 5, 1933, Prohibition ended. That afternoon on CBS radio, the Reverend Howard Hyde Russell, the seventy-eight-year-old founder of the league, offered the league's response to this turn of events. He said, "This is no dry funeral; only a period of mistaken public opinion, warped and twisted by the conspiracy of a 'refuge of lies,' of false propaganda and political party duress . . . the question is What shall drys do next? . . . If we cannot get the whole loaf, we accept a half loaf, a slice, crust or crumb."

The effect on Bermuda and the Bahamas was almost immediate. The new prosperity dried up, quite literally. Hotels and branches of off-island banks closed, while wharves emptied. Few tourists returned, and the Depression, held off from the hapless islands by their booze-inflated economies, finally had its way with them. As had happened after the Civil War, bust followed boom, and the islanders returned to more mundane tasks of fishing, farming where they could, and hoping for better times. Like other parts of the world not directly affected by the coming combat of World War II, this slump would only be alleviated when both the British and American militaries would funnel millions of dollars into both island groups.

The continued existence of dry towns and counties here and there, however, assure us of the truth of Russell's statement. But even as with Queen Lill's establishment, the town and county lines of such places are usually filled with liquor stores and bars.

Nevertheless, alcohol has retained its somewhat shady place in the official imagination. Taxes on liquor and tobacco, for example, are routinely dubbed "sin taxes," while those on condoms and contraceptives are not. Blue laws forbidding sale of liquor on

Sundays remain in many areas—in New York State, it was only in 2003 that the Sunday ban was lifted, and over the governor's veto at that. Even so, the law also requires liquor stores to close one day a week; thus, they must choose some other day if they choose to be open on Sunday. Quite a few U.S. states maintain liquor monopolies; although a probable violation of the Constitution as regarding freedom of commerce, these establishments are often defended on moral grounds.

Perhaps the most glaring example of alcohol's continuing bad reputation in the United States is the age requirement for drinking, twenty-one years. The voting age is eighteen, the age of sexual consent is seventeen or eighteen (depending on the state), one may join the armed forces as early as seventeen; in many places a girl may have an abortion without her parents' knowledge or consent as early as twelve. But apparently, none of these activities are as important as drinking alcohol, since the latter act apparently requires more maturity than voting, having sex, risking one's life for one's country, or terminating a fetus. That this is an idea shared by the federal government may be seen by the Minimum Drinking Age Act passed by Congress in 1984, which required all states to increase their minimum drinking age to twenty-one or lose out on federal highway funds. Desirous of revenue and unconcerned about the views of their eighteen- to twenty-one-year-old voters, maverick states speedily complied. But it does lead one to wonder if these youngsters are too young for drinking, are they not too immature as well for those other activities?

Government aside, there also remain religious groups who are opposed to alcohol. The Methodists were traditionally very much opposed to any drinking at all, perhaps reflecting John Wesley's and other early Methodists' work among the gin-ridden poor in eighteenth-century England, as well as the frontier conditions referred to earlier. So strong was the denomination's support for all anti-saloon activities that the WCTU was considered for a long time to be "the Methodist Church in action." Although their militancy has for the most part dimmed, they still generally serve grape juice rather than wine for their communion services, and the 2000 *Book of Discipline* of the United Methodist Church declares: "We affirm our long-standing support of abstinence from alcohol as a faithful witness to God's liberating and redeeming love for persons." (Paragraph 306.4f)

Doubtless due to experiences similar to Wesley's, Quaker founder George Fox (1624–1691) forbade alcohol to members of the Society of Friends. While many today continue to believe that total abstinence is a religious witness and that drinking defiles a God-given body, others do not object to moderate use of it. But rare is the Quaker college, school, or meetinghouse that permits booze on the premises.

Of all the best-known religious groups in America, perhaps the most famous for insisting on strict abstinence from alcohol are the Mormons, or Church of the Latter-day Saints. Where Quakers, Methodists, and other groups refrain from alcohol due to strictures imposed by their founders, the Mormons believe the ban to come from God Himself. This practice of abstinence derives from an 1833 revelation to Joseph Smith, known as the "Word of Wisdom" (the common title for a revelation that counsels Latter-day Saints on maintaining good health, published as *Doctrine and Covenants*), which states "that inasmuch as any man drinketh wine or strong drink among you, behold it is not good, neither meet in the sight of your Father." (Section 89:5)

Methodists, Quakers, and Mormons are, in varying ways, among the most influential of American religious sects. Taken together with our underlying Puritan heritage, it is not surprising that few Americans who have not traveled abroad find the national attitude toward alcohol strange. Certainly college and university administration crusades against on-campus alcohol use contrast strangely with their views on co-ed student housing; as with federal law, the one extracurricular activity of the young that seems to require regulation by their elders in academia is drinking. One wonders what the younger versions of those administrators would have said to their current selves way back in the days of the Free Speech Movement.

Nevertheless, it appears, for the moment, that demon rum has triumphed over its enemies. But some would argue that the increasing bans on tobacco from every public place show that Prohibitionism lives on beyond the superannuated memberships of the WCTU and the Prohibition Party. Then again, others might find significance in the fact that the same U.S. president who spearheaded the return of demon rum to legality, also successfully ordered America's citizens to surrender their gold.

Three years after Prohibition's end, however, the most popular rum drink served in speakeasies appeared in court again—this time as a plaintiff rather than a defendant. As noted, Havana had become a prime refuge for drink during Prohibition. There, at such bars as Sloppy Joe's and La Flordita, Americans discovered Bacardi rum. Moreover, they found with it a new cocktail, named after its prime ingredient: the "Bacardi Cocktail." Combining the signature rum, lime juice, simple (or sugar) syrup, and grenadine, produced a drink that reflected both deliciousness and sophistication. Back in New York, topers who had been to Havana ordered a Bacardi Cocktail with whatever rum the bootlegger servicing their favorite speak could find.

After the "noble experiment" ended, the Bacardi family was furious to find that Manhattan bartenders commonly advertised the drink by name but mixed it as they chose. Moreover, they feared that they and their company's prestige would suffer from being associated with such irregular fare, to say nothing of the royalties to which their name entitled them. In 1936, seeking a restraining order to prevent anyone from serving the Bacardi Cocktail without its original rum, Bacardi approached the New York Supreme Court for justice. Although their opponents argued that the term had, through more than a decade of use, simply become a generic name, the court ruled in Bacardi's favor. The judges declared that "the Court finds as a clear, preponderating, and even that which would be exacted in a criminal situation, beyond a reasonable doubt, that Bacardi rum left out of a Bacardi Cocktail is not a Bacardi Cocktail, and that otherwise it is a subterfuge and fraud." In response, Bacardi hired billboards throughout the United States advertising the court ruling. Together with the nationwide publicity generated by the case, Bacardi became a household word—a last, if unexpected product of Prohibition.

Rumless Hot Buttered Rum

For those who want to relive those dry days.

HOT BUTTERED RUM
BATTER #1:
1 pound dark brown sugar
$^1/_2$ pound salted butter
1 teaspoon ground nutmeg
1 teaspoon ground cinnamon
1 teaspoon ground cloves
1 teaspoon ground white
  cardamom
1 teaspoon vanilla

HOT BUTTERED RUM
BATTER #2:
$^1/_2$ cup brown sugar
$^1/_2$ cup white sugar
$^1/_2$ pound butter
1 pint good quality vanilla
  ice cream

In either case, blend all ingredients in a food processor or mixer, and store in the fridge or freezer. To make a drink, add 1 or 2 tablespoons of batter to a mug of very hot water.

Bacardi Cocktail

$1^3/_4$ ounces Bacardi rum
$^3/_4$ ounce lime juice
Bar spoon of Simple Syrup
  (see page 23)

Dash of grenadine

Shake ingredients with cracked ice; strain into a chilled cocktail glass. Squeeze the juice of a small lime wedge into the drink, and then drop the fruit into the drink.

Cuban Black Bean Soup

1 pound dried black beans
1 cup chopped onion
1 tablespoon butter
    (or margarine)
6 cups water
12 ounces lean ham, cut into
    chunks
2 bay leaves
$\frac{1}{2}$ teaspoon dried thyme

$\frac{1}{2}$ teaspoon dried oregano
$\frac{1}{2}$ teaspoon salt
2 whole hot red chili peppers
1 beef bouillon cube
1 cup green bell pepper,
    chopped
2 tablespoons dark rum
    (optional)

Sort and soak beans overnight; drain and discard soak water. In a 4-quart pot, sauté onion in butter or margarine until tender but not browned. Add soaked beans, water, ham, bay leaves, thyme, oregano, salt, and red chili peppers. Bring to boil; reduce heat. Cover and simmer until beans are tender, 1 to 2 hours.

Remove one cup of the beans from the stew and mash in a bowl with a potato masher or fork. Add dissolved bouillon and mashed beans to stew; stir to thicken. Remove ham and dice. Remove bay leaves and red chili peppers, and discard. Add diced meat, green pepper, and rum (if desired) to beans. Cover and simmer 15 minutes. Serve beans over rice and top with sour cream if desired.

Chapter 12

"Over the Top": Rum and the Army

I KNEW a simple soldier boy
Who grinned at life in empty joy,
Slept soundly through the lonesome dark,
And whistled early with the lark.

In winter trenches, cowed and glum,
With crumps and lice and lack of rum,
He put a bullet through his brain.
No one spoke of him again.

. . . .

You smug-faced crowds with kindling eye
Who cheer when soldier lads march by,
Sneak home and pray you'll never know
The hell where youth and laughter go.

—Siegfried Sassoon, "Suicide in the Trenches"

The year 1900 found Europe triumphant. Although, two
years before the United States had ejected Spain from the
ranks of the Great Powers by snatching Cuba, Puerto Rico,
and the Philippines (thus ensuring its own promotion to exalted

status), were not the Americans Europeans themselves? The Queen Mother of Spain had warned that if the other Europeans did not help the Spanish in the 1898 war, the Americans would one day own them, but who listened? Although the Continent was dividing into two major antipathetic blocs, they drew together, with the Japanese and the Americans, to punish China for the Boxer Rebellion.

Despite the rattling of sabers, the jousting for colonies, the growing arms race, and the seemingly never ending crises in the Balkans, the first decade of the twentieth century was an optimistic time. It was true that the industrial proletariat in each country suffered much, and often turned to godless prophets for promises of this-worldly salvation. But surely technology would eventually solve their difficulties. For it was an age of scientific wonders. The telegraph and the telephone were slowly binding the world together in a communications web. Steamships and canals were uniting the continents as never before, and ambitious plans for such railways as the Orient Express, the Berlin to Baghdad, and the Cape to Cairo promised to do the same for the land. In all the European colonies, an infrastructure comparable to that in the home countries was being built, and it was confidently predicted by no less an authority than the 1911 *Encyclopaedia Britannica* that a worldwide civilization was emerging. Poverty and war would soon be banished, and humanity faced an incredibly rich and glorious future. Glittering courts in London, Vienna, Berlin, St. Petersburg, and elsewhere seemed to promise that the best of the past would be preserved.

But, as in H. G. Wells's *War of the Worlds*, all of this activity was unknowingly facing an enemy. That foe was not Wells's octopus-like and technologically advanced Martians, but the hatred and duplicity, the nationalisms and greed of humanity itself. Underneath the surface of a continent that had known only small wars since Napoléon Bonaparte's apocalyptic defeat at Waterloo, the previously mentioned qualities festered, and the bureaucracies and peoples of Great Britain, France, Russia, Germany, Austria-Hungary, and Italy quietly hungered for war. Although none of their leaders were evil men, in the sense of Josef Stalin, Adolf Hitler, Mao Tse-tung, or any of a hundred with which succeeding generations have had to deal, they were shortsighted, to say the least. Whether it was to prove themselves, to right old wrongs, or simply to bring about a regeneration of society through external conflict, Europeans were spoiling for a fight. They would have their wish.

The assassination of Archduke Franz Ferdinand unleashed a juggernaut, as Austria-Hungary declared war on Serbia, Russia declared war on Austria-Hungary, Germany declared war on Russia, and France declared war on Germany, each seeking to defend its ally. Thinking it could outflank the French defenses, Germany invaded Belgium, violating a treaty and bringing Great Britain into the war. Mobs of civilians enlisted and soon were on their way to the front, clad in brilliant uniforms. They soon learned, however, that a century of progress meant that technology had altered war as well. After the failure of the Germans to take Paris and their being beaten back some few miles, the Allies and the Central Powers sat down to face each other over a network of bloody trenches extending from Switzerland to the North Sea. For the next four years, fruitless attempts to break through the enemy's trenches were punctuated by new inventions (poison gas and the tank) and the accession of new combatants—Italy, Romania, and Greece for the Allies, Bulgaria and Turkey for the Central Powers. All that occurred was the extension of combat into new areas and the correspondingly increased suffering of soldiers and civilians alike.

It is difficult for us of the twenty-first century, used as we are to such horrors, to imagine the psychological effect of this horror on our grandparents' and great-grandparents' generations. As the handful of surviving veterans continues to dwindle, the Great War departs living memory. But the wholesale slaughter, the constant stink of dead and unwashed bodies, the parasites and disease, marked forever those who lived through it.

As it happened, for the British—and the Canadians, Australians, South Africans, New Zealanders, Indians, Africans, and West

Indians who answered the call to fight for king and empire—solace was provided in the traditional way, through our old friend, rum. Traditionally, British soldiers on campaign had been issued rum, in similar manner to their confreres in the Royal Navy. During the Boer War, Canadian troops under British command received a half-gill (less than a half-pint) ration of rum, three times a week.

Each battalion was issued its own supply of rum, drawn from the three hundred gallons given each twenty-thousand-man division. The tot was generally issued after an offensive, rather than before, although it also accompanied breakfast during very cold weather; summer was dreaded because it meant the end of the regular rum ration. The breakfast ration was not large—one or two table-spoonfuls per man. The rum arrived in earthenware jars marked "SRD." These mysterious initials were interpreted as "Service Rum Department" or "Special Red Demerara." Wine and brandy were daily given the French and German troops regardless of the season, and the latter also received occasional rum rations.

One of the most inspiring and painful events of the war on the western front was the Christmas truce of 1914. As is well known, German troops began singing "Silent Night" in their own language, and British troops emerged from their trenches to join them For a few hours, the combatants played games, sang carols, and shared food and drink. On Christmas Eve, the British Royal Flying Corps dropped a Christmas pudding on a German airfield at Lille; the following day the Germans responded by dropping a bottle of rum.

The regular soldier loved his rum. According to Canadian veteran Arthur Ament, "Each morning, while in the trenches, we were given a ration of rum that was not much larger than a thimbleful, but if you could down it and immediately say thank you, you qualified for a second shot. However, this rarely happened with me because I could feel the rum right down to my big toe."

Canadian military historian Tim Cook, in his article "Demon Rum and the Canadian Trench Soldier in the First World War," has gathered an impressive number of firsthand accounts of the importance of rum to the war effort. "People tend to focus on the buddy system that soldiers fought for their pals in the trenches," Cook said in an interview. "Well, the thing I found while reading through their diaries and letters is this little three-letter word kept popping up—rum."

He quotes Canadian infantryman Ralph Bell, who wrote that, "when the days shorten, and the rain never ceases; when the sky is ever gray, the nights chill, and trenches thigh deep in mud and water; when the front is altogether a beastly place, in fact, we have one consolation. It comes in gallon jars, marked simply SRD." Cook mentions an anonymous soldier who declared, "If we hadn't had our rum, we would have lost the war."

The usual horrors of the trenches were multiplied whenever the high command came up with another idea for breaking the enemy line, as at the Somme in 1916 and Passchendaele in 1917. M. A. Searle of the Eighteenth Canadian Battalion, one of the infantry-men who defended the mud at Passchendaele, declared, "Most of us carried on . . . because of not limitless but more than ordinary issues of rum." Fellow survivor of that battle, Private G. Boyd of the Eighth Battalion, recounted, "If we had not had the rum we would have died."

Rum was initially given to men at dawn and dusk. Anticipating an assault at those times, the thirsty soldiers fell out with rifles at the ready. All being peaceful, sergeants issued two ounces of overproof rum to each soldier. Although this practice ceased during the second year of the war as both sides realized that each was on high alert, the rum ration remained.

To prevent hoarding, the rum was issued only in the presence of an officer or noncommissioned officer (NCO); any surplus was poured out onto the ground. Few libations of this sort found their way to earth, however, partly because the NCOs' cronies were allowed to drink the remainder, and partly because, as one official memorandum mentioned, "the individual man is in all cases free to refuse the issue of rum if he so desires, but this option is only exer-cised in a few instances."

Since the pounding of the guns, the horrors witnessed, the

general misery, and the ever present prospect of death were not what one might call restful, rum also served as a powerful soporific. The overproof lulled the soldiers to sleep, blotting out the daily round of atrocities.

Rum was issued to the battalions; each quartermaster then portioned it out to the companies. Since men under punishment were excluded, and only those in good standing were allowed their ration, rum was a powerful disciplinary tool. The beverage was also used as a reward for service above and beyond the call of duty. Reconnaissance men, for example, would receive a mug of rum after a raid.

Extra rum could be obtained for extra work, such as carrying the wounded or repairing trenches. Rum was particularly welcomed by those who dug graves. Private Ernest Spillett of the Forty-sixth Canadian Battalion wrote in a 1917 letter about removing the corpses from his unit's last engagement, "I am [so] used to these sights they don't have to prime me with rum before I can handle a man; although I have and do certainly drink it sometimes on those jobs but usually afterwards, to take the taste of dead men out of my mouth."

One of the most stressful periods in trench warfare was awaiting the order to go "over the top." Initially, the army authorities preferred, as already mentioned, to wait until after an assault to issue the rum. But, as George Bell of the First Canadian Battalion wrote, "A good stiff 'tot' of rum served to buck up the spirits of those wavering." Eventually, officers and NCOs would travel about the forward firing line, ladling out extra rum. Operational orders for the Canadian corps' attack on Vimy Ridge pointed out that "the comfort, efficiency and fighting value of the troops are greatly increased by the issue of fortified alcohol."

This sort of warfare resulted in obscene casualties and horrible wounds. When found alive, soldiers' wounds were dressed and a shot of rum was administered. If still alive when at last they made it to a field hospital for a quick operation, a sedative was administered. If the hospital was well supplied, this would be morphine; if not, the anesthetic was generally rum. Soldiers also believed, however, that rum acted as a preventative for colds and the flu and staved off shell shock. One soldier wrote in his postwar memoirs, "There are not one, but numberless occasions, on which a tot of rum has saved a man from sickness, possibly from a serious illness. Many a life-long teetotaler has conformed to SRD and taken the first drink of his life on the battlefields of France, not because he wanted to, but because he had to."

There was a risk in issuing rum before the fight, however. According to Cook, one Canadian soldier wrote, "Under the spell of this all-powerful stuff, one almost felt that he could eat a German, dead or alive, steel helmet and all." While this was a powerful motivation, it had its drawbacks. At Amiens in 1918, Lieutenant Lunt of the Fourth Canadian Battalion was passing out rum on the firing line when he encountered a boy so frightened that his teeth chattered. According to Cook, "Lunt plied him with four double rum shots before the shakings stopped. When they finally attacked, Lunt remembered seeing the young lad stumbling forward in a drunken daze before he was shot in the face." In some units, therefore, rum was withheld, but any officer rash enough to do so toward the end of the war had trouble on his hands.

The rum ration was issued at the whim of the battalion commanding officer. Lime juice and pea soup might replace the alcohol, much to the disgust of the men. One of these was Victor Odlum, the commanding officer of successively the Seventh Canadian Battalion and then the Eleventh Brigade. A child of Protestant missionaries, the teetotalling Odlum denied his troops their rum ration, winning the epithet "Old Lime Juice" from his men. Since he was of an extremely warlike disposition, and was not reluctant to send his men "over the top," their dislike of him began to smack of mutiny. In response, his superior, General David Watson, overruled him, initiating the rum ration in February 1917.

Much of the slang, song, poetry, and culture of the soldiers revolved around the rum ration. A favorite drink was called "Gunfire," which was strong tea laced with rum. Such maxims as "one swallow doesn't make a rum issue" became quasi immortalized. The letters "SRD" were constantly lampooned as "Seldom Reaches Destination," "Sergeants Rarely Deliver," "Soldiers' Real Delight," or "Soon Runs Dry." Rum was also frequently mentioned in soldiers' songs, such as in "The Old Barbed Wire":

> If you want to find the sergeant-major,
> I know where he is, I know where he is.
> If you want to find the sergeant-major,
> I know where he is,
> He's boozing up the privates' rum.
> I've seen him, I've seen him,
> Boozing up the privates' rum,
> I've seen him,
> Boozing up the privates' rum.

But as we saw in the last chapter, the forces of temperance had seeped across the northern border; by 1917, all the Canadian provinces save Québec had enacted Prohibition. Much to the annoyance of the men in the trenches, antisaloon types wanted to end the rum ration to the Canadian soldiers. The reaction of the latter, risking their lives for Crown and country, might be expected. According to infantryman Harold Baldwin, "Oh you psalm-singers, who raise your hands in horror at the thought of the perdition the boys are bound for, if they should happen to take a nip of rum to keep a little warmth in their poor battered bodies, I wish you could all lie shivering in a hole full of icy liquid, with every nerve in your body quivering with pain, with the harrowing moans of the wounded forever ringing in your ears, with hell's own din raging all around."

In 1918, reinforcements arrived from the soon to be seat of Prohibition, the United States. While the doughboys faced (albeit for a much shorter time) the same rigors as their British and French allies, they were given, in accord with their government's policies, far less with which to face them internally. Rather than the rum of the former or the wine of the latter, since "issues of intoxicants to soldiers were contrary to the American policy . . . quantities of soluble coffee were substituted." The making of regular coffee required too much in the way of fire; vigilant German sharpshooters would see the smoke. As "it was found necessary to give hot drinks to the men before they went over the top or after they had undergone periods of exposure," the soluble coffee was provided. The solidified alcohol supplied to heat the coffee was as close as American soldiers would get to any kind of issue of spirits.

The western front was not the only place where the forces of the British Empire had their tot in hell. In 1915, the Ottoman Empire entered the war on the side of Germany and Austria-Hungary. In an attempt to knock Turkey out of the war, it was decided to seize the Gallipoli Peninsula. This place secured, Constantinople would be sure to fall quickly. But the Turks who manned the place were dug in, and the Australian, New Zealand, and British troops who were landed there spent months of torture. Regardless, rum played for them the same role it did for their brothers on the western front. Even today, alongside the bullets, shell fragments, dentures, fountain pens, and tobacco tins that local farmers still find in their planting, the most common relics are pieces of the rum jars.

We find in the diary of Lieutenant Frank M. Coffee of the Australian Imperial Forces (who was killed in action on November 18, 1915) the journal entry of September 13, 1915:

At Quinn's Post a shell landed on a parapet just after the morning rum ration had been issued. It took twenty minutes to dig one man out of the mess; but when they did get him out all right, the first thing he said was: "who the h—l stole my ration? Damn them, they upset my bottle!" But not a word about the shell! All he cared was that it had spilt his rum for him. Can you beat men like that? It is quite true that they lack in discipline; but it is a question whether or not their pure audacity has not more than compensated for that disadvantage.

The sugar colonies were not unaware of the needs of the empire's forces. The women of Jamaica organized Flag Day fund-raisers, a War Relief Fund, and sewed woolen garments for soldiers. Other funds included the Gleaner Fund and the Palace Amusement Company's Palace War Fund, for which thousands of pounds were collected. Over four thousand packages of fruits, seventy-one bags of sugar, forty-nine cases of ginger, four casks of rum, and two cases of playing cards were shipped to military hospitals in France and elsewhere; some of this largesse was distributed locally to men manning Jamaica's coastal forts. For that matter, the French colonies of Martinique, Guadeloupe, and Reunion began producing rum at a furious rate for their ally's military. Apart from drinking, rum was also used in the making of explosives. Nevertheless, even the French soldiers developed a taste for it. Production of rum in the French sugar colonies doubled, and they enjoyed a period of prosperity—all too brief. On Guadeloupe, where today there are a mere nine rum distilleries, there were fifty in 1918. After the war, returning French soldiers had developed such a thirst for rum (and introduced their friends at home to it) that metropolitan French distillers of brandy took fright. They pressured the French government to pass a law limiting importation of rum from the colonies—mercantilism in reverse! The new law took effect on December 31, 1922.

In the United States, however, whiskey was in short supply. Many distilleries were forced to change from whiskey production to gunpowder. The whiskey became accordingly scarce; here too, rum would creep back into the picture.

At last, on November 11, 1918, the enemy fire ceased. At Woodrow Wilson's insistence, Germany became a republic (Wilson had indicated to a starving Germany that there would be no peace until the kaiser and the other German princes were removed), and the Habsburgs were exiled, while their empire was partitioned. The American president's god-child, Yugoslavia, was erected on its ruin. Thus, the way was paved for Hitler, central Europe became a power vacuum, and Russia had become communist; the foundation was laid for much of the bloodshed and horror that would characterize the rest of the twentieth century.

In a sense, however, the damage to Europe was even deeper than it appeared. Not only would war and holocaust follow, but also the European sense of mission died in the trenches. Although the colonial empires would survive intact until after World War II, the ideologies—whether religious or secular—that underlay them were severely damaged. By 1970, the Europeans had departed from almost all of their colonies, leaving behind an infrastructure that would decay if untended and in many cases an artificially constructed technocratic class that had neither traditional nor European values. In any case, the great adventure of which rum had been the lifeblood was over.

Or was it? For while the European empires were no more, on their foundations a global civilization was rising. In 1915, the center of world finance shifted from London to Wall Street, where it has remained ever since—in that same year, for the first time in its history, the United States shifted from being a debtor to become a creditor nation. For a time after World War II, there was some question as to whether the United States or the Soviet Union was to guide/force the globe into its image. But the fall of the Soviet Union gave an answer to that riddle. Another question took its place: Can the United States actually accomplish the goal of shaping the world? The answer will be provided on the pages of newspapers, on television, and over the Internet, as events unfold.

But for rum, the eclipse of Europe meant far less than did the repeal of Prohibition in America. As we shall see, the drink of empire made itself at home in *Pax Americana*. If it was no longer to be the soldiers' and sailors' relief, it would soon find another role.

Between the Sheets

The name does not go back to World War I, but the formula does.

Juice of $1/4$ lemon $1/2$ ounce Cointreau
$1/2$ ounce brandy $1/2$ ounce light rum

Shake with ice and strain into cocktail glass.

Sweet Potato Pudding

A favorite of Jamaican troops in World War I.

$^{1}/_{2}$ cup Jamaican rum
2 pounds raw sweet potatoes,
   peeled and grated
3 cups coconut milk
   (see instructions)
2 cups brown sugar
2 teaspoons almond or vanilla
   extract

3 cups plus 3 tablespoons
   (1 pound) all-purpose
   flour
$1^{1}/_{2}$ teaspoons cinnamon
$^{1}/_{2}$ teaspoon grated nutmeg
1 cup raisins
1 teaspoon salt

Soak raisins in rum for 3 hours. Peel and grate the sweet potatoes into a large mixing bowl. Instead of grating the potatoes, you can use a food processor with the fine shredding blade attached. Although the initial appearance of the potatoes will be different than if using the grating method, however, the texture of the finished pudding will be identical.

To make coconut milk: Crack open a dry coconut and remove the meat from the shell with a knife. Grate the coconut meat into a bowl. Add water to the grated coconut, and squeeze coconut to extract milk into the water. Strain out the solids. If necessary, add enough water to make 3 cups.

An easier way to make the coconut milk is to use a blender. After removing the coconut meat from the shell, cut the meat into small pieces, and place half the meat in blender jar with enough water to cover it. Grate until coconut is very finely chopped; if necessary, add more water to allow the mixture to circulate in the blender jar. Strain coconut mixture into a bowl to remove the solids and repeat process with remainder of the coconut. Squeeze the grated coconut to extract as much milk as possible.

Preheat oven to 350°. Mix coconut milk, brown sugar, and almond extract together. Add to the grated potatoes and mix until blended. Mix flour, cinnamon, and nutmeg together. Stir flour mixture into potatoes, then add rum and raisin mixture. Pour mixture into 9-inch or 10-inch round pan. Bake at 350° for 2 hours, or until pudding is firm.

Chapter 13

"Rum and Coca-Cola": A Symbol of Exotic Sophistication, 1933 to the Present

Since the Yankees come to Trinidad
They have the young girls going mad
The young girls say they treat them nice
And they give them a better price
They buy rum and coca-cola
Go down Point Cumana
Both mother and daughter
Working for the Yankee dollar

—Rupert Westmore Grant (Lord Invader),
"Rum and Coca-Cola" (1943)

While Europe struggled (ultimately without success) to recover from the horrors of World War I, and the United States was locked in a life-and-death struggle with demon rum, more Americans traveled overseas than ever before. Of course, there had always been genteel travelers to Europe of the Henry James type. But now the trickle became a flood, as artistic types sought freedom from the perceived triumphant

247

Puritanism of their native land, and less lofty folk simply looked for places they could drink in peace.

Art Deco in architecture and jazz in music began to epitomize the height of sophistication for Americans; so, too, did violating Prohibition and embarking on foreign travel. Cuba offered all four in abundance, as did, to a lesser degree, the rest of the West Indies. They were exotic, they were wet, and, above all, they were cheap. So hordes of Americans boarded ships and planes (newly emergent air travel being another touchstone of glamour) for points south.

The gowned lady dripping with jewels and sitting at a table with a man in a white linen suit became a powerful icon. Under the tropic moon, this couple would sit in a club with slow fans whirling languidly, parrots screaming from their cages, a band playing tangos, and native waiters impeccably dressed and fetching round after round. This was an image seared into the national conscious-ness by film after film (and yes, this new invention was already shaping the American self-image). But what was this exemplary couple quaffing? Much to the delight of the Bacardi Company, which had felt severely threatened by the Eighteenth Amendment, it was any one of a dozen or more rum-based drinks.

Most likely, at first, they were drinking Cuba Libres, a drink whose origin we saw first in the Spanish-American War. More complex than the rum and cokes with which they are often con-fused, the Cuba Libre requires Coca-Cola and rum, to be sure. But first a lime wedge must be rubbed on the rim of a highball glass, and then gin and bitters are added to the rum and coke. According to the official Bacardi description (and we may defer to Bacardi, since it was almost certainly Bacardi rum that was used for the first Cuba Libres):

The world's most popular drink was born in a collision between the United States and Spain. It happened during the Spanish-American War at the turn of the century when Teddy Roosevelt, the Rough Riders, and Americans in large numbers arrived in Cuba. One afternoon, a group of off-duty soldiers from the U.S. Signal Corps were gathered in a bar in Old Havana. Fausto Rodriguez, a young messenger, later recalled that a captain came in and ordered Bacardi rum and Coca-Cola on ice with a wedge of lime. The captain drank the concoction with such pleasure that it sparked the interest of the soldiers around him. They had the bartender prepare a round of the captain's drink for them. The Bacardi rum and Coke was an instant hit. As it does to this day, the drink united the crowd in a spirit of fun and good fellowship. When they ordered another round, one soldier suggested that they toast ¡Por Cuba Libre! in celebration of the newly freed Cuba. The captain raised his glass and sang out the battle cry that had inspired Cuba's victorious soldiers in the War of Independence.

One might add that in 1965, according to his sworn deposition, Rodriguez certified that the Cuba Libre was first mixed at a Cuban bar in August 1900 by a member of the U.S. Signal Corps; Rodriguez called him "John Doe."

Mind you, the invention of Coca-Cola had spurred an awful lot of experimentation as far as mixing it with alcoholic fluids went. According to H. L. Mencken in *The American Language*, "The troglodytes of western South Carolina coined 'jump stiddy' for a mixture of Coca-Cola and denatured alcohol (usually drawn from automobile radiators); connoisseurs reputedly preferred the taste of what had been aged in Model-T Fords."

While the Cuba Libre maintained its position among drinkers after Prohibition and through the Depression, World War II gave it a tremendous boost when the Andrews Sisters recorded their 1944 song "Rum and Coca-Cola." In fact, it became America's national drink during the war, partly due to the song (the Andrews Sisters sold seven million records), but also because U.S. mainland distillers of other liquors (like whiskey, bourbon, and rye) were ordered to limit their production in order to manufacture industrial alcohol for the war effort, thus increasing the demand for rum, which was produced outside the continental United States and thus exempted from the territorial mandate.

The "Rum and Coca-Cola" story had another twist. Morey Amsterdam, a comic best known to later generations for his portrayal of Dick Van Dyke's pal on the *Dick Van Dyke Show*, claimed authorship of the lyrics and music of the song. He copyrighted it and promoted it in the United States, sold it to the Andrews Sisters, and looked forward to enjoying his share of the seven million sales.

Truth be told, Amsterdam had actually plagiarized the lyrics and tune, which he had heard on a trip to Trinidad in 1943. That was the year that the distinguished Calypsonian Lord Invader (real name Rupert Westmore Grant) began singing the tune, under the name "Rum and Coca-Cola." It was an instant hit, particularly among the U.S servicemen based in Trinidad, whom it was satirizing (Calypso was notorious for poking fun at contemporary figures). In 1945, Invader sued Amsterdam and Leo Feist, Inc. (his publisher) for plagiarism. He won; although Amsterdam's lyrics were milder than the Invader's, they were recognizably the same song. The trial lasted three years, and it took Invader another seven to collect the $132,000 awarded him by the court from the defendants. Amsterdam was bankrupted, and the Invader himself, highly respected as a musician, died in New York in 1961.

But Amsterdam was not only sued for plagiarizing the lyrics; apparently, he stole the music as well. The second suit was brought by Maurice Baron, a music expert, who claimed that the song was plagiarized from a book published by him, *Calypso Songs of the West Indies*. The actual title of the tune was "L'Année Passée," composed by Lionel Belasco in 1906. A tune in French patois, it was a lament for an aristocratic Franco-Trinidadian girl who was seduced and then pimped by a worthless lover. Belasco in 1941 submitted some of his songs to Baron for publishing. One of these was "L'Anné Passée." Baron had hired Olga Paul to translate the lyrics into English; the next year "Rum and Coca-Cola" appeared under Morey Amsterdam's name. Amsterdam maintained that while entertaining American soldiers on the base at Chaguaramas, Trinidad, he had heard his military driver sing a song to the tune of "It Ain't

Gonna Rain No Mo'." This, he claimed, inspired him to write "Rum and Coca-Cola." But Baron was able to prove through scores of witnesses and expert testimonies (including that of Belasco himself, who came to New York for the trial) that Amsterdam had plagiarized the tune as well as the lyrics. An appeal was defeated, and Amsterdam's finances suffered accordingly.

It is hard to think, while drinking rum and coke, that such a song could have made so much trouble!

But rum had far more arrows in its quiver than Cuba Libres. A local legend was in the making to the north, on the island of Newfoundland. Demerara rum had long been a mainstay of the Newfoundland diet. As a last gasp of the old Triangle Trade (now strictly bilateral), salt fish was traded to the West Indies in exchange for rum. The Newfoundland Colonial Government (the island would not become a Canadian province until 1949) took control of the traditional liquor business in the early twentieth century and began selling this rum in an unlabeled bottle. This nameless state might have persisted but American servicemen coming to the Island during World War II changed all that.

The American commanding officer of the first detachment assigned there had his first taste of Newfoundland hospitality. He followed his host's example, downing his drink in one gulp, and let out a tremendous shriek that echoed in the neighborhood and instantly brought neighbors as well as some of his command to his rescue. One old American sergeant pounded on the door shouting, "What the cripes was that ungodly screech?" The Newfoundlander who opened the door replied, "The screech? 'Tis the rum, me son."

As word of the incident spread, the soldiers, determined to try this mysterious "Screech" and finding its effects as devastating as the name implied, adopted it as their favorite. The opportunistic liquor board subsequently pounced on the drink's name and reputation and began labeling Newfoundland Screech, which became the most popular brand on the island. Today, the government-owned Newfoundland Liquor Corporation continues to bottle

Jamaican rum under the name of Screech, although they also dispense authentic Demerara as Old Sam's rum.

Perhaps the second most popular rum drink is the daiquiri, which takes its name from a small town in the east of Cuba—not very far from the first Bacardi distillery. After the Spanish-American War of 1898 ejected the Spanish, Americans descended on the island to exploit its natural resources. Among these were the iron mines near Daiquiri. One of the engineers assigned to the mines was Jennings Cox. His granddaughter declares that Cox ran out of gin when entertaining fellow Americans. Rather than giving them rum neat, he added lime juice and sugar to the beverage. The drink took the name of the village and local Americans came to prefer it to gin.

It might have stayed in Daiquiri forever, but in 1909 Admiral Lucius W. Johnson, an American naval medical officer, visited Cox. Enchanted with the daiquiri, Johnson brought the recipe and gallons of local rum back to Washington, D.C., where he introduced it to his club, the Army and Navy. Moreover, Johnson, like a sort of alcoholic Johnny Appleseed, propagated the cocktail in all the ports he visited over a distinguished career. Forever grateful to the admiral for his good deed, the club named its second-floor bar the "Daiquiri Lounge," which boasts a brass plaque honoring Johnson's contribution to humanity.

Prohibition drove the daiquiri back offshore, however. The renowned "Cocktail King," the bartender Constante Ribelague, gave it refuge at Havana's La Floridita. Moreover, Ribelague improved it by substituting syrup for sugar; his version first attracted the notion of the literary public in F. Scott Fitzgerald's 1920 masterpiece *This Side of Paradise*. Ernest Hemingway also popularized it, but then Papa never met a rum drink he disliked.

The stuff was served with cracked ice and became yet another symbol of sophistication. Readers of Irwin Shaw's *Rich Man, Poor Man* will recall that daiquiris were used by the dissipated hometown aristocrat in the book's first chapter to impress easily impressible young ladies. In that tradition, the daiquiri was John F. Kennedy's favorite aperitif. Thus clothed in the middle-wattage glimmer of Camelot, it reached new heights—heights from which it was destined to fall.

Innumerable variations were developed on the original recipe, such as strawberry daiquiris. At Mountain Top, the famous bar and cafeteria perched on the fifteen-hundred-foot-tall St. Peter's Mountain on the island of St. Thomas, U.S. Virgin Islands, the banana daiquiri was born, with the addition of half a banana to the mix.

But the daiquiri was fated to become a common man's drink. Louisiana is hot in the summer—extremely hot. But the daiquiri, with its sweet cold taste, was destined to find a niche in the Cajun folk culture. Around 1981, the first of innumerable drive-through "daiquiri huts" opened. In time, the idea spread throughout the South, and the daiquiri became as ordinary a part of the southern summer as iced tea.

Puerto Rico eventually challenged Cuba's supremacy in the world of rum cocktails with a powerful weapon: the *piña colada*. It was invented in 1954 by Ramon "Monchito" Marrero, a bartender at the Caribe Hilton Hotel in San Juan, Puerto Rico. Marrero's self-proclaimed goal was "to capture all the flavors of Puerto Rico in a glass." For three months, he tried various recipes, before settling on what he called the "piña colada" ("strained pineapple"). His winning formula combined coconut cream, pineapple juice, and rum served over ice and garnished with a pineapple chunk. Marrero was blessed with success, serving his cocktail to thousands of hotel guests, including John Wayne and Gloria Swanson. In 1978, Puerto Rico declared the piña colada its national drink, while singer Warren Zevon confessed in his song "Werewolves of London" to having seen a werewolf with perfect hair drinking one at Trader Vic's.

The latest rum drink to come into fashion is also the oldest: the *mojito*. Again owing its origin to the indefatigable house of Bacardi, this was originally a nonalcoholic drink comprised of sugar, yerbabuena (a local variety of mint) leaves, lime juice, ice, and soda water, called the *draque*. But when Don Facundo Bacardi added his rum and renamed it the mojito, it became for the Cuban peasant what the daiquiri has turned into for the southerner. Hemingway embraced it, as only he could. In recent years, it has emerged as a very trendy drink, indeed. Available at the toniest clubs and bars, it has avenged the daiquiri, so to speak.

World War II completed the work of European self-destruction begun in 1914 and cemented America's place as the senior partner in a mutually hostile world diarchy. This pre-eminent place was assured by the United States being the most prominent and powerful ally on the second front of the war, opened by Japan in December, 1942. It was as bloody or worse than the fight being waged against Germany and its European allies. But thousands of American servicemen discovered Hawaii and the South Pacific as a result. While this occurrence had its effect on the locals by adding spam to the list of island favorites, it also added Polynesia to the list of exotic locales in the American popular imagination. In 1947, James Michener released a book based on his experiences during the war, *Tales of the South Pacific*. Two years later, Richard Rodgers and Oscar Hammerstein used it as the basis for their Broadway show *South Pacific*, which was made into a movie eight years later. With its mythical island of Bali Hai and its story about whites in a tropical paradise, it caught the imagination of a country hungry for the exotic. The Tiki craze was born.

Of course, given that most Americans' geographical knowledge was and is sketchy, the already existing national fantasy of the Caribbean was conflated with the new one of Polynesia. But generic "tropical" motifs invaded domestic architecture and Tiki lamps multiplied in the backyards of newborn suburban America (itself also largely a creation of World War II). Don Ho and Hilo Hattie sang island melodies. Backyard bars supported Hawaiian shirt–clad hosts dispensing tropical drinks (duly festooned with miniature paper umbrellas) to similarly attired guests, while ribs for the puu-puu platters roasted on the barbecue. It was, in fact, the sort of lifestyle immortalized by such writers as columnist Jack Smith of the *Los Angeles Times*. "Polynesian" restaurants serving Chinese food washed down with potent and heretofore unheard of rum drinks multiplied across the country. In large part, the culinary and bibulous aspect of the Tiki program was originated by two extraordinary men: Don the Beachcomber and Trader Vic. Not surprisingly, both men started their respective "tropical" adventures before World War II in California, the one part of the country already oriented toward the Pacific.

Ernest Raymond Beaumont Gantt was born in Louisiana, where he learned to cook spicy Cajun food at his mother's side. A stint in Jamaica led to his discovery of Jamaican rum; so enamored of the stuff was he, that to the day of his death he called it "the nectar of the gods." After his family moved to Texas, he worked in his mother's restaurant, earning enough money to travel around the globe for two years. In 1932, he arrived in Los Angeles without a dime in his pocket. There he became a bootlegger for the short period Prohibition had left to live.

Shortly after its unlamented demise, Gantt built himself a bar (which he called the Beachcomber) in a thirteen-by-thirty-foot space connected to the McCadden Hotel. He went to work combining rum with various fruit juices, coming up with unheard of mixtures. A few days after he opened, a well-dressed man came into the bar and ordered a Sumatra Kula from the drink list behind the bar. After finishing it and saying that "it was the first really good drink he'd had for a donkey's year," he ordered another. After the third, he introduced himself as Neil Vanderbilt, a roving reporter for the *New York Tribune*. Promising to return with friends, Vanderbilt showed up with a small group including Charlie Chaplin. Asked for his best drinks, Gantt mixed five of his new cocktails. The friends departed after three rounds. Gantt's career was made.

During that career, he created over seventy-five tropical rum drinks: these include the Zombie, Missionary's Downfall, Cobra's

Fang, Vicious Virgin, Scorpion, Test Pilot, Three Dots and a Dash, the 151° Swizzle, and many more. The Hollywood crowd took him to themselves and started calling him "Don," in tribute to his brief bootlegging stint. Changing his name to "Donn Beach," he moved to a new and larger location across the street from the first Beachcomber's Bar. The name was changed to Don the Beachcomber Bar and Restaurant.

So popular did his first place prove, that in short order he opened another Don the Beachcomber Bar and Restaurant in Chicago. After service in the air force during World War II, Beach set down at Waikiki, where he opened yet another Don the Beachcomber Bar and Restaurant. This incarnation was a complex of several large thatched huts on the property where Liberty House now sits along Kalakaua Avenue.

Probably the most enduring of Beach's inventions is the Zombie. He invented it in the late 1930s as a cure for hangovers. Its delicious taste hides its alcoholic contents (three kinds of rum, a 151 floater, and a fruit brandy). Back in the early 1980s, I was a member of the Five Zombie Lunch Club, at the storied Nine-Oh, near the University of South Carolina campus; membership was dependent on completing the aforenamed meal and still being able to function. The fruity taste of the drink led many unwary souls to suppose it an easy task. In any case, seemingly every bar has its own more or less potent recipe.

Beach's greatest rival—he would say student—was Victor Jules Bergeron Jr. (a.k.a. Trader Vic). Beach often called him "his greatest imitator." Whatever the case, Victor Jules Bergeron Sr. was both a waiter at San Francisco's Fairmont Hotel and an owner of a grocery store on San Pablo Avenue in Oakland. His son, Victor Jr., helped out with the store and lived with his family upstairs. From this upbringing he grew up to love food; the loss of a leg in a childhood accident gave him a conversation piece he used for the rest of his life.

The same year that the Beachcomber arrived in Los Angeles, Vic opened a bar across the street from his father's store. Calling it

Hinky Dink's, he dished out Americanized Polynesian food and rum-based "tropical" drinks. Again in eerie parallel to his southern California rival, patronage by the press (in this case columnists Herb Caen and Lucius Beebe) launched the establishment on the road to success. Of course, San Francisco's position in those days as America's leading port in the Asiatic and Pacific trade meant that there was a built-in constituency. In 1936, Caen declared that the "best restaurant in San Francisco is in Oakland." By this time, Vic had become "The Trader," and Hinky Dink's was renamed Trader Vic's. According to the Trader himself, his establishment's South Pacific theme "intrigues everyone. You think of beaches and moonlight and pretty girls. It is complete escape."

By 1946, spurred by the Tiki boom referred to earlier, Trader Vic's had become nationally renowned. That year, Lucius Beebe wrote in his introduction to *Trader Vic's Book of Food and Drink:*

> Trader Vic's is . . . more than an Oakland institution. Its influence is as wide as the Pacific and as deep as a Myrtle Bank punch. Vic's trading post is long on atmosphere, and it is possible for the ambitious patron with a talent for chaos to get into more trouble with obsolete anchors, coiled hausers of boa-constrictor dimensions, fish nets, stuffed sharks. . . . Hawaiian ceremonial costumes, tribal drums, boathooks and small bore cannon than the waiters can drag him out of in a week.

Eventually, Trader Vic opened twenty-five Polynesian-style restaurants around the world, and several Señor Pico Mexican restaurants. His son, Lynn, ran the company after his father died, and remains chairman emeritus of Trader Vic's Restaurant Company.

The rivalry between Don the Beachcomber and Trader Vic remains today in one question: Who invented the Mai Tai? Both men claimed credit in their lifetimes, and their heirs and successors continue the dispute. According to the Trader Vic faction, he invented the drink at the restaurant in 1944 and introduced it to

Hawaii in the 1950s. Said to be Tahitian for "the very best," Mai Tai remains the slogan for his entire operation.

The Beachcomberites, on the other hand, assert that it was one of the many drinks originally created at the McCadden Street bar by Beach in 1933. They maintain that during a dinner conversation with columnist Jim Bishop and Beach, the Trader "finally admitted the truth about the Mai Tai." In a letter to Don Chapman of the *Honolulu Advertiser*, Bishop wrote, "In probably 1970 or 1971 Donn and I were with Vic at Vic's in San Francisco. In the 'friend-foe' relationship Donn and Vic had, Vic said in effect that night, 'Blankety blank, Donn, I wish you'd never come up with the blankety blank thing. It's caused me a lot of arguing with people.' Then Vic looked at me and said, 'Jim, this blankety . . . blank did do it. I didn't.'"

As far as Beach's fans are concerned, that settles it: "If you happen to see Trader Vic listed as the originator of the Mai Tai on a drink menu, just remember Jim Bishop's letter and Vic Bergeron's own words, then think of another original, 'Don the Beachcomber,' who in 1933 following the repeal of Prohibition opened Beachcomber's Bar in Hollywood, and along with several other original exotic tropical rum drinks, created the Mai Tai."

In contradiction to Bishop's letter, however, Vic fired his own salvo with this squib:

Let's Set the Record Straight on the Mai Tai
Victor Bergeron
San Francisco, 1970

Earlier this year, a long time friend from Tahiti, Carrie Guild (now Mrs. Howard Wright), sent me a column from a Honolulu newspaper which once again has raised the argument over where the Mai Tai was born and who originated it.

I originated the Mai Tai and have put together a bit of the background on the evolution of this drink, which has earned worldwide identification and acceptance. There has been a lot of conversation over the beginning of this drink. Many have claimed credit, includ-

ing Harry Owens. The people who now own Trader Vic's in Honolulu (which at this time has no connection with the Trader Vic
operations on the mainland) claimed it was originated in Tahiti. . . .
This aggravates my ulcer completely. The drink was never introduced by me in Tahiti except informally through our good friends,
Eastham and Carrie Guild.

In 1944, after success with several exotic rum drinks, I felt a new
drink was needed. I thought about all the really successful drinks;
martinis, manhattans, daiquiris. . . . All basically simple drinks.

I was at the service bar in my Oakland restaurant. I took down a
bottle of 17-year-old rum. It was J. Wray Nephew from Jamaica;
surprisingly golden in color, medium bodied, but with the rich pungent flavor particular to the Jamaican blends. The flavor of this
great rum wasn't meant to be overpowered with heavy additions of
fruit juices and flavorings. I took a fresh lime, added some orange
curacao from Holland, a dash of Rock Candy Syrup, and a dollop of
French Orgeat, for its subtle almond flavor. A generous amount of
shaved ice and vigorous shaking by hand produced the marriage I
was after. Half the lime shell went in for color. . . . I stuck in a
branch of fresh mint and gave two of them to Ham and Carrie
Guild, friends from Tahiti, who were there that night. Carrie took
one sip and said, "Mai Tai—Roa Ae." In Tahitian this means "Out
of This World—The Best." Well, that was that. I named the drink
"Mai Tai."

This drink enjoyed great acceptance over the next few years
in California and in Seattle when we opened Trader Vic's there in
1948. In 1953 the Mai Tai was brought by me to the Hawaiian
Islands, when I was asked by the Matson Steamship Lines to for-
malize drinks for the bars at their Royal Hawaiian, Moana and
Surfrider Hotels. Any old Kamaaina can tell you about this drink
and of its rapid spread throughout the islands.

In 1954 we further introduced the Mai Tai when we included it
among other new drinks in bar service for the American President
Lines. It is estimated that several thousand Mai Tais are served daily
in Honolulu alone, and we sell many more than that daily in our
eighteen Trader Vic's restaurants throughout the world. I have let
Eddie Sherman, the columnist on the above mentioned Honolulu

Star Bulletin, know who originated this drink and think it is time the general public knows that these are the facts of the evolution and growth of the Mai Tai.

In fairness to myself and to a truly great drink, I hope you will agree when I say, "Let's get the record straight on the Mai Tai."

Whichever story is true, there is no doubt, at least, about the drink's potency. Its mix of light rum, triple sec, lime juice, orgeat, syrup, and Grenadine remains an enormous favorite with the public, thus justifying the intense paternity struggle.

Trader Vic's restaurants are still in existence, although a number (such as the one formerly in New York's Plaza Hotel) have closed. In the United States, there are still five: Atlanta, Chicago, and three in California, in Beverly Hills, Emeryville (almost the original, and flagship of the chain), and Palo Alto. But overseas is where the strength of the chain lies. There are three in Germany and one each in Great Britain and Spain. They have been quite successful in the Far East, boasting two in Japan, one in Taiwan, and one in Thailand. But most surprising is their great success in the Near East. Bahrain, Egypt, and Oman each have one, while the United Arab Emirates has three! There is even one in Beirut—a tribute to that city's recovery from the years of Lebanon's civil war.

Alas, however, like all else, the Tiki craze had its day, although in certain favored refuges, such as Hollywood's Tiki Ti, it survives. For that matter, like the fondue fad at about the same time, it occasionally has fitful revivals. Moreover, one relic has survived in bars far removed from any other influence—the tiki-tiki umbrellas in tropical rum drinks. Where do these come from? Not surprisingly, from Trader Vic's, although they have not been served there since the 1940s. According to the Trader's son, Victor J. "Joe" Bergeron III, they stopped using them when importation of the little parasols from factories in the Far East was halted by the outbreak of war. Bergeron says that his father took the idea (again not surprisingly) from Don the Beachcomber. He, in turn, Bergeron believes, took the idea from Chinese restaurants. So in all likelihood, the umbrella is a Chinese-American invention. If Trader Vic's will not use them, many others do.

But regardless of Tiki's fate, rum is not bound to it, as the recent popularity of the mojito makes clear. Mixed with anything or taken neat, it remains the emblem of the global civilization we all inhabit. Whether the United States remakes the world in its image, some other power supplants it, or the whole edifice crumbles, rum will remain—infinitely adaptable, infinitely enjoyable.

From being a harsh liquor, good only for slaves, pirates, and the lower orders in general, rum has become a gourmet libation, useful both for the production of refined cocktails and haute cuisine. So true is this that rum has been embraced by no less than the Slow Food Movement, an international organization grouping connoisseurs who demand only the best for their palates. Juan Bureo, writing in their journal, *Slowine* sums up the recent history of the beverage thusly:

Rhum Boulevard

Beyond the three nautical miles which constituted the limit of American territorial waters, one particular stretch of water became impossible to control and eventually became known as Rum Boulevard, the scene of thousands of nightly crossings by motor boats of every shape and size. Cuba was not the only place to benefit from the prohibition laws but it did have the advantage of lying just a stone's throw from the Florida Keys. Some Americans just upped and went directly to the source in Havana, where they could drink in peace. The Cuban capital turned into America's local bar and was regarded as such for years to come in North American drinking lore. Indeed, the age of rum can even be viewed as a romantic one. After Fidel Castro rose to power, Cuba's biggest rum producer moved to Puerto Rico, where it remains to this day as the world's number one exporter, while Bacardi is the largest producer of ron ligero. North America is its biggest market, but Bacardi also holds sway over all of the most important European markets bar one. In France, fortunately, that magnificent spirit from the French West Indies, rhum agricole, remains the number one rum.

Today, the decline in rum production witnessed in the twentieth century on the islands which originally created it seems to have slowed down. Jamaica, Barbados, Trinidad, Antigua, the Bahamas and Guyana have joined together to form an association to protect their common interests. On the other smaller islands of the West Indies, the amount of rum distilled is insignificant. The former English colony of Guyana, which gained its independence in 1966, is still a major producer, exporting, mostly to Europe, a rapid-fermentation rum which is highly prized and used in the very best blends.

Rhum agricole, which comes from the French overseas territories, is a spirit unto itself. Generally of a very high quality, it is, in our opinion, likely to survive thanks to the popularity it enjoys in France. Also of note is the surprising but interesting fact that Spain and Portugal have recently begun to produce rum and are the only countries in Europe to manufacture sugar cane spirit. (from "Rum," *Slowine* no. 1, January–March 2001)

The irony here is that it is precisely rhum agricole which the French infantrymen took to the trenches in World War I. But irony is the stuff of history and the stuff of life. Rum has much to recommend it, in taste, in tradition, and above all, in how it stimulates the imagination. If, for all of life's faults and injustices, our lives are at all comfortable in this modern globalizing world of ours, rum must claim its share of the credit. There are nobler substances that run through our history—and nastier ones as well. But rum has been a constant: sometimes an enemy, often a friend, usually a comfort.

So the next time you hold a glass of rum or a rum cocktail in your hand, think of all who came before you, who made it possible for you to lift the beverage to your lips. Planters and slaves, pirates and sailors, World War I Tommies and voodoo priestesses, rum-runners and African kings, missionary priests and Yankee traders all played their part, hate them or love them, in bringing this nectar to you. And as you drink, know that you yourself are joining their company.

The Cuba Libre

3 ounces Coca-Cola
Lime wedge
1 ounce rum

2 ounces gin
2 dashes of bitters

Rub the rim of a highball glass with the lime. Fill with ice. Add rum and fill with Coca-Cola. Drop in the lime squeeze.

Mai Tai

THE ORIGINAL FORMULA:
2 ounces 17-year-old J. Wray
    Nephew Jamaican rum
$^1/_2$ ounce French Garnier
    orgeat

$^1/_2$ ounce Holland DeKuyper
    Orange Curaçao
$^1/_4$ ounce rock candy syrup
Juice of 1 fresh lime

Hand shake and garnish with half of the lime shell inside the drink and float a sprig of fresh mint at the edge of the glass.

FIRST ADJUSTED MAI TAI
FORMULA:
1 ounce 15-year-old J. Wray
    Nephew Jamaican rum
1 ounce Coruba or Red Heart
    Jamaican rum

$^1/_2$ ounce Trader Vic Formula
    orgeat
$^1/_2$ ounce Holland DeKuyper
    Orange Curaçao
$^1/_4$ ounce rock candy syrup
Juice of 1 fresh lime

Mix and serve as in the original formula.

SECOND ADJUSTED MAI TAI
FORMULA:
1 ounce Trader Vic's Jamaican
    Rum (15- or 8-year-old)
1 ounce Martinique rum
    (St. James or Trader Vic's)

1 ounce pre-mixed Curaçao,
    orgeat, and rock candy
    syrup
Juice of 1 fresh lime

Mix and serve as in the original formula.

PRESENT-DAY MAI TAI
FORMULA:
2 ounces fine dark rum

4 ounces Trader Vic's Mai Tai
Mix
Juice of 1 large lime

Mix and serve as in the original formula.

SOURCE: www.tradervics.com.

Zombie

Cracked ice
1 ounce light rum
1 ounce dark rum
$1/2$ ounce Grenadine
$1/2$ ounce triple sec
1 ounce apricot brandy

2 ounces orange juice
2 ounces bottled sour mix
Splash Rose's lime juice
151-proof rum
Ice cubes
1 lemon slice

Fill a mixing glass with cracked ice. Add light and dark rums,
Grenadine, triple sec, apricot brandy, orange juice, sour mix, and
lime juice. Shake well and strain into a Collins or highball glass
filled with ice cubes. Top with a dash of 151-proof rum and garnish
with a lemon slice.

Original Daiquiri

1.3 ounces of light rum
0.7 ounces of lime juice

0.2 ounces of Simple Syrup
(see page 23)

Shake with shaved ice, serve in cocktail glass.

Frozen Blue Daiquiri

2 ounces white rum
$1/2$ ounce Blue Curaçao

$1/2$ ounce lime juice
$1/3$ cup of ice

Put the entire ingredients into a blender. Blend at medium speed for
about 20 seconds. Pour into an old fashioned glass.

Banana Daiquiri

4 parts light rum   1 part banana liqueur
1 part white Creme de Cacao   1 sliced banana

Pour all of the ingredients except for the banana into the blender.
Start to blend, then add banana.

Pina Colada

2 cups coconut milk   1 cup rum, preferably golden
3 cups pineapple juice   1/2 cup sugar
2 cups crushed pineapple   1 teaspoon clear vanilla
1/2 cup shredded coconut,
      sweetened

Combine all ingredients in a large bowl. Blend in batches using a
blender. Serve over ice.

Piña Colada Bread

2 1/2 cups flour   1/3 cup corn oil
1/2 cup sugar   1/4 cup rum
2 teaspoons baking powder   1 8-ounce can crushed
1/2 teaspoon baking soda   pineapple in unsweetened
1/2 teaspoon salt   juice
2 eggs   1 cup flaked coconut
1/2 cup light corn syrup

Combine flour, sugar, baking powder, baking soda, and salt in a
medium bowl. In a large bowl, beat eggs, corn syrup, corn oil, and
rum until well blended. Gradually stir in flour mixture just until
moistened. Stir in pineapple with juice and coconut. Pour into a
greased and floured 9 × 5 × 3-inch loaf pan.

Bake 60–65 minutes in a 350° oven, or until a wooden skewer
inserted in the center comes out clean. Remove from oven and
leave in pan for 10 minutes to cool, then move to a wire rack to cool
completely.

Rum-and-Pepper-Painted Fish
with Habañero-Mango Mojo

2¹/₂ tablespoons black
   peppercorns
12 whole cloves
³/₄ cup white rum
¹/₂ cup sugar
¹/₂ cup low-sodium soy sauce
2¹/₂ tablespoons grated lemon
   rind
2 tablespoons fresh lemon juice

1 tablespoon vegetable oil
4 6-ounce grouper fillets
   (or other firm white
   fish fillets)
Habañero-Mango Mojo
   (see recipe below)
Black Bean and Fruit Salsa
   (see recipe below)
Lime wedges (optional)

Heat a nonstick skillet over medium-high heat until hot. Add peppercorns and cloves, and cook 1 minute. Place mixture in a spice or
coffee grinder; process until ground fine. Place mixture in a
saucepan. Add rum, sugar, soy sauce, and lemon juice; bring to a
boil. Reduce heat; simmer, uncovered, 25 minutes, or until reduced
to ¹/₂ cup. Strain pepper "paint" through a fine sieve over a bowl;
discard solids. Set aside.

Preheat oven to 450°. Wrap handle of skillet with foil; heat oil in
pan until hot. Brush pepper paint over one side of fish. Place fish,
paint side down, in skillet; sauté 3 minutes or until dark brown.
Turn fish over; place skillet in oven.

Bake 7 minutes or until fish flakes easily when tested with a fork.
Serve fillets with Habañero-Mango Mojo and Black Bean and Fruit
Salsa (recipes below); garnish fillets with lime wedges, if desired.

Habañero-Mango Mojo

1¹/₂ cups ripe mango, peeled
   and cubed
¹/₄ cup dry white wine

2 tablespoons orange juice
1–1¹/₂ teaspoons Habañero
   pepper sauce

Combine ingredients in a blender or food processor, and process
until smooth.

Black Bean and Fruit Salsa

½ cup ripe mango, peeled and
  cubed
1 cup papaya, peeled and diced
½ cup pineapple, cubed
½ cup red onion, diced
½ cup canned black beans,
  rinsed and drained
1 teaspoon Habañero pepper
  sauce

1 tablespoon fresh cilantro,
  minced
1 tablespoon fresh lime juice
1 tablespoon extra-virgin olive
  oil
1 teaspoon ground cumin
½ teaspoon black pepper,
  freshly ground
1 clove garlic, minced

Combine ingredients in a large bowl and toss gently to coat fruit
pieces.

Makes 4 cups.

Chapter 14

Varieties of Rum: A Historic and Libational Survey

Rums are produced all over the world, as our historical survey suggests. What follows does not claim to be comprehensive, but simply offers a look at some of the more common varieties of the drink. There are in fact four main classifications of rum: first comes very dry, light-bodied rum generally produced in the Spanish-speaking countries—Puerto Rican rum is today's outstanding example. The next is a medium-bodied rum. Then follows the rich pungent rum produced in the English-speaking islands and countries—the best example of this is Jamaican rum. Lastly comes the aromatic Indonesian Batavia arrack rum from Java.

Golden rums (also known as amber rums), such as Barbados and Demerara, are medium-bodied rums. Most of these are aged in oak casks, which gives them their unique flavor.

Dark, rich, full-bodied, pungent rums, usually produced in the English-speaking islands and countries such as Jamaica, are traditionally caramel-dominated rums. The best are produced mostly from pot stills and are frequently aged in oak casks for extended periods. The richest of these rums are consumed straight up.

However, this distinction does not mean that Puerto Rico produces only light-bodied and Jamaica only full-bodied rums. Both countries can and do produce both types, although they are renowned for their own traditional type.

As with fine wines, rums are labeled by their area of origin and legally cannot be classified by type; subtle differences in rums come from their growing area (weather, soil type, humidity, and so on) and the effects these have on the sugar cane—again as with wine. Molasses carries and concentrates these characteristics. As with many whiskies, rums are blended to achieve consistent taste and quality. Still other factors that affect the final product are the distillation process itself (aguardientes, coming from the middle distillate), the aging process (how long, what type of barrel, charred or not, and so on), and the flavoring additives in special rums.

So informed, we are now ready to begin our tour of some of the world's great rum labels! The list is hardly exhaustive, but it will get you started on your own exploration!

Anguilla

Pyrat XO Reserve—Planters Gold

This rum is blended to be elegantly smooth and delicious. Its amber color indicates its flavorful sippability. It is blended to be enjoyed over ice with a twist of lemon or combined with almost any high-quality mixer.

Pyrat Pistol

The Pistol bottle and blend are similar in flavor to the Pyrat XO Reserve—Planters Gold. It is slightly lighter in body and very drinkable. The Pyrat Pistol was inspired by a bottle size often carried on old English sailing ships. The Pyrat Pistol size is presented in branded wooden boxes of six Pyrat "pistols."

Pyrat Cask 23

This is a very fine, aged, dark amber rum similar in color and body to a rare cognac. Cask 23 is a rare limited-production rum. It is packaged in an incense cedar box and a numbered hand-blown decanter.

Antigua

Cavalier Rum

Cavalier Rum is a blend of both gold and light rums. Very full bodied and yet smooth.

English Harbour Rum

English Harbour Rum is a very full-bodied gold rum.

Australia

Bundaberg Black

Originating in 1985, Bundaberg Black owes its origin to Dr. Lou Muller, the distillery's master distiller. He set aside one vat of Bundaberg Rum and allowed it to age slowly at the distillery. Bundaberg's best seller, this dark rum features a hint of molasses, toasted cedar, and a butterscotch finish. As with all Kimberley and Bundaberg Rums, it is a product of the cane fields of Queensland State.

Bundaberg U.P.

Bundaberg U.P. is a light, golden rum with a strong yet mellow taste.

Bundaberg Rum O.P

Bundaberg Rum O.P is an overproof version of Bundaberg U.P., virtually identical except for the higher alcoholic content.

Kimberley Cane Spirit

Kimberley Cane Spirit is a young rum aged for two years in a wood cask. It is light with a fresh taste.

Kimberley Cane Spirit O.P.

Kimberley Cane spirit O.P. is similar to the above, save for the higher alcohol content.

Barbados

Mount Gay Rum Eclipse Rum

Mount Gay Rum Eclipse Rum, the granddaddy of all rums, was invented almost three hundred years ago. It is a golden rum, with a very complex aroma at once floral and fruity. Light bodied, it is good either neat or in cocktails.

Mount Gay Rum Extra Old Barbados Rum

Mount Gay Rum Extra Old Barbados Rum is a blend of old spirits, carefully selected from Mount Gay's rum reserves. Amber brown in color, it is dry, surprisingly light bodied, and very smooth.

Bermuda

Gosling Brothers Black Seal Rum

Gosling Brothers Ltd. imports and blends three-year-old rums from around the Caribbean to produce Black Seal, a well-aged, extremely dark rum. It is an essential ingredient in Bermuda fish chowder, the Bermuda Rum Swizzle, and the Dark 'n Stormy, Bermuda's favorite cocktail.

Brazil
Cachaça Rainha do Vale

Cachaça, like rum, is a cane spirit, but rather than being distilled from molasses, it is distilled directly from fermented cane juice. Unlike the majority of cachaças, which are un-aged and clear in color, Cachaça Rainha do Vale is aged in wood casks for approximately eighteen months, resulting in a light gold libation with an alcohol content of 46 percent.

British Virgin Islands
British Navy Pusser's Rum

British Navy Pusser's Rum, as noted in chapter 2, is the same blend of five West Indian rums served sailors for three centuries; it is still blended in accordance with the Admiralty's specifications of 1810. Another remaining tie with the Royal Navy was the custom of Great Britain's Queen Mother Elizabeth (until her death in 2003) of mixing a tub of grog—Pusser's Rum and water—for the commissioning of her daughter's warships. Somewhat reminiscent of brandy, Pusser's boasts both smoothness and a full rich flavor; it is perfect for sipping neat, although remaining distinctive in cocktails.

Costa Rica
Marques Rum

This rum is extremely light and delicately flavored. It is strong, with an alcoholic content of 40 percent.

Magallanes Centenario Rum

A blended amber rum mixed from very old beverages. Even though it has an alcoholic content of 40 percent, it is very mellow.

Old Rum (ron Viejo)

The Old Rum has a light aroma and a unique flavor, due to its derivation from cane spirit. Its alcoholic content is also 40 percent.

Cuba

Note: While delicious, Cuban rums cannot be imported legally into the United States and its possessions. Moreover, Cuban distilleries were seized from their rightful owners and the profits therefrom go to prop up the oppressive Castro regime. Politically aware drinkers will bear this in mind.

Silver Dry Rum

Silver Dry Rum is derived from the blending of aged eau-de-vie (fermented from molasses), which is matured for at least eighteen months, with sugar cane alcohol. This produces a light, strong, white rum, tasting like *guarapo* or sugar cane juice. It has a clear but slightly syrupy look. Light tasting, it is ideal for typically Cuban cocktails such as mojitos and daiquiris.

Anejo 3 Years

Blended from eau-de-vie and sugar cane alcohol, the young rum is then aged for three years—hence its name: Anejo 3 Years. Having a light straw color, it has a pleasant vanilla-ish flavor. It goes well in cocktails, on the rocks, or neat.

Anejo Reserva

Anejo Reserva is made from various Cuban rums of different ages, with specific proportions of young and more mature rums. Amber in color, it is strongly flavored and is drunk as a liqueur—often with a Havana cigar (which alas suffers under the same strictures).

Anejo 7 Years

Anejo 7 Years is the oldest product in the Havana Club range. Its manufacture is similar to that of Anejo 3 Years save, of course, that it is aged four more years. It, too, is amber in color, with a very clear taste, and is often drunk like a liqueur.

Czech Republic
Bum Pražské Gardy

Bum Pražské Gardy is an exclusive variety of Czech rum aged in larch-wood cisterns. Its suffix *gardy* refers to its being chosen as the official drink of the Prague Castle Guards; it was so baptized at their vow-taking by former Czech president Václav Havel. It, too, boasts an alcohol content of 40 percent.

Dominican Republic
Ron Barceló Añejo

A typical Dominican light rum, this variety is aged for two years and is quite smooth.

Ron Barceló Gran Añejo

Aged for a longer period than the foregoing, this rum is amber in color and fuller bodied.

Barceló Gran Añejo Blanco

Although possessing the same general characteristics of the Barceló Gran, Blanco has, through technology, been deprived of its color. Its taste and aroma is virtually identical to Barceló Gran.

Ron Barceló Dorado

Aged for over a year, this is a light rum of amber color.

Ron Barceló Blanco

Of the same formula as the previous rum, it, too, has had its color removed.

Ron Barceló Imperial

A high familiar of limited production, numbered bottle, and made reserve totally by hand. It is, without a doubt, the noblest reserve of the Dominican rum.

Grenada

Pure White Rum

Made from blended cane syrup and cane juice by Clarke's Court, Pure White is Grenada's most popular white rum. With a 69 percent alcohol content, it is used not only for punches or drunk straight (or with a dash of Angostura bitters), but also as a food preservative.

Superior Light Rum

As a less lethal alternative to Pure White, Superior Light Rum was developed in 1991. A mere 43 percent alcohol-by-volume proof, it is known for a fresh taste and less unpleasant mornings-after.

Westerhall Plantation Rum

A smooth-sipping rum that owes its unique character to a unique process. A "flavor rum" is distilled in copper kettles from cane juice, blended with "smoothing" rum, and then aged in oak casks. This is an amber rum.

Westerhall Superb Light

This special three-year-old blended rum is smooth and light. It was created particularly for cocktails.

Rum Sipper Strong Rum

A light-bodied overproof white rum used for sipping when chilled. Also excellent in tropical drinks like daiquiris, planter's punches, and others.

Jack Iron

An aged overproof light rum. Bottled at 70 percent alcohol-by-volume proof, it is recommended as a mixing rum with cola or tonic water.

Westerhall Strong Rum

Bottled at 70 percent alcohol-by-volume proof, this is a traditional, overproof pot still rum. A pure cane juice rum, Granadans often drink it neat, but others may prefer it in rum punches and exotic cocktails.

Guadeloupe

Rhum Coeur de Chauffe

A white rum made from cane juice rather than molasses. With a 50 percent alcohol content, it is recommended for cocktails, where its strong flavor will be appreciated.

Rhum Vieux 1993

This rum is aged in oak casks for an additional three years. At 40 percent alcohol by volume, it is drunk neat.

Guyana

5-Year-Old XM Rum

A Demerara Rum famous for its smooth flavor, which is derived from fruit. This blended rum is 40 percent alcohol by volume.

XM Classic Light

Although this rum is 40 percent alcohol by volume, it is light in both taste and color and is often drunk neat.

XM Classic Dark

Also 40 percent alcohol by volume, this blended Demerara Rum is dark in color and rich in flavor. Very good in cocktails.

El Dorado 25-Year-Old Demerara Millennium Rum

This is a very smooth, mellow, scotch-like rum, aged in oak casks for twenty-five years. It is an extremely unique beverage.

El Dorado 12-Year-Old Rum

Aged in oaken casks for twelve years and blended to achieve a smooth strength and a rich, full-bodied taste, this is a rum of superb amber color and full, fragrant aroma.

Haiti

Rhum Barbancourt

Rhum Barbancourt is a superior premium four-year-old white rum distilled twice in copper pot stills. Made directly from sugar cane juice, it has a slightly alcoholic nose, a smooth, rich taste, and a warm finish.

Rhum Barbancourt Estate Reserve

This fifteen-year-old rum is copper colored with a dry oaky flavor and a lengthy aftertaste.

India
Sikkim Snow Lion White Rum

This is a rum redistilled from a well-matured dark rum to remove the color and some flavor. It is designed to be used in a wide variety of cocktails.

Trafalgar White Rum

Trafalgar White Rum is distilled from molasses; despite its color, it is very aromatic and heavily flavored.

Jamaica
Appleton White Jamaica Rum

Appleton White Jamaica Rum is smooth, brilliantly clear, and light bodied with a subtle taste and delicate aroma. It has a fruity bouquet with the aroma of coconut and pear, perfumed with lychee. Good neat or in cocktails.

Appleton Special Jamaica Rum

This rum is a blend of traditional pot still rums and lighter character modern-column still rums. These rums are aged separately in oak barrels and afterward are hand-blended to produce a medium-bodied golden rum that has a delicate and fruity bouquet with a hint of exotic spices—ginger, nutmeg, and vanilla.

Appleton Estate V/X Jamaica Rum

A blend of several marks of rum, with the heart of the blend being slowly distilled in small batches in the company's old copper pot stills. Once distilled, the rums are aged in small oak barrels. Finally, the master blender combines the rums of the various marks and ages in large vats. It has a golden color and a rich aroma. Its bouquet is a blend of dry fruits such as apricots and oranges with a hint of vanilla.

Madagascar

Dzama White Rum

This white rum, at 42 percent alcohol by volume, has an expansive, fruity, and sharp aroma, with a soft and fruity taste.

Dzama Black Rum

A dark rum at 43 percent alcohol by volume, it is extremely mellow, with a powerful aftertaste.

Dzama 52

Dzama 52 (named after its alcohol-by-volume percentage) has a strong, powerful, and penetrating aroma. Recommended for both summer punches and winter hot toddies, it can also be used as a digestif.

Martinique

Clement Rhum Blanc 50

Again named after its alcohol content, this rum has a delicate aroma of sugar, flowers, and oranges. In the French West Indies, it is the preferred ingredient for Ti-punches, but it is also used for planter's punches and other fruit-based drinks.

Clement Rhum Blanc 55

A more intense version of the foregoing, its higher alcohol content makes it perfect for stronger punches. It is renowned for lowering inhibitions and assisting conversation.

Clement Rhum Vieux 3 Years

An amber-colored beverage, it is drunk like cognac. But Martinique locals also use it in a special variety of Ti-punches and add it as a floater to their planter's punch.

Clement Rhum Vieux 10 Years

Similar to the foregoing, save that its taste conveys a hint of almonds.

Depaz Rhum D'Ore

This is a white rum that is aged for one year in oak casks. After its maturation, coloring is added. It is drunk like cognac, which it resembles in taste and appearance.

Depaz Vieux Rhum VO

Slowly aged in oak casks, this VO (Very Old) rum is well balanced and presents an excellent aromatic taste. Its alcohol content is 40 percent.

Depaz Vieux Rhum VSOP

Aged for four years in oak casks, this rum acquires a wonderful balance and a superb harmony in its aromas: slight oaken notes and potpourri perfume. Its taste carries a hint of plum jam. It is often used neat as a digestif.

Nepal

Khukri XXX Rum

Khukri XXX Rum has a subtle and complex nature. It is distinguished by its lingering aroma and by a smooth and balanced flavor with a hint of oak wood.

Réunion

Most of the rums produced on the island are called "traditional." This means that they are distilled by private individuals. Both cane juice and molasses may be used to produce what is called "Traditional Rum from Réunion," which is a simple white rum. A number of other types of beverages are produced from this beverage.

Vieux Rhum

This is the traditional white rum aged in oak barrels with a maximum capacity of 650 liters for a minimum of three years. The tanins and other essences drawn from the wood give to the product its brown color and its characteristic taste.

Maturé Rhum

This is a copper-colored beverage that is aged in oak casks for only a few months.

Ambré Rhum

This traditional rum owes its color to the addition of caramel. The practice is legal but strictly regulated.

According to the raw material used and the processes of fermentation and distillation employed, one can make other standard rums:

Light Rhum

This rum has an alcohol content that ranges between 20 and 40 percent (unlike darker rums, which range between 40 and 80 percent alcohol). Its more neutral taste makes it popular in cocktails.

Grand Gout Rhum

This is a rum with a very assertive taste, enriched in aromatic compounds. This improved rum is used to cut rums whose flavor is too neutral.

BIBLIOGRAPHY

Arkell, Julie. *Classic Rum*. London: Prion Books, 1999.

Ayala, Luis. *The Rum Experience*. Round Rock, TX: Rum Runner Books, 2002

———— and Margaret Ayala. *The Encyclopedia of Rum Drinks*. Round Rock, TX: Rum Runner Books, 2002.

Barbados Rum Book. Oxford: Macmillan Education, 1985.

Barr, Andrew. *Drink: A Social History of America*. New York: Carroll & Graf, 1999.

Barty-King, Hugh, and Anton Massel. *Rum Yesterday and Today*. London: Heinemann, 1983.

Brown, John. "The Rum Rebellion," *Military History* (February 2003), 12–14.

Caribbean Rum Book. Oxford: Macmillan Education, 1985.

Carrington, Selwyn H. H. *The Sugar Industry and the Abolition of the Slave Trade, 1775–1810*. Gainesville: University of Florida Press, 2002.

Dunn, Richard S. *Sugar and Slaves: The Rise of the Planter Class in the English West Indies, 1624–1713*. Chapel Hill: UNC Press, 1972.

Hamilton, Edward. *The Complete Guide to Rum*. Chicago: Triumph Books, 1997.

————. *Rums of the Eastern Caribbean*. Culebra, PR: Tafia, 1995.

Foster, Peter. *Family Spirits*. Toronto: Macfarlane Walter & Ross, 1990.

Hurston, Zora Neale. *Mules and Men*. New York: HarperCollins, 1990.

————. *Tell My Horse: Voodoo and Life in Haiti and Jamaica*. New York: HarperCollins, 1990.

Morrison, James, and J. Moereira. *Tempered by Rum: Rum in the History of the Maritime Provinces*. Halifax: Pottersfield Press, 1988.

Nassau, Rev. Robert Hamill, M.D., S.T.D. *Fetichism in West Africa: Forty Years' Observation of Native Customs and Superstitions*. New York: Charles Scribner's Sons, 1904.

Pack, James. *Nelson's Blood: The Story of Naval Rum*. Annapolis: Naval Institute Press, 1982.

Rediker, Marcus. *Between the Devil and the Deep Blue Sea: Merchant Seamen, Pirates and the Anglo-American Maritime World, 1700–1750.* Cambridge: Cambridge University Press, 1987.

Roberts, Adolphe. *The French in the West Indies.* Indianapolis, IN: Bobbs-Merrill, 1942.

Salinger, Sharon V. *Taverns and Drinking in Early America.* Baltimore and London: Johns Hopkins University Press, 2002

Saxon, Lyle, Edward Dreyer, and Robert Tallant. *Gumbo Ya-Ya.* New Orleans: Pelican, 1987.

Schermerhorn, Richard, Jr. *Schermerhorn Genealogy and Family Chronicles.* New York: Tobias A. Wright, 1914.

Tallant, Robert. *Voodoo in New Orleans.* New Orleans: Pelican, 1983.

Thomas, Hugh. *The Slave Trade.* New York: Simon and Schuster, 1997.

Turley, Hans. *Rum, Sodomy, and the Lash: Piracy, Sexuality, and Masculine Identity.* New York: New York University Press, 1994.

Williams, Joseph J., S.J. *Voodoos and Obeahs: Phases of West India Witchcraft.* New York: Dial Press, 1932.

INTERNET SITES

Ministry of Rum: www.ministryofrum.com

Peter's Rum Pages: www.rum.cz/main.htm

The Rum Shop: www.rumshop.net

Black Seal Bermuda Rum Recipes: www.goslings.com/recipes.html

INDEX